# The History of Greek Vases

Attic black figure cup
by Exekias, from Vulci. c. 525 BC
*See [309], p. 284*

John Boardman

# THE HISTORY OF GREEK VASES

Potters, Painters and Pictures

*358 illustrations*

**Thames & Hudson**

*in memoriam*
ROBERT COOK

First published in hardcover in the United States of America in 2001 by
Thames & Hudson Inc., 500 Fifth Avenue, New York, New York 10110

Library of Congress Catalog Card Number 00-108863

ISBN 0-500-23780-8

Printed and bound in Singapore by C.S. Graphics

# Contents

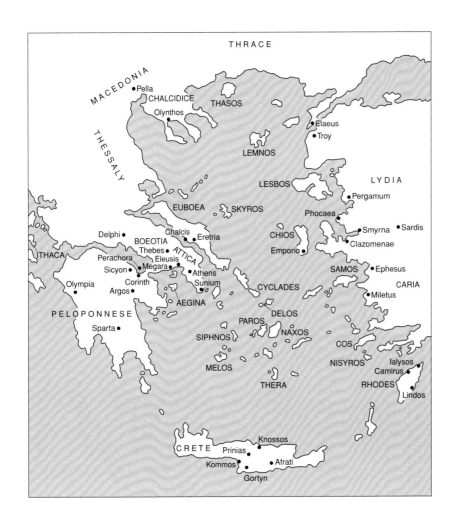

**Map 1**
The Aegean World

**Map 2**
South Italy and Sicily

# Preface

Greek pottery is one of the most spectacular and familiar crafts of classical antiquity. This is the more remarkable because the raw material could not be commoner or cheaper. Only oriental ceramics seem to have commanded comparable importance in the culture and trade that they served over several centuries A D, and they were not the important field for figure decoration that Greek pottery became. Some classes of European pottery have been decorated with ambitious painted scenes, from Faenza to Sèvres, but were never in such common use. Several Central American wares are informatively decorated but were not widely traded even in the New World. So this is an odd phenomenon. Study of it has more to teach us about Greek antiquity, especially from the eighth to fourth centuries BC, than study of any other ancient medium for art, including sculpture. This is a product of, on the one hand, its plenty and ubiquity, on the other hand, the attention paid to its decoration, which offers a subtle but direct commentary on the attitudes and preoccupations of the day, as well as a great deal of engaging narrative.

In this book I survey the record of the Greek pottery industry from roughly the tenth century BC to the second. This is not, however, the only period of significant pottery production in Greece. Any commodity in such common and universal use was being made throughout the life of all civilised, and most primitive, communities, but the chosen period for Greece embraces the most elaborate and informative products of the craft. There had been, it seems, a certain penchant in Greek lands for elaborately decorated pottery long before, in the Bronze Age: first by the non-Greek Minoans of Crete, and then their successors in control of both Crete and the mainland, the Greek-speaking Mycenaeans. After them came a recession, followed by renaissance, and at this point, in the eleventh/tenth century BC, a virtually new story of crafts and art in Greek lands begins. After the fourth century BC, however, painted decoration for pottery became sparse and relief decoration mainly debased, both dependent on metal models; hence my concentration on the earlier centuries. The geographical area involved is that of the Greek mainland, islands, the eastern shores of the Aegean (western Asia Minor, Turkey), and to some degree the colonial world of the Greeks on the shores of south Italy and Sicily, the Black Sea and north Africa.

The subject is hardly a new one, and there is no shortage of reference books. In the World of Art series of our publisher I have written four which deal with the main classes of painted pottery down to the fourth century, and there is one (by Dale Trendall) for South Italian Greek wares. These books will be often referred to since they are very generously illustrated, but I have tried to make the illustration of this volume as self-sufficient as I can. For the non-painted wares the sources are more dispersed.

The volumes mentioned treat the subject art-historically, by style, date, place of origin and, where possible, artist. Other relevant matters are dealt with, in passing, and it is the purpose of the present book to go on to consider these more carefully, to provide a history of the craft that goes beyond the physical appearance of the vessels. They have then to be considered in their relationship to the prosperity and fortunes of the cities that produced them as well as of the people who made and designed them. Methods of manufacture need to be explored as well as the processes of trade, since they were widely dispersed through and beyond the Greek world, and they have much to tell beyond the simple matter of their own distribution. Their function as containers, fine objects, even as purveyors of messages that the scenes upon them might embody, needs consideration, while the scenes themselves provide a mighty subject that ranges the whole field of art, society, religion and mythology, more comprehensively than any other medium of their day. This 'iconography' of Greek vases has been dealt with in detail in monographs and dictionaries; here I try to explain how the scenes were composed, and to elicit what they meant to viewers and buyers in antiquity, rather than merely providing a key to the recognition of stories and figures. The aim then is to provide both more and less than the standard histories of the subject, to try to explain what might too readily be taken for granted or ignored. So there is a lot of information, leading to comment and speculation, which I take to be more useful than alleged explanations without presentation of evidence.

Though the clay vases were among the cheapest of the products of ancient craftsmen, study of them is, for the historian and archaeologist, among the most rewarding. They are plentiful, in excavations they can provide close dates, and in their iconography they reflect on almost all the other arts of Greece, visual and literary. Sculpture is more grandiose and truly monumental but restricted in its range and messages, more a public or civic art;

other media are either mainly banal (clay figurines) or in their way élitist (jewellery, gem engraving, fine metalwork), less representative of the experience of the ordinary (or extraordinary) Greek, and very seldom so informatively decorated. Other media such as wall or panel painting are lost. But one of the problems must be to elucidate the relationship of this craft to other crafts practised by other (or even the same) craftsmen, in terms of both shapes and decoration.

'Craft', 'art': it must be understood that we are not dealing with 'Art', let alone 'Art for Art's Sake', in the modern sense, but there are vases which can match in artistry of technique, design and execution, the best of any period or place, and this is not the least claim that they have on our attention. Ancient art was essentially functional, but exercising functions forgotten today or served in other ways. There was no 'Art Market' as such for Greek vases, or indeed for anything before Roman times. Our 'artists' served their public rather than the self-esteem of collectors.

The vases themselves were much prized when they were first found in any numbers, in Italy in the eighteenth century. Etruria and the areas south of Rome, around Naples, had been an especially ready market, and the use there of built tombs has ensured better preservation of whole vases than the burial practices of the Greek homeland. The vases were admired for their finish, their shapes which appealed to and helped form the neo-Classical fashions of the day, and especially for their figure scenes which could be related to classical literature, which was the acknowledged source and inspiration of much western thought. They commanded relatively high prices, though not always as high as their imitations, such as those by Wedgwood. They have remained valuable, some even moving into the Fine Art range of prices. Any collection of classical art is bound to include them, and they can be displayed in various ways. When New York bought its famous Euphronios crater it had a room to itself, lacking only, as Professor Trendall wryly remarked, a *prie-dieu* before it. The new exhibition in the Louvre has them presented both individually and in groups, well lit and backed with modern electronic resources for the curious to discover more about them, if they wish. In Oxford most are now exhibited only in a back room rather like cans of peas in a supermarket, to disguise their individual appeal. The difference is between them being in the hands of a scholar who had to justify considerable expenditure (von Bothmer); a museum curator mindful of the richness of his collection and his public and educational duty (Pasquier); and a curator careless of what he regards as the 'detritus of antiquity' or 'unrecyclable junk' (Vickers). The motivation of the former two is easier to understand than that of the latter. I hope this book will help readers to a balanced view.

Other revisionist views about the importance of Greek decorated pottery and the methods of study have also come to the fore in recent years, in keeping with a trend in much current scholarship, critical but not constructive, and seldom well based on knowledge of the subject and its ramifications. These chapters answer some of these in passing, not directly, since a free exposition of the evidence is as good an answer as any. For much that is discussed here the evidence is clear, even if the theory always is not. But there has also been a far more valuable shift of interest, away from painter attribution and the iconography of myth, the traditional art-historian's playground, and into enquiry about the craft as a trade, about the meaning of the figure scenes and their social function, if any. This is valuable, and where properly practised it complements the older approaches without in any way replacing them – indeed, as we shall see, it depends on them. It is, however, remarkable how much scholarship of a hundred years ago anticipated much that is thought novel today.

It is necessary to present some continuous history of the craft and this is attempted in Chapter 1. Here I describe the vases with an eye to the political and social fortunes of each centre of production and period, mentioning those other aspects of the subject which will be picked up again in later chapters, and doing no more than summarize the development of style, the range of decoration or the role of individual painters. This complements the more stylistically focused handbooks. Later chapters range more widely, and sometimes in depth, over subjects generally avoided or treated summarily in books for the public and student, but which are crucial to understanding. The Epilogue strikes a more personal note.

# Chapter 1:    A History of Greek Vases

*Introduction*

It would be reasonable to assume that every major town in Greece, and many a minor one, would have had its own potters' yard. Few have been located, but then they were generally in areas which have not attracted the attention of excavators, as do temples and cemeteries, and their products would have engaged the archaeologist more than the art historian. Only with the growth of the ancient trade in pottery, and the development of attractive lines in decorated vases in certain towns which could then corner a market, did this relatively domestic situation change, and at any time a local potter of plain wares might be tempted to try his hand at something more exotic. Thus, by the fifth century BC, a figure-decorated vase normally meant an Athenian one. This implies the existence of a complex but not necessarily well organized production and distribution service. So this becomes as much a story of business acumen as of developing styles in potting and painting. There was diversity in other wares to meet special needs or to reflect local taste and interests, and there was no shame attached to copying the ideas of others. Copyright is a modern concept.

Before the fifth century this diversity was impressive, with the styles of different towns freely inspiring imitation or competition, and open even to the influence of foreign arts. Thanks to good archaeological control of the material it is now possible to trace this record in Greece in more detail than we can with most ancient wares, until the advent of mass production of potter-stamped vessels in the Roman period. Regional diversity in the early period might tell us something too about life in the different production centres. That a distinctive pottery style was in some way a deliberate or even accidental form of corporate identifier, like coinage, seems fairly improbable, given that much seems to stem from individual potter/painter choice, or can be explained by propinquity to dominant centres of production, though it was of course always conditioned by the market and local tradition. Not too many Greeks would have been very conscious of such a factor unless some commercial consideration intervened. These vases are only incidentally expressions of identity or ambassadors of state; if it had been otherwise, we may be sure that these functions would have been quite as unmistakable as they are on, for example, coins or the imperial arts of eastern empires. There was no such thing as a 'Greek state' in our period, but there was intense local pride and frequent horrendous warfare, Greek against Greek. Thus, we do not look on vases for any obvious declaration of the militancy of Sparta, or of democracy and philosophy at Athens, or of rare poetic expression in Ionia. These are not instruments of propaganda, for all that we may find them subtly reflecting on common attitudes to these matters, mainly through the choice and presentation of mythological subjects, rather than of the everyday. Yet the artists' products, in all media, were designed for and acceptable to populations whose fortunes had been in part conditioned by such considerations. Loyalty was to the home town, not the country.

This chapter attempts a summary history of the record of pottery production and especially pottery decoration in Greek lands. It does not repeat the more detailed stylistic accounts to be found in other handbooks, nor does it altogether rely on them, though readers will be helped by their far more numerous pictures. Various matters of technique, trade, and the like, will be discussed later in this book (and where some points may need repeating from this chapter), for their problems rather than just to demonstrate the evidence, or they can be studied in books dedicated to such matters. They can contribute much to our understanding of the subject and appreciation of the vases.

A few words are needed about terminology. 'Geometric period' and 'geometric style' are not necessarily co-terminous, but they are roughly so. Where I write of periods, geometric means roughly late ninth century to around 700 BC; orientalizing, late eighth century to about 600 BC; archaic, late seventh century to around 475 BC; classical, the fifth and fourth centuries; Hellenistic, late fourth to first centuries BC. I use conventional names for vase shapes; these are often in fact wrong, as will be shown in later chapters, but they are the terms familiar in all the books. I have given rough dates in the picture captions but they should not be taken as more than a guide to relative placing, another matter for a later chapter. But I do not believe that they are far from the truth or in any way misleading.

*Beginnings*

The Greek liking for highly decorated pottery, and especially figure-decorated pottery, was not shared by many other ancient peoples, yet it goes back to their Bronze Age, down to around 1100 BC, a period not considered in this book because after it there was

1. Late Minoan 'pilgrim flask' from Palaikastro (Crete). 16th c. BC. H. 28cm. (Heraklion)

2. Late Mycenaean crater from Marion (Cyprus). This style is best represented in Cyprus. 14th c. BC. H. 41.9cm. (London 1911.4–28.1)

3. Sub-Mycenaean stirrup vase, for oil, from Athens. The top is a 'false spout' supporting the two stirrup handles. 11th c. BC. (Kerameikos)

effectively a new beginning in the craft. The non-Greek Minoans of Crete had made colourful and highly decorative wares [1]. The Mycenaean Greek potters of the mainland learnt from them, but were generally more restrained. Most of the decoration was abstract, floral or marine, with little by way of other animal or human subjects except with the later Mycenaeans [2]. At all times there was production of storage vases: the stirrup vases with narrow spouts for oil are the most characteristic [3], and huge

pithoi, like barrels, for bulk storage of solids or liquids, painted or plain, most familiar from the storerooms of Knossos. The Minoan palace economies encouraged such usage since they controlled distribution of major commodities. However, with the decline of the palaces in the twelfth century BC, which seems accompanied by a decline in population and even some measure of change in its composition (more Greek-speakers from the north, it may be), the more elaborate pottery, as well as other more sophisticated arts, disappear from all Greece.

The pattern of life was now of fewer, smaller communities. The political pattern was one dictated by geography, and the prosperity of the towns by the relative poverty of the land, much of it forested and unfit for either pasture or agriculture, and with no major mineral resources. It is hardly surprising that Greece was never bonded into one nation, except as the result of pressure from outside, and then only superficially, from Macedon, then Rome. The unity was one of language and religion only, but on occasion this could be supremely binding. No wonder they were always ready to travel. At the start of our period there had been some expansion in the form of groups who had travelled east across the Aegean (as some had shortly before to Cyprus), often to sites already known to or occupied by Greeks in the Bronze Age. The most important of these settled in Ionia and the Dodecanese, on the coast and offshore islands of Anatolia, modern Turkey. Isolation did not mean unawareness, however, nor lack of communication, in such a small country and across a sea studded with islands.[1]

We pick up signs of renewed interest in pottery as a major and not simply utilitarian craft in Athens and its countryside villages, extending to Eleusis in the west, Marathon in the north east, Sunium in the south. This countryside (*chora*) was extensive – Attica; which is why 'Attic' will be used at least as often as 'Athenian' to describe the vases, though the latter is kept for matters expressly relevant to the city, and for the early period it should not be assumed that any political dependence at all is implied by 'Attic'. For our concerns it was more a matter of demand and geography.

This renewal is surprising inasmuch as it is marked by qualities of fine potting which immediate predecessors had not matched, as well as a new precision in the disposition and execution of decoration. Throughout the history of Greek art the craftsmen can be seen to be 'doing their best', and if their best could not be exercised on anything grander than pottery, then that is where

4. Attic protogeometric amphora, from a grave (12) in the Kerameikos, Athens. 10th c. BC. H. 52cm. (Kerameikos)

5. Attic protogeometric jug, from the Kerameikos, Athens. 10th c. BC. H. 29cm. (Kerameikos 2022)

we have to judge it. In Greece, however, this set a pattern of behaviour even for more prosperous days. Where the last of the Mycenaeans ('sub-Mycenaeans') had reduced the old floral patterns to roughly drawn concentric arcs and dots [3], the new potters drew carefully, and with newly devised multiple brushes on something like a compass, to produce the concentric circles and semicircles characteristic of the 'protogeometric' period [4–6]. The black paint achieves a deeper, more regular gloss than hitherto, which indicates greater care in preparation and in the firing, not different pigments: Greek pots are long to be essentially 'black and white'. The shapes serve a wide domestic range: cups and larger bowls (craters) which were used, among other things no doubt, for the mixing of wine and water in the Greek manner; jars (amphorae with two variously placed handles) for storage, and water jars (hydriai) with pouring handles, as well as smaller specialist shapes – narrow-mouthed jugs for oil [5], boxes. These all attract the same protogeometric patterns. The production is well documented all over Greece, with minor regional preferences for some shapes and decoration. Athens is taken to have been the

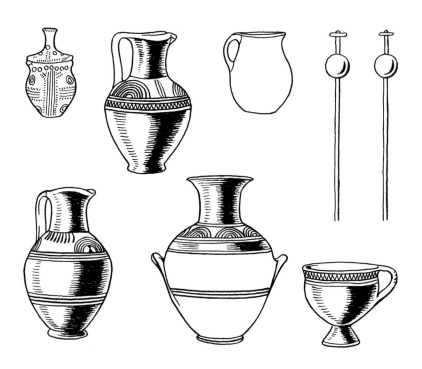

6. Protogeometric pottery from a grave (37) in the Kerameikos, Athens, with two bronze dress pins and an incised monochrome vase (top left). Late 10th c. BC. (Kerameikos)

model mainly because its products are more diverse and elaborate, and its pottery seems to have travelled well. A potter could learn quickly enough by observation, but we are in some danger of overvaluing the apparent Attic lead in the craft. There were other important areas displaying some common characteristics – in the Peloponnese (south Greece) and especially in central/northern Greece, apparently centring on Euboea where a major site at Lefkandi, between the better known towns of Chalcis and Eretria, has been discovered in relatively recent years.[2]

There seems to be little completely undecorated fine ware from these potteries, although there was plenty of plain cooking ware. However, there was in circulation a number of mainly small, plain vases with impressed decoration (top left on [6]). They have been thought to be of foreign inspiration (from the north) or to have served for special exotica, even drugs, though the evidence for much drug-taking in early Greece is too sparse to be convincing. These monochrome vases are a continuing but minor phenomenon in central and southern Greece down to the sixth century, and they are exceptional for being both fine and unpainted.[3]

At this point we need to be aware of the possible limitations of our evidence. Almost all the pottery that has survived from this period comes from graves, and we are invited to assume that what was put into them was representative of what was being used day by day. This is probably correct, although we cannot be sure whether there was a tendency to select the better, decorated vases for the grave, or to retain them for continued use. Some special practices can already be detected in Athens in the use of different shapes for male and female burials. But these probably still reflect domestic usage rather than cult: wine vases for men, water vases for women. The other major source, mainly in later periods, is from the deposits of votive offerings in sanctuaries, where we can expect a good mix of the humble and the grandiose, depending on the affluence of the donor and his desire for conspicuous display of wealth and piety; the very richest might not have given pots at all, and what they did give may not have survived. Among the votive pottery from Athens' Acropolis we may even detect the potters' own dedications of their work in later years, while a local shrine near Corinth's potters' quarter has yielded a whole series of painted clay plaques demonstrating devotion as well as many aspects of the potters' lives and work [173]. What goes into a grave is a more private matter, but also dictated by the need to satisfy the survivors' feeling of loss, and possibly some demonstration of status, which may have been better shown outside the grave or before burial, and provision for the passage to the land of the dead if not even the afterlife; all rather ill-defined but sanctified by slowly changing traditions. There is little here which is peculiar to Greece in the matter of placing pottery in graves.[+]

*The Geometric Style*

Given the nature of early Greece there was remarkable uniformity among the protogeometric vases, suggesting free passage of goods within Greece, although this is little evident in the finds. With the ninth century there was in Athens a significant increase in the range of patterns on the vases, gradually replacing the circles and half-circles, and leaving more of the vase in the pale clay ground rather than black, which had been preferred towards the end of the protogeometric. The 'geometric' patterns are sometimes quite complex and they introduce the typically Greek maeander, key-pattern, swastikas and the like, and many devices filled with hatching [7–9]. The inspiration could easily be wickerwork, which may even be influential on some shapes, such as the flat round 'wool-basket' boxes (pyxides; centre on [9]) and some dishes [281]. The patterns are also of the type readily executed in weaving, which is probably another source. They remain current throughout the geometric period, down to around 700 BC, with the expected regional variations. Through the period there is a

**7.** Attic geometric amphora from a grave (41) in the Kerameikos, Athens. Early 9th c. BC. H. 69.5cm. (Kerameikos)

**8.** Attic geometric pyxis, from Athens. Early 8th c. BC. H. 94cm. (Acropolis)

**9.** Attic geometric pottery from a grave (50) in the Kerameikos, Athens; including a pomegranate vase and a model horse carrying amphorae (top row, second from left and right), model cocks and a miniature basket (bottom row, left and right). After mid-8th c. BC. (Kerameikos)

**10.** Cypriot dish showing a loom. 8th c. BC. W. 26cm. (Bonn inv. 3107)

**11.** Detail of the tapestry pattern on an Attic geometric pitcher (full H. 77cm.). Mid-8th c. BC. (Athens 812)

gradual increase in the number of identified settlements in Greece, and indications of a steady rise in population.

The new patterns for pottery are also current in Cyprus, a source which we shall not otherwise dwell on, but it should be mentioned here, since there is growing evidence that the island had more Greek-speakers from around 1000 BC on than has been thought, and although their material culture was more Levantine than Greek there are obvious signs of continuing contact with Greece. A Cypriot eighth-century vase is decorated with a loom bearing a cloth patterned with many of the typical schemes seen on Greek and Cypriot vases of the period; a fair indication of probable origins for the patterns on pottery [10].[5] If weaving was women's work this might suggest that vase decoration too could have been in the hands of women. The potting seems normally to have been a man's job in our period in Greece, but in many early societies pot-making was women's work, largely because they were the prime users and it was an at-home task. Much of household or kitchen pottery was handmade, built in coils of clay, and required some strength, but well within the capability of women. The bands of pattern on [11] are strongly reminiscent of weaving.

In the eighth century human and animal figures are added to the decoration, mainly in friezes and panels. Figures had been exceptional before, except on some vases in Crete where there

**12.1,2.** Cretan protogeometric crater, from Knossos, with confronted sphinxes and a bird, and (detail) two lions tearing a warrior. See *EGVP* fig. 23 for whole scene. 10th c. BC. H. 31.4cm. (Heraklion)

**13.** Attic geometric grave-marking amphora by the Dipylon Painter, from Athens. The laying-out of a woman; two mourners appear to hold up the shroud. On the neck are friezes of grazing and reclining animals. Mid-8th c. BC. H. 1.55m. (Athens 804)

seems to have been less of a break with the Bronze Age past and a more direct awareness of eastern arts [*12*]. In the hands of an artist like the Athenian Dipylon Painter (scholars have to invent names like this for the anonymous) and his fellows the figures are heavily geometricized, yet able, through pose and gesture, to act out quite complicated scenes, though none of true story-telling content, rather than scene-setting [*13, 14*]. For the bigger vases preparation for burial is the prime subject, often with intriguing detail [*208*], beside some fighting scenes which might relate to

**14.** Attic geometric grave-marking crater, from Athens. The laying-out (*prothesis*) – the chequered shroud is cut away to show the man lying on his bier; mourners, hands to heads, at either side; notice the children – one on a lap at the foot of the bier, two on the bier; and courtyard animals. Honorific procession of chariots and warriors with 'Dipylon' shields below. Mid-8th c. BC. H. 1.22m. (New York 14.130.14)

the status of the deceased [*207*], and chariot processions, of mourners or intimating funeral games. The grander vases for female burials have funeral scenes and patterns only [*13*]. We shall look again in Chapter 6 at the way the geometric figures and scenes develop. Other vase shapes in Athens offered more variety than the protogeometric, though basically for the same purposes, with occasional essays in vessels shaped like animals (quadrupeds, ducks), and still for the most part known to us only from cemeteries. The smaller vases often have more varied figure scenes upon them [*15*] or early intimations of observation of eastern decorative schemes [*16*]. At the end of the period more detail, by drawing or added white, begins to make the figures more informative [*17, 18*] and even the generic scenes become more ambitious

**15.** Attic geometric kantharos. The main frieze has – a warrior and woman; a duel; two lions tearing a man (see [12]); a lyre-player with women carrying jugs. See *EGVP* fig. 65 for other side. Late 8th c. BC. H. 17cm. (Copenhagen NM 727)

**16.** Attic geometric cup, with a procession of bulls, which is a common motif on Syrian bronze bowls of the period and recurs often on this shape in Attica. Late 8th c. BC. (London market)

**17.** Detail of women mourning, from the neck of an Attic geometric amphora. About 700 BC. (New York 10.210.8)

**18.** Detail of warriors, from the neck of an Attic geometric amphora; the shields have white-painted devices. About 700 BC. (Copenhagen, Ny Carlsberg I.N. 3187)

**19.** Drawing of the shipwreck shown on the neck of an Attic geometric oinochoe. Late 8th c. BC. (Munich 8696)

**20.** Corinthian oinochoe, from Ischia, grave 1187. About 700 BC. (Ischia)

**21.** Argive geometric crater, from Argos. The devices below the horses recall yokes and wheels, and the mazy centrepiece, with the other patterns, water. See *EGVP* fig. 127 for other side and detail. Late 8th c. BC. H. 47.3cm. (Argos C201)

**22.** Panel on an Argive geometric crater. Dancers; a man in a high headdress tames a horse; fish, pebbles and a waterbird indicate the presence of a river (the zigzags). Late 8th c. BC. (Argos C240)

[*19*]. The most significant evidence for specialist production, however, lies in the very large (five feet high) grave-marking vases decorated with funeral scenes. The Attic potter has moved out of purely domestic production into something more truly monumental and for something serving more than the usual requirements of pottery – display.[6]

The geometric patterns and figures were adopted for vase decoration over much of the rest of Greece,[7] though there were places, such as Corinth, where pure pattern, sedulously executed, was usually deemed sufficient [*20*].[8] There are some large vases too, but they are storage pithoi, like big barrels, not like the craters and amphorae that marked rich Athenian graves, and they are differently decorated. This reminds us that we need not take Athens as the model for all Greek behaviour and taste in this craft. The political geography of Greece was taking shape, with many small states, never as large as the Mycenaean kingdoms, but often embracing several townships, with one in control. Athens' influence in Attica was probably the most extensive, but there was Argos and its Argolid which included the old cities of Mycenae and Tiryns, Corinth with wide influence in the north-east Peloponnese, the cities of the Euboean Straits. The pottery of each state was distinctive, with minimal variation if there were local potteries but with the 'state' style dominant. Broad similarities of pottery style in the townships of, for instance, Boeotia, or in the islands of the Cyclades, probably reflect more on geography than on any loose political confederations.

At Argos and in the towns of the Argolid we find large patterned pithoi and craters with broadly composed motifs and scenes of men and horses [*21*], not funerals, and wavy patterns that seem to suggest watery subjects; to Homer Argos was a land of horse-rearing, and 'thirsty'.[9] The elements of decoration follow

*24*

simple formulae, but in combination, as on [22], come close to making 'real' pictures. Cretan vases are almost all pattern; Boeotian have some oddly disorganized geometric figures [23]; the islands long favour high-necked forms [24]. It is probable that the majority of these larger pots were not grave-markers; indeed they might have been for domestic use before becoming coffins, often for children or for cremated remains, and their decoration seems not to be determined by their ultimate use.[10] Euboea remains an important centre for the craft, and it is in these years that Euboean states explore both western and eastern Mediterranean shores: the opening phases of the colonizing movement and of developing trade with non-Greek states. Politically and commercially Euboea is more important in this period than Athens, which seems busy but introspective. The Cesnola crater [25], found in Cyprus, is prime Euboean work, but even more important are the pendent-semicircle skyphoi [26] which retain a form of protogeometric decoration down to around 750 BC, and are markers for Euboean exploration in the east, the results of which we now address.[11]

**23.** Detail of a Boeotian geometric hydria, showing the laying-out of a woman, with mourners and warriors. See *EGVP* fig. 106. About 700 BC. (Louvre CA639)

**24.** Detail from a Theran geometric amphora, from Thera. See *EGVP* fig. 94, whole vase. Early 7th c. BC. (Copenhagen NM VIII.324)

**25.** Euboean geometric crater (the Cesnola crater), from Cyprus. The goats at a tree in the centre panel are an oriental motif. After mid-8th c. BC. H. 1.15m. (New York 1874.51.965)

26. Euboean sub-protogeometric cup, from Lefkandi. About 800 BC. H. 6.7cm. (Eretria, Lefk S59/2)

The achievements of Greek geometric art, presaged already in the protogeometric and best judged by us in the pottery, have a message for us of greater significance than just another chapter in the history of a craft. From this time on Greek art began to take a course quite different from that of the older cultures of the near east and Egypt, however much it was from time to time invigorated by contact with them, and never more so than in the period we are about to consider. This is, in a way, where classical Greek culture begins, and the same divergence from the record of neighbours can be traced in literature, where Hesiod, Homer and the early lyric and elegiac poets parted from the eastern traditions that they also had shared, and developed a new treatment of word and thought that was to lead to the achievements of fifth-century tragedians and philosophers as surely as the art of the day was to lead to the Parthenon.[12] There is much even in the pre-classical arts to mirror these new attitudes.

*The Orientalizing Styles*
Greek curiosity about the east, especially Syria and the approaches to the great empires of Mesopotamia, and some probable immigration of specialist craftsmen (metalworkers, not potters) from the east to Crete and central Greece, fuelled the so-called Orientalizing Revolution of the eighth and seventh centuries BC. Some time before the mid-eighth century the Greeks of the Euboean Straits had even settled a town at the mouth of the River Orontes (Al Mina), to facilitate trade – there could have been no

27. Protocorinthian aryballos.
See *EGVP* fig. 166 for other sides.
About 700 BC. H. 6.8cm.
(London 1969.12–15.1)

28. Protocorinthian cup (kotyle),
from Aegina. Early 7th c. BC.
H. 12cm. (Aegina)

29. Protocorinthian aryballos.
Early 7th c. BC. H. 6.6cm.
(Boston 95.511)

other reason – while Phoenicians from the coastal cities to the south were beginning voyages to Greece and beyond, and spreading knowledge of their more egyptianizing arts which were never much to Greek taste.[13] The new interest made little enough difference to pottery production at home. A very few shapes were copied, notably the eastern bronze, round-bottomed cauldrons with swing handles, and, in Crete and Rhodes, eastern and Cypriot oil flasks [*283*]. Metalwork was more influential and this, at one remove, affects pottery shapes and decoration.

Pottery is so closely determined by daily needs that the ways of life of different peoples may often make the pottery of one unacceptable to another, except sometimes for display or novelty value. The latter was important in later years, mainly to the west in the Mediterranean world, and it may be that even pottery, if it looked exotic enough, could form part of that gift-exchange which expressed status and became an informal process of trade. In the east there was no real demand for Greek pottery rather than other Greek goods or services which are now less easily identified: slaves and mercenaries. For one thing, much of the pottery served Greek drinking habits, and these involved use of largish cups with handles and flat bases [*26*], where the easterners long before, and long since, preferred handleless cups which were generally smaller. So the Greek eighth-century clay cups that are found anywhere in numbers in the east were for the use of Greeks, and not a serious trade item, although isolated examples travelled far, to Assyria and Palestine, in the hands of Greeks or others.[14]

30.1,2,3.
Protocorinthian olpe, the 'Chigi vase', from Veii (Etruria). The black bands on lip and body carry florals and animals in white and red (mostly gone). The top frieze is a hoplite battle, with the ranks closing, and a boy piper. The centre frieze has a cavalcade, two-bodied sphinx, lion hunt and Judgement of Paris (names are inscribed: Alexandros (=Paris), just the tip of Hermes' caduceus wand, Hera (name gone), Athena, Aphrodite (the winner)). These are the only figures that might have puzzled the Etruscan buyer. The frieze below has a hare hunt. Some details in *EGVP* fig. 178. Mid-7th c. BC. H. 26.2cm. (Rome, Villa Giulia 22679)

In decoration of pottery there were considerable changes as a result of observation of eastern decorative forms. These were to be observed not on eastern pottery but on bronzes and ivories, many of which were decorated by incision or in low relief with figures far more detailed than the black Greek geometric silhouettes. Moreover, floral and animal patterns (mainly friezes) had long been a major element of eastern design, and these gradually began to displace the geometry of most Greek pattern [27–29]. One of the eventual results was that greater detailing allowed identification of figures as heroes or gods, could even better distinguish the sexes, by closer definition of attributes and dress. Sometimes inscriptions were added – the alphabet had been learned from the east in the early eighth century. Eastern schemes of combat could be re-identified as Greek myth. Gradually, pottery became a field for scenes that were more than statements of cult or husbandry,

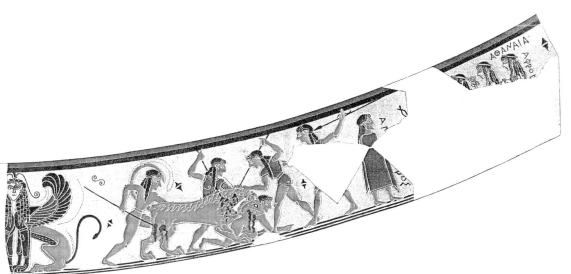

and offered both generic and specific myth and divine subjects. It became for the Greeks, in other words, a medium for communication of narrative, as well as a visual commentary on their life and beliefs. Since their myth-history was central to their attitudes to life and worship, their pottery becomes for us a source of evidence often more detailed than any surviving texts, and certainly relating far more closely to the experience of the ordinary people.

The eastern floral patterns never quite broke the Greek artist's dedication to geometry, but they did inspire some original variations on eastern themes, in interlaces of lotus and palmette which acquire a geometry of their own, and later developed into wholly Greek floral creations which in time even found their way east again to their sources, transmuted. On seventh-century Greek pottery these changes manifested themselves in different ways in different places. We are challenged to discover why this was so. To a minor degree it may have been a matter of the influence of different eastern sources, but this applies mainly in the East Greek world and Crete; everywhere else Corinth seems to have set the pace for these new orientalizing patterns, and to a lesser extent at first, Athens.[15]

In Corinth the most elaborate vases are the smallest, flasks for perfumed oil (aryballoi), and these attracted the new decoration first [27], followed shortly in the decoration of the typically Corinthian cup shape – the kotyle [28]. As a result Corinthian orientalizing ('Protocorinthian') tends to be miniaturizing and is the first to introduce the finely incised figures — the 'black figure' technique which was to dominate most pottery decoration eventually [29].[16] But it was also more deeply committed to the eastern friezes of animals, and a monotonous animal-frieze style soon set in. The Chigi vase of the mid-seventh century is in friezes, some of animals, even with small hunting scenes painted in red and white on the broad black dividing bands [30].[17] In the main friezes the use of red and brown washes introduces an unfamiliar element of polychromy to our subject; an effect achieved from about this time also on larger works in fired clay for the decoration of buildings, all Corinthian-inspired. The Chigi vase also demonstrates a far finer conception of vase decoration. One frieze deploys several different scenes, including narrative, with no physical divisions between them [30.3]; another is wholly occupied by two battle lines approaching each other (at the top). This is a fairly large vase compared with the aryballoi, though the individual friezes are shallow – the tallest about 4cm. The same style is seen even more delicately on the tiny oil vases, some of which are enhanced with moulded

**31.** Protocorinthian aryballos, the 'Macmillan aryballos', by the same painter as [*30*], from Thebes. Moulded lion-head spout. The main frieze is a hoplite rank breaking up in battle; below it, riders, and a hare hunt. Drawn out in *EGVP* fig. 176. Mid-7th c. BC. H. 6.8cm. (London 1889.4–18.1)

**32.** Protocorinthian olpe. After mid-7th c. BC. H. 34cm. (Munich 8764)

animal or human heads at their tops. This is almost the potter/painter as jeweller [*31*]. The majority of the production, however, is dedicated to animals [*32*].

The new technique and decoration were soon influential, but other pot-painters, especially in Athens and the Cyclades islands, saved their most elaborate work for larger vases. So we have already a divergence of interests among Greek potters and painters, with Athens retaining something of the monumentality of its geometric, Corinth the delicacy and precision of its earlier products. In the islands the geometric styles died hard, but before the mid-seventh century Athens and the Cycladic island schools were producing large vases, known to us principally from cemeteries, decorated with big-figure subjects. These were usually drawn in outline, not incised silhouette as in Corinth, and sometimes with some modest colour contrast through use of diluted or pigmented clay slips. The subjects are divine and mythological, the florals more unruly than the neat Corinthian interlaces.

Athenian potters had moved warily into the new fashion, at first combining geometry with a little more linear detail and even incision [*33*]. The most characteristic of the 'Protoattic' orientalizing vases of Athens are of the mid-seventh century and earlier, in the so-called Black and White style, with big mythological subjects [*34*].[18] This was not, of course, the only style for pottery decoration and there was specialization for grave goods, it seems, in smaller shapes [*35*].[19] Several of the Cyclades islands seem each

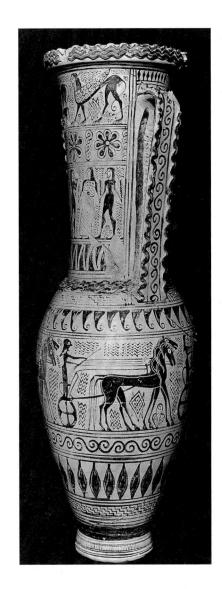

**33.** Early Protoattic amphora. Relief 'snakes' at lip, shoulder and handles, for a funeral vase. A little black figure incision on the manes. Another view, *EGVP* fig. 189. Early 7th c. BC. H. 80cm. (Paris, Louvre CA2985)

**34.1,2.** Protoattic 'Black and White' amphora, from Eleusis, where it served as a child's coffin. On the neck Odysseus and two companions blind the giant Polyphemos, who clutches the inebriating cup. The frieze on the body has the decapitated gorgon, her two sisters pursuing Perseus, who has her head (the missing part), with Athena protecting him. Pre-mid-7th c. BC. H. 1.42m. (Eleusis)

**35.** Group of Protoattic vases, the contents of an offering ditch beside a burial in Athens. Apart from the kotyle (second left) the shapes are somewhat bizarre, funeral furniture. Mid-7th c. BC. (Kerameikos)

to have had their own style [36, 37], sometimes very short-lived, as if the creation of a single potter or his family. It is not easy to place them and most are known from examples which had been taken to the central, sacred island of Delos, either for dedication there, or as grave goods, which were all dug up in the sixth century BC and conveniently redeposited together in a pit on the nearby island Rheneia. The latest of the styles, running into the sixth century, is from Paros: long called 'Melian' for the prolific finds on the island of Melos — a reflection on the many mistakes of attribution in the past, not all of which may yet have been uncovered [36].[20] Crete has several different workshops; it is a large island. At Knossos the favourite grave vase was big and ovoid. As early as the late ninth century there had been a brief experiment with orientalizing patterns (the 'Protogeometric B' style) while all around was geometric. And from the early seventh century there is a small group of polychrome vases with flowers and birds in reds, blues and blacks on a white slip [38]. Crete seems to have been more exposed than most of Greece to the direct effect of immigrant craftsmen, from Syria and Cyprus, and its orientalizing patterns are less stereotyped than those of the mainland [39].[21]

The East Greek world, Ionia and its islands, with Dorian Rhodes in the Dodecanese, took yet another line.[22] The geometric style lingered to the mid-century, by which time a different animal-frieze decoration was being adopted. This is known as the 'Wild Goat Style', defined by its commonest actor shown in friezes walking or grazing, but with other orientalizing animals and monsters, often set heraldically either side of elaborate floral compositions of volutes and palmettes. The favourite shape for the best

**36.** Parian ('Melian') amphora, from Melos. A fight over armour watched by women, on the neck. On the body Apollo and two women (Muses?) in a chariot drawn by winged horses, greeted by his archer sister Artemis, with a stag. Detail in *EGVP* fig. 250. After mid-7th c. BC. H. 97cm. (Athens 3961)

**37.** Cycladic jug (Parian?) with a griffin-head as neck, from Aegina. Mid-7th c. BC. H. 41.5cm. (London A547)

**38.** Drawing of a Cretan polychrome grave pithos from Knossos. The colours are red, blue and black on white. Early 7th c. BC. H. 53cm. (Heraklion Fortetsa 1383)

**39.** Pattern from a Cretan flask from Knossos. Pre-mid-7th c. BC. (Heraklion)

**40.** Milesian Wild Goat oinochoe, the 'Marseilles' or 'Levy oinochoe'. Late 7th c. BC. H. 39.5cm. (Paris, Louvre CA350)

decoration here is the broad jug (oinochoe, 'wine-pourer') [*40*], while the drinking cups (bird bowls) clung to geometric pattern [*41*] for over a century. The decorative style of both cups and jugs seems to represent a common style in the eastern Aegean, and it is proving none too easy to distinguish sources though new finds and location by clay analysis are now resolving many doubts. For long most of the Wild Goat vases were called Rhodian because Rhodes had proved the first prolific source in excavation [*42*]. Exceptions to the rule of animal decoration are very few but can be

**41.** North Ionian 'bird bowl'. Late 7th c. BC. W. 14cm. (Oxford 1928.313)

**42.** Dish from Camirus (Rhodes). About 600 BC. W. 32cm. (Paris, Louvre A352)

**43.** Plate from Camirus (Rhodes). Menelaos fighting Hector over the body of Euphorbos. Outline style with much colour but the bird-blazon is black figure. About 600 BC. W. 38.5cm. (London 1860.4–4.1)

conspicuous [43]. Samos and Miletus have proved major centres of production, while Chios had its own variants with a distinguished following in the sixth century.

In these areas the traditional repertoire of pottery shapes was still being made, occasionally admitting the finer decoration for the more favoured shapes, big or small. But by now we have to look farther afield also. Not to Cyprus, which, however Greek it may have been, remained wedded to pottery styles which were partly derived from the geometric shared with Greece, partly from other, eastern sources, including some exotic abstractions of animal forms.[23] From around the mid-eighth century the Greeks were

**44.** Western Greek crater, signed by Aristonothos, from Caere. A warship (left) fights a merchant ship (with marines on board). Other side with the blinding of Polyphemos, *EGVP* fig. 282. Mid-7th c. BC. H. 36cm. (Rome, Conservatori)

founding colonies in South Italy and Sicily, in an important enterprise to settle and trade. These were individual ventures, not corporate. The colonists took their pottery with them and stimulated a demand for more of the same from their mother cities, or from carriers of the few wares very widely popular with Greeks (mainly Corinthian), but many also started to make their own decorated vases.[24] These copy homeland styles, but many soon deviate and produce distinguished versions, though never too far from whatever was current and fashionable in the homeland [*44*].[25] They even have some influence locally, as in Etruria. And there are other effects far from home, where the western waters were being explored by Phoenicians at the same time and beside the Greeks. Thus, there are eastern shapes of dish made on Ischia, in the Bay of Naples, where there was the first Greek western settlement; some are plain, as for easterners, but some are decorated as Greek geometric and must have served the Greeks. And in western Phoenician trading posts, in south Spain, west Sicily and at Carthage, Greek cups and their decoration are locally produced, many perhaps for such Greek residents as there might have been since they would not have suited most easterners.[26]

The potter's role had clearly much changed from being a producer of utilitarian wares, for storage or cooking, to purveyor of pictorial objects which might win foreign markets and entertain, even instruct, buyers at home or abroad. Most wares never travelled beyond their home towns, except with the occasional emigrant or visitor. Corinth was among the first to have her pottery distributed far from the expected Corinthian areas of interest or settlement, but this reflects as much or more on the Corinthians' maritime enterprise in other matters as on the quality of their pottery. The contents may have been part of the attraction – perfumed oil – but it was not only the flasks that travelled. Larger or open shapes, like jugs and cups, also travelled for use but not as containers. Fine-walled cups were not the sort of cargo to treat carelessly, and the difficulties of packing and transport reflect on the value to the trade. Pottery was indeed becoming a real trade item, and so of interest to any merchant and not simply a source of subsistence for the potter and his family. This subject will be looked at more closely in a later chapter, but it affects our view of the work being produced and of the roles of potter and painter. The signatures of the craftsmen begin to appear on the pots as early as the inscriptions naming figures in the scenes, and from different motives, of which pride is more probable than advertising.

### Relief and Plain Pottery

There are other classes of pottery to be considered before continuing the narrative, some of them mainly a product of this period only. First are large pithoi, thick-walled and decorated in relief. If they were also painted, it was done after firing and the paint has generally not survived. The decoration was executed by impressing patterns, or moulding figures which were then applied to the surface. Some have truly modelled and carved figures upon them. Crete is a major source from the eighth to sixth centuries [45],[27] but the most imaginative have been found on the island of Tenos, elsewhere in the Cyclades [46], and in Boeotia [47]; the link is not

**45.** Relief vase from Crete. A winged goddess between sphinxes; and panels with horsemen, all from the same mould. Mid-7th c. BC. H. 1.25m. (Jerusalem, Israel Museum)

**46.1,2.** Relief vase, from Mykonos. The neck has the Trojan Horse; the body, panels with scenes of slaughter at the Sack of Troy (as the detail). Early 7th c. BC. H. 1.34m. (Mykonos 2240)

**47.** Detail from the neck of a relief vase, from Boeotia. Perseus, with his magic cap and bag slung from his arm, looks away from the petrifying Medusa as he decapitates her. She has a horse-body – she mated with Poseidon as a horse. Mid-7th c. BC. (Paris, Louvre CA795)

**48.** Drawing of a relief vase from near the sanctuary of Artemis Orthia at Sparta. Mid-6th c. BC. H.pres. about 46cm. (Sparta)

**49.** Fragment of a relief vase, from Chios. A merman swims holding an octopus. Late 6th c. BC. H. 20cm. (Chios 1431)

clear but might be a migrant potter. They are decorated with elaborate figure scenes of cult and myth which seem outside the usual repertory of the painted vases of their day.[28] In the sixth century some more ambitious vases from Sparta seem to be close copies of metal vases to judge from details of their shape [*48*], although metal vases of any size did not attract all-over figure decoration, and this can often be seen to be the potter's additive.[29] There are stray examples of the genre all over Greece (as [*49*]).[30] All seem to represent specialist production, though usually only for a local market, and not necessarily from the usual potter establishments. We need to remember that pots were not the only fired clay objects of antiquity. Large clay roof tiles, architectural members (metopes), and, with the sixth century, architectural decoration for upperworks and roofs, were in demand, and with the latter we intrude also on the work of the coroplast making clay figures, some small, some up to life size.[31] These too are unlikely to have formed part of the ordinary potter's business, though many are seen to be painted by the regular pot-painter, and kilns and workshops were probably shared. For special commissions, as for a temple, new kilns were probably constructed at the building sites.

Storage and carriage vases, for liquid (oil or wine) or solids, become important by the end of the geometric period, and a class of nearly spherical vases with narrow mouths made in Athens and Euboea are important indicators of early trade in their contents, usually, it seems, oil [50].[32] The wine and oil trade especially became a major source of profit in Greek lands, and by the sixth century there are already distinctive local shapes being created for their carriage [51]. These are generally ovoid, but unlike the long-established eastern form (which is normally neckless and with smaller loop handles), becoming more conical with time, needing therefore to be supported on a base, when not stacked on their sides for transport. They soon become the commonest finds from domestic sites and shipwrecks, right through the Roman period. Many local varieties from the fourth century on have stamps on their handles, indicating source or date. The pots are of high quality for the job they had to do, and in Egypt some were kept to serve for water storage, and even imported empty. Not all parts of the ancient world were blessed with such good clay or potting skills as the Greeks enjoyed.[33] Only the earliest of these amphorae have some decoration, and of the simplest. These too are likely to have been from specialist potteries.

**50.** Attic oil amphora, from Marmari (Cyprus). H. about 65 cm. (Nicosia 1961/viii-18/2)

**51.** Series of 6th- to 5th-century BC wine amphorae, made in Chios, from Athens. (Athens, Agora)

*Black Figure in Corinth and Athens*

We return to the expiring orientalizing styles in pottery decoration of the later seventh century, where the interests in myth narrative and the demands of an animal-frieze style continued to compete. In other respects Greece of the years since the protogeometric period had become steadily more populous, and signs of reduced population which have been suspected in some places, such as seventh-century Athens, may simply be a misreading of the incomplete evidence. At least one of the reasons for brisk colonizing on distant shores, in the west and later round the Black Sea, must have been a surplus and often ambitious population. The relationship of a city with its countryside (*chora*) and often with other dependent towns and villages had become better defined, as well as its independence from its neighbours despite their shared religious and material culture. The Greek *polis*, that overworked term for the Greek city-state beloved of taxonomic historians and some archaeologists, had arrived, though variety was as evident as conformity in every walk of life and politics. But there could hardly be much variety in such a small country, even though the 'country' of Greece was barely perceptible until a common threat enforced some recognition of what was and was not Greek, and criteria other than the shared language and religion emerged. The *polis* is, as much as anything, defined by what it is not: totally unlike most eastern cities, some of which may have managed their own economy and religion but were politically dependent on the current superpower (Assyria, Babylonia, Egypt, Persia) and paying tribute in goods or service to sometimes alien states and gods. In Greece it was never a matter of tribute, just local taxes. Only the Phoenician cities seem comparable, or those on the less well policed fringes of the eastern empires. The independence of the Greek cities explains much about their political development as well as about the development of their arts, undisturbed by considerations of imperial styles and propaganda, and evolving in an atmosphere where individual taste and invention could still count for something.

While these social and political changes left the economy of the smaller townships unchanged, together with whatever local provision there may have been for pottery needs, the potters in larger towns, and especially those with trade or colonial connections, found themselves in a commercially interesting situation. Corinth remained a big exporter of pottery, not only to colonial areas but also within Greece, even to Athens. It seems that the Athenians may have been prompted by this success to emulate

**52.** Decoration of an amphora by the Nessos Painter. About 600 BC. H. of frieze 35cm. (Berlin 1961.7)

Corinth, but the first intimation of this is the painters' acceptance of the Corinthian black figure technique, and with it the animal-frieze style of decoration. Athenians, however, retained an interest in decorating large vases – too large perhaps for the fine incising technique of black figure to appear to its best effect, so there was a tendency to double lines in the drawing for emphasis [*52*].[34] There was little or no market for big decorated vases, yet some began to get around the Greek world by about 600 BC, despite the fact that Athens had no colonies of her own. Presumably quality told, with customers and so with carriers.

The Corinthians' vases were long wedded to the animal-frieze style for the bulk of the production, but there was an increasing use of mythological subjects to decorate major areas.[35] The backs of vases and secondary friezes might be left to the animals, just as in the seventh century the bigger vases in the rest of Greece had their backs left plain or covered with squiggles. The animal-frieze vases are often competent and colourful [*53*], but easily degenerate into weary processions of elongated bodies, economizing in the

**53.** Corinthian oinochoe. Early 6th c. BC. (Charterhouse School)

**54.** Corinthian crater. Heracles rescues Hesione from a sea monster (*ketos*). The monster head seems inspired by a fossil monster head such as are found in Aegean cliffs. Pre-mid-6th c. BC. (Boston 63.420)

**55.** Corinthian amphora. Heroic battles; no identified occasion, as often on Corinthian vases, though all figures are named. Before mid-6th c. BC. H. 35cm (Copenhagen NM 13531)

56. Corinthian cup. Suicide of Ajax, impaled on his sword (contrast [82,267,268]). Watching are Diomedes, Odysseus, Phoinix, Nestor, Agamemnon, Teukros and (the Lesser) Ajax. Early 6th c. BC. W. 20.3cm. (Basel BS1404)

time taken to draw heads.[36] The figure scenes include a good range of subjects with no very distinct pattern of choice emerging [54, 204, 233].[37] Several, such as the chariot scenes, and even on the larger and more elegant craters, seem generic [55][38] rather than depicting specific mythical or human occasions. All shapes are decorated, the larger ones used at the drinking party being favoured for export, with some large cups, where myth often displaces the animals [56].[39] There is still a brisk production of oil-filled aryballoi and alabastra for female and male (athletic) cosmetics. Most of these small vases are very plainly decorated, and

57. Corinthian aryballos. Heracles slays the Hydra, with the help of Iolaos; Athena, behind, holds a flask (for the Hydra's poison-blood with which Heracles will tip his arrows; it is too small for refreshment!). About 600 BC. (Basel BS425)

are met by the hundred (some Boeotian graves contained dozens each), but there are exceptions with elaborate figure decoration, generally larger and often flat-bottomed [57, 294].[40]

In the first half of the sixth century it would be easy, too easy, to tell the story of the craft in Greece in terms of a trade war between Corinth and Athens, each vying to attract the prime attention of carriers and customers. This may be to adopt too sophisticated an approach to the role of pottery as a trade item and to its appeal, but it was obviously a crucial factor for the potters themselves. Most obvious is the way Athenian potter/painters take more note of Corinth, copying some shapes (cups and craters) together with their decoration, and even observing to some degree their colour schemes. Corinth too begins to adopt a reddish background to the finer figure scenes and some think that this is in imitation of Attic, though it seems just as likely to be an aesthetic choice, giving a better colour range beside the usual black, deeper red and white on the figures, and more necessary when the clay itself was almost white, unlike the Attic pink/red. Meanwhile, in Athens, the more colourful schemes of Corinth were adopted and copied, notably for a ware which was deliberately aimed at an export market, in Etruria. These are the so-called Tyrrhenian amphorae which combine a popular Attic shape of neck amphora with a Corinthian scheme, well liked in Etruria, of gaudy myth and animal friezes [58, 59, 263].[41] There is no little speculation about some activity by Corinthian potters in Athens, possibly encouraged by the reforms of the lawgiver Solon, who was said to have promoted the immigration of craftsmen. When names on vases become more plentiful we shall see that the Athenian potters' quarter was probably well staffed by immigrant Greeks, metics (*metoikoi*) and even slaves, who lived beside the citizens but without full rights. We can see from the evidence of other arts too that the archaic craftsman could be vagabond.

Strangely, figure decoration on Corinthian vases stops around the mid-sixth century. It is very hard to see this as a result of any hypothetical trade war, since the quality of production was at a high and export remained brisk long afterwards. There was no major epidemic in the potters' quarter, unless it was confined to painters, since pots go on being made in quantity, and exported, but they are plain and very simply decorated, without figures. Certainly, more Greeks were making their own decorated vases, and in a broadly corinthianizing style, but not enough to freeze out the imports. I cannot credit a change of heart or manner of Corinthian life to account for the demise of the figure-decorated

58. Attic Tyrrhenian amphora, by the Timiades Painter, from Vulci. Heracles attacks the Amazon Andromache. Pre-mid-6th c. BC. H. 39.4cm. (Boston 98.916)

59. Attic Tyrrhenian amphora (detail), by the Kyllenios Painter, from Caere. The birth of Athena, emerging from the head of Zeus, who is attended by the goddesses of childbirth, the Eileithyiai. At the left: Dionysos, Hephaistos with his wood axe and a crippled foot, and Hermes announces 'I am Hermes of Kyllene'. Pre-mid-6th c. BC. (Berlin 1704)

vases. In the next generation the city was important in the development of panel painting, to judge from references in later authors, but all the pot-painters could not have suddenly defected to a senior craft, while Athenian vases are increasingly imported.[42] Clay is still painted with figure scenes, as on miniature clay altars [60],[43] and there was a continuing demand for Corinthian terracotta revetments for buildings, but the latter called for other and minor painting skills. Possibly a combination of the causes mentioned, and of others we cannot even guess, was the reason, but if anyone was to profit from the change, it was the Athenian potter.

Most Athenian vases down to around 570 BC bear the stamp of Corinth to varying degrees, copying shapes and decoration but

60. Corinthian miniature clay altar, from Skione (north Greece). A satyr. Late 6th c. BC. H. 11.5cm. (Harvard 60.491)

61. Attic standed dinos by Sophilos. The main scene is of the Wedding of Peleus and Thetis (as on [62,64]), with divine guests. About 575 BC. H. 71cm. (London 1971.11–1.1)

62. Attic crater, by Kleitias and Ergotimos, from Chiusi. The friezes show: hunt of the Calydonian Boar; chariot race at the Games for Patroklos' funeral; divine guests arrive for the Wedding of Peleus and Thetis (as on [61]); Achilles pursues Troilos and Polyxena outside the walls of Troy (at right); on the foot, pygmies fight cranes. See [63, 64, 202]. About 575 BC. H. 66cm. (Florence 4209)

very seldom to the point at which there can be doubt about where they were made. There is a growing interest in myth scenes, besides the banal animal friezes, in work by the painter Sophilos [61][44], and, leading the way in his more ambitious work, by the KX Painter, one of the painters of cups with komast (dancer) figures. Then a potter-and-painter partnership, Kleitias and Ergotimos, started making big craters decorated with several friezes of myth scenes, front and back, and minimal animal display. Fortunately one of their works has survived complete – the François Vase [62–64, 202], named for its finder, and found in Etruria.[45] There were other such which we know only from fragments, some of the finest vases being from the Acropolis at Athens where, no doubt, the very best were to be seen displayed as dedications; but one such crater reached Egypt.[46] The François Vase has

63. Drawing of detail from [62]. Melanion and the huntress Atalanta, Peleus and Meleager, hunt the Calydonian boar; even the dogs are named.

64. Drawing of detail from [62]. Peleus, the groom, at the right, before an altar over which is the potter's signature; then, Chiron the centaur, who will educate Peleus' son Achilles, and who brings game for the feast; Iris with her caduceus wand as messenger of the gods; Demeter, Chariklo (Chiron's wife) and Hestia; an alert Dionysos shouldering a wine jar (decorated like the SOS amphorae [50]).

six friezes of figures covering the whole vase, front and back, and pairs of panel scenes repeated on the handles. There are no less than 270 figures on it in ten myth scenes, and 121 inscriptions. It offers the fullest statement of some of the subjects known from other vases, and some very original treatment of others. The clay vase has come into its own as a field for really ambitious narrative, but attempts to detect a pattern in the choice of so many subjects for the François Vase have proved inconclusive.

The way now lay open for the production of vases devoted wholly to figure scenes, though the animals are not quite exorcized for another fifty years or so, even if relegated to subsidiary areas or trivial pots. Not all the painters were Kleitiases, though some, such as Nearchos, are as good, and at all scales, from the near-monumental votive cup from the Acropolis [65] to the

miniaturist obscenity on a Corinthian shape [66].[47] As an antidote I show an example by the Polos Painter, who produced many smallish vases with animals and sphinxes, in a summary though decorative style, which travelled far and in numbers in the Greek world [67]. By now over two hundred of his vases have been identified, against barely a score by Kleitias, and these mainly in isolated fragments.

Now too the export of Athenian vases begins on a rapidly growing scale: to Greek colonial areas, outside them to neighbouring Etruria, and to other parts of Greece. The volume is impressive and what it implies will be considered in more detail later in this book. The quality is sometimes extremely high. There is, however, little obvious regard for any special interests of the market. Some Etruscan shapes are copied and the products aimed at Etruria, notably by the potter Nikosthenes [187], a continuation of the enterprise shown by the makers of the Tyrrhenian amphorae. But there are no concessions or specialities that we can distinguish in the scenes chosen, and it is the potter who observes sometimes, and copies, not the painter. Though potter and painter must often have been one, we are now in a period when specialization begins to set in. We must, however, judge that the home market was still the one which dictated, or was conditioned to approve, the product.

There is a full range of shapes now, many catering for the symposion (cups and craters) and serving of liquids, many water jars (hydriai), several for the handling of oil (pelikai), while Athens begins to compete with Corinth and east Greece in producing the containers for perfumed oil, developing its own distinctive shape (lekythoi) with larger bodies than their rivals, but not necessarily a better product within [68, 69].[48] The cup shapes particularly have

**68.1,2.** Attic lekythos by the Amasis Painter. A wedding procession. The couple in a cart, with the best man, led by the bride's mother with torches to the new home, where the groom's mother, with torches, awaits them. After mid-6th c. BC. H. 17.1cm. (New York 56.11.1)

**69.** Attic lekythos by the Amasis Painter, from Vari. This seems a sequel to [68]. On the shoulder a bride receives guests; on the body, work at the household loom. After mid-6th c. BC. H. 17.2cm. (New York 31.11.10)

**70.** Attic 'Siana cup' by the Heidelberg Painter, from Camirus. Bellerophon on Pegasos confronts the Chimaera (lion with goat's head on back, like a wing, and a snake tail), with anonymous onlookers. About 575 BC. H. 14cm. (Paris, Louvre A478)

**71.** Attic lip cup by the Tleson Painter. The potter's signature, as son of the painter Nearchos [65,66], between the handles. Mid-6th c. BC. H. 16.1cm. (New York, Callimanopoulos Collection; once Castle Ashby)

**72.** Attic band cup by the Tleson Painter, from Taranto. Cock fight. Mid-6th c. BC. H. 14cm. (Munich SL462)

become more interesting. Early in the century they looked rather as the Corinthian, and soon also borrowed their decoration of komast dancers. Then a deeper East Greek shape ('Siana' cups, from a site on Rhodes) was adopted, with miniaturist friezes except where they are allowed awkwardly to overlap the lip [70]. Soon the cups grow more elegant with broad shallow bowls and high feet, attracting fine miniaturist work (the Little Masters)[71, 72]. These seem to be copies of eastern open bowls, but provided with the necessary Greek handles and feet [270].[49] There are a few special shapes also, such as vases for burials, often with funeral scenes upon them (loutrophoroi). These are strictly for local use.

One special shape and class deserves separate treatment. From before the mid-sixth century on, vases were made to contain the prize oil for successful athletes in the Panathenaic Games [73]. They were appropriately decorated with a striking Athena on one side, flanked by cocks on columns (perhaps a reference to their combative nature) and an event from the Games (even musical) on the other. They begin with the reorganization of the Games in the second quarter of the sixth century, and are labelled as prize vases. They go on, in the same traditional black figure technique, into Hellenistic times [74–76].[50] In the fourth century they bear the date (by magistrate's name) of when the oil was collected; the Athena starts to face right, not left, and her dress is stylized in an exaggerated archaizing manner. These are from the usual potteries for decorated vases, but were bespoke by the state and must have proved profitable commissions for potters. In the later sixth to fourth centuries most of their painters can be recognized as leaders in their craft, and their work on other shapes can be detected. Half the vases with known proveniences have been found in Attica, but they also travelled, not necessarily with the victors since the vases themselves and certainly their contents (prime oil) were valuable. This provokes questions of the possibility of a secondhand market for decorated pottery, which we shall pursue in Chapter 4.

Corinthian black figure could produce masterpieces such as the seventh-century Chigi vase and many fine later craters. These are in a different mode from the best of the Athenian, starting with Kleitias and going on to the beginning of the fifth century. Attic black figure is technically excellent: the potting and shape are carefully planned and executed, the details pared to almost mathematical precision, and the paint is fired to an excellent black gloss. The panel comes to mean more than the frieze for figure compositions.

**73.** Panathenaic amphora, the 'Burgon amphora', from Athens, one of the earliest of the series. Inscribed: 'I am one of the prizes from Athens'. The other side has a two-horse chariot racing: *EGVP* fig. 296. Pre-mid-6th c. BC. H. 61.3cm. (London B130)

**74.** Panathenaic amphora from the workshop of the Kleophrades Painter. On the other side a four-horse chariot racing. Early 5th c. BC. H. 65cm. (Malibu 77.AE.9)

**75.** Panathenaic amphora by the Berlin Painter, from Vulci. The back, with runners approaching the turning post. Early 5th c. BC. (New York, Callimanopoulos; once Castle Ashby)

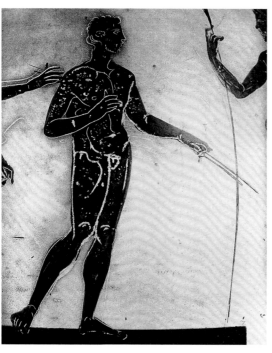

**76.1,2,3.** Panathenaic amphora, of the Kuban Group, from Taucheira (Tocra, Cyrenaica). The shield device is of the statue group of the Tyrannicides in Athens (*GSCP* figs. 3–9). The athlete and trainer from the reverse show how the black figure technique adapts to the more realistic drawing of the day. Late 5th c. BC. H. 57cm. (London B605)

**77.** Attic column crater by Lydos. Hephaistos returning to Olympus in the company of satyrs and maenads, handling snakes, grapes and wineskins. Mid-6th c. BC. H. 56.5cm. (New York 31.11.11)

The figure decoration ranges from the miniaturist to the monumental, from the tiny figures on the new, long-stemmed Little Master cups, to panel amphorae with figures often up to 25cm high. Some names deserve mention. A painter who signs himself *ho Lydos*, the Lydian, must have come from the East Greek area but was trained and worked in the Athenian tradition, sometimes close to Kleitian standards [77], sometimes still practising the looser animal style.[51] Amasis may have come from much the same area, well in touch with Egypt (whence his name was derived, for whatever reason), and makes his own contribution to the developing Athenian tradition with finesse and what we judge to be no little humour [68, 69, 78, 79].[52] Exekias is made of sterner stuff, and seems to represent archaic art in vase painting coming of age, and aspiring to more than mere decoration and narrative [80–82, 198, 203, 309].[53] He is innovative in his subject matter and, in some features of figure drawing, able to impart a degree of pathos into

**78.** Attic 'eye cup' by the Amasis Painter. An 'eye-siren'. After mid-6th c. BC. (Boston 10.651)

**79.** Attic amphora by the Amasis Painter. Dionysos with men and women (*not* satyrs and maenads). The women's flesh is outlined, not painted white. After mid-6th c. BC. H. 44cm. (Basel KA420)

**80.** Attic amphora by Exekias, from Vulci. Tyndareos and Leda greet their sons, the Dioskouroi, Kastor and Polydeukes and the horse Kylaros. After mid-6th c. BC. H. 61cm. (Vatican 344)

scenes, the most obvious being his choice of the moment of Ajax preparing his suicide rather than the bloody impalement (as [56]), and introducing a touch of emotion in the way he draws the hero's features, even if by no more than a furrowed brow [82].

These are artists working in a period of tyranny in Athens, a regime not 'tyrannical' especially in our sense, but one in which affairs were arranged by a single forceful politician (Peisistratos) and his family. It is a period of maximum activity in trade, including pots, and in public works, temples and fountain houses, activity which seems characteristic of other archaic 'tyrant' cities. The new Athens reflects on her new status in new treatment of old myth

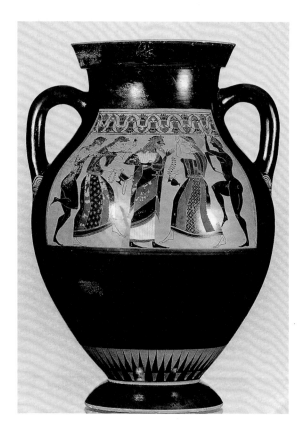

81. The other side of [80]. Achilles and Ajax dice; Achilles throws four, Ajax two.

82. Detail of an Attic amphora by Exekias. Ajax plants his sword in the ground, contemplating suicide. After mid-6th c. BC. (Boulogne 558)

and in the invention of new stories, a process demonstrated also in art, and best seized on the vases, as we shall see in Chapter 6.

Peisistratan family rule ended in 510 BC to be replaced by a measure of democracy which was to develop into its full classical form in little over fifty years. This occasioned some shift of subject emphasis for the vase painters but otherwise is unmarked in the potters' quarter. By 510 BC new groups of artists are developing more robust black figure decoration on the usual shapes (the artists around the Antimenes Painter, then the so-called Leagros Group) [83, 84]; and there is an interesting series of big cups, skyphoi, with a variety of colourful scenes [85].[54] One of the painters from this group, the Diosphos Painter, working into the fifth century, has an odd style; it is not very precise but more painterly than most on Greek vases since his brush seems more important to him than his graver, and he imparts a new life to his spindly

**83.** Detail of an Attic hydria of the Leagros Group, from Vulci. A fight with Amazons, possibly at Troy since it would be appropriate that Achilles bears the body of the queen Penthesileia (see on [*126*]). Note the bowman at the right with Scythian cap and battle axe; these often figure in heroic fights. Late 6th c. BC. (London B323)

**84.** Attic hydria of the Leagros Group, from Vulci. At the shoulder the battlements of Troy with an archer, warriors and mourning women. On the body, at the left a chariot emerges from a city gate, too late to rescue Troilos whose body is being brandished by Achilles at the right, in a sanctuary of Apollo. By the Skaian gate is the famous tree, Athena discouraging Trojan pursuit, while the sad greybeard must be Priam, mourning his grandson.
Late 6th c. BC. H. 47.5cm.
(Munich 1700)

**85.** Attic skyphos by the Theseus Painter. Heracles, unusually dressed as an ordinary Athenian but the lionskin atop, receives a libation from Athena; the satyr is appropriate for a divine festive occasion. About 500 BC.
H. 17.5cm. (London 1902.12–18.3)

**86.** Attic amphora by the Diosphos Painter. Eos (Dawn) flies with the body of her son Memnon from the battlefield at Troy. Early 5th c. BC. (New York 56.171.25)

**87.** Attic phiale in the 'Six technique' of red and white over black. About 500 BC.
Diam. 19.8cm. (Rhodes)

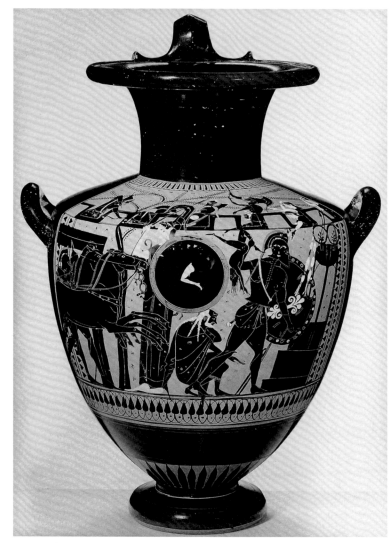

figures [*86*] as well as having a special way with myth.[55] He reminds us that there could be more than one way of using the black figure technique. He is also adept with figure decoration rendered in white and red on a plain black background, a variant technique for black figure of some popularity around the turn of the century, notable on other vases in what is called the 'Six technique' [*87*].[56]

By about 520 BC a new technique for drawing on vases had been adopted in Athens, red figure, and consideration of this I leave for later in this chapter. It did not immediately replace black figure in Athens and there is still distinguished work done in the older technique into the early fifth century, but it soon degenerated on products which might better have been left plain black, and disappeared by about the mid-fifth century except for traditional vases like the Panathenaic amphorae. The political and military events of the last hundred years of Athenian black figure had no effect on trade. There was no explicit reference in the decoration of the vases to the joys of democracy, to dismay at invasion and loss of their city to the Persians, to celebration of victory or, later, of a form of limited empire of a type unfamiliar to the new Greece. Such hints of all this that can be detected in the decoration of the vases were disguised in ways explained below, in Chapter 6. At any rate, a major part of the production may have gone overseas or to other parts of Greece, especially in the latter case the black figure, since the home market was conservative in its taste.

### Other Black Figure

The story of the potter's craft through the sixth century may seem dominated by Corinth, then Athens. Elsewhere, however, there were flourishing, if not so prolific potteries, some of which could also claim a share of the market outside their home towns. Some simply continue older traditions, adjusting to the new leading styles of Corinth and Athens in varying ways – Laconian, much East Greek. Others seem to have been generated by enterprising

**88.** Laconian cup by the Hunt Painter. Note the broken throwing spear (with loop attached) in the field above. After mid-6th c. BC. W. 19.5cm. (Paris, Louvre E670)

potters, sometimes immigrant, who add a figure-decorated range of vases to an otherwise workaday output. These may be one-man or family affairs and usually lasted for only one or two generations, but they offer some of the most interesting work, attractive for its originality and sheer quality.

Sparta (Laconia) had a reputation for austerity in antiquity and its citizens prospered under a fairly militaristic regime bolstered by a large slave population (helots) and serviced by immigrants (metics) from other parts of Greece. To the latter is usually attributed any artistic flair visible, and there was a great deal, but we may doubt whether the pure Spartiates were incapable of making their own art. In pottery, after an unenterprising orientalizing production, the last three quarters of the sixth century saw the work of an accomplished series of painters who had adopted the black figure technique and practised it especially on cups. The work is dull but careful, though one artist, the Hunt Painter, took an original view of cup interiors, treating them like portholes through which to view myth and life, effectively eschewing any attempt to adjust figures to the circle [88], which we can see was a major accomplishment of the Greek artist. The rest of the scene was probably in his head if anywhere, though the pictures look like excerpts. Laconian vases reached the old Spartan colony at Tarentum (Taranto), and Etruria in Italy, Samos, with which there were political affiliations, and north Africa (Greek colonies in Cyrenaica and the Greek trading town at Naucratis in Egypt), associations which sometimes influence subject matter [89].[57]

**89.1,2.** Laconian cup by the Arkesilas Painter, from Vulci. King Arkesilas of Cyrene, a hunting cat beneath his chair, under a sun-awning attended by monkeys, supervises the weighing of wool (?), which is being stacked in bales below. The shape is related to the Attic lip cup, but differently patterned. Mid-6th c. BC. W. 29cm. (Paris, Cab.Med. 189)

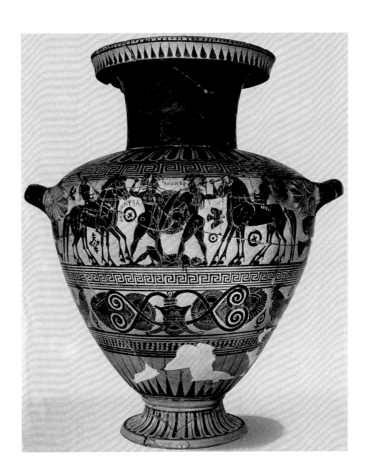

**90.** Laconian hydria by the Hunt Painter, from Rhodes. A battle of named but otherwise unknown heroes. After mid-6th c. BC. H. 43cm. (Rhodes 15373)

The only other major shape accorded figure decoration was the hydria [*90*]. Laconian black figure barely survives into the fifth century but there was brisk production also of plain black or striped vases, of all shapes and well finished, which also travelled well. We shall consider other Greek fine but plain black wares later.

Boeotia, in central Greece, has a mixed record of mainly short-lived black figure workshops, one of them specializing in animal-frieze bowls (lekanai) [*91*] and with the kantharos a popular shape [*92*]. It was an area with a bad reputation in Greece for matters of the intellect; through all the black figure period potters went on making bowls decorated with the old orientalizing flying birds (upside down, for easier painting). There is evidence there too for the work of immigrant potters and painters from Corinth and Athens. In the latter case their hands can be recognised on Attic shapes in Attica, then on Boeotian corinthianizing shapes in Boeotia. This movement of painters must have been quite common but can seldom be so clearly documented.[58] There was atticizing black figure too on the island of Euboea [*93*], and a related style can be detected in production in north Greece.[59]

**91.** Boeotian lekane.
Later 6th c. BC. W. 38.6cm.
(Columbia, Miss., 59.71)

**92.** Boeotian kantharos.
Other side, *EGVP* fig. 442.
Mid-6th c. BC. H. 18.8cm.
(Munich 419; inv. 6010)

**93.** Euboean amphora, from
Eretria. The wedding procession
of Peleus and Thetis.
Mid-6th c. BC.
(Athens 12076+16184)

94. Chian chalice, from Taucheira. Mid-6th c. BC. H. 17.7cm. (Tocra 785)

95. Interior of a Chian chalice from Pitane (Aeolis). White and red on black. Mid-6th c. BC. (Istanbul)

96. Samian head kantharos. Other views, *EGVP* fig. 330. Mid-6th c. BC. H. 21.4cm. (Munich 2014)

East Greece was going through a troubled period politically, dominated first by Lydians, then (after the 540s BC) Persians, but nevertheless making important contributions to the story of Greek art, mainly in areas other than pottery decoration – in architecture with the Ionic order, and in sculpture. Chios produced a fine ware, almost eggshell thin, covered by a thick white slip to take the painting which could be highly coloured, and specializing in a local shape, the chalice [*94, 95*]. It was the only East Greek centre that took much notice of the type of myth scenes that were the norm in Corinth and Athens, and may have been no little influenced by a long Anatolian tradition in wall painting, not yet matched in mainland Greece so far as we know. Their artists practised both outline drawing, with colour, and black figure, and the unusual, even exotic appearance of the vases guaranteed them a wide distribution throughout the Greek world, abetted by the well-attested activity of Chian traders. There is good reason to think that Chian potters had clay brought to Naucratis in Egypt to make plain votive vases for the local sanctuaries.[60] Naucratis plays an important part in this story; founded by East Greeks in the Nile Delta before the end of the seventh century, it was a mainly Greek town of merchants, with their own temples, importing, among other things, fine wares for local use and further distribution through an Egypt which was not conspicuously receptive.[61]

Samos, Chios' neighbour island, has a different record, and around the mid-sixth century produced a series of miniaturist Little Master cups and other fine and original wares [*96, 97*].[62] The detail looks like black figure but in fact the thin lines are reserved in the silhouette, not incised, a laborious technique but

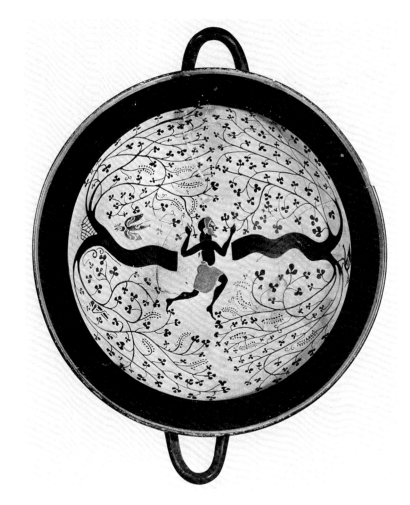

97. Samian(?) cup, from Italy. A man between two vines. On one (left) a bird is flying to feed its chicks in the nest, being approached by a snake and a locust; on the other a heron perches. Mid-6th c. BC. W. 23cm. (Paris, Louvre F68)

98. Milesian 'Fikellura' amphora, from Fikellura (Rhodes). After mid-6th c. BC. H. 34cm. (London 1864.10–7.156)

99. Milesian 'Fikellura' amphora, from Rhodes. After mid-6th c. BC. (Rhodes)

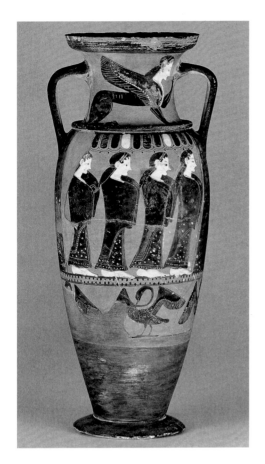

**100.** Clazomenian amphora, from Tell Defenneh (Egypt). The source is a rich one for the class, probably the site of a Greek mercenary station overrun by the Persians in 525 BC. After mid-6th c. BC. H. 53.6cm. (London 1888.2–8.71a)

**101.** Rhodian situla from Tell Defenneh (see [100]). A winged merman holds snakes. After mid-6th c. BC. H. 53.6cm. (London 1888.2–8.1)

one met also in Miletus, one of the most powerful of the mainland Ionian cities. There, the Wild Goat Style died hard, but from the 570s on a distinctive style called Fikellura (from an early find of the vases on Rhodes) developed, mainly for amphorae and hydriai, with some fine free-field compositions, elegant friezes and spirals with florals, and figure work with the reserved lines I have just remarked [98, 99].[63] Farther north on the mainland, around Smyrna and Clazomenae, the Wild Goat Style adopted black figure, which for a while lingered beside the outline-drawn animals, in separate friezes for each technique. Here too the techniques, outline Wild Goat and black figure (and even some red figure), were applied for the decoration of the rims, and sometimes lids, of big clay sarcophagi. There was also a colourful if rather wooden, purely black figure style associated with Clazomenae [100].[64]

In Dorian Rhodes and neighbour islands to the south the old manner lingered, especially for plates and dishes, and there is some black figure on a shape borrowed from Egypt (the situla), of which examples may also have been made by Greeks in Egypt [101].[65]

**102.** Chalcidian crater by the Inscription Painter. At Troy Hector bids farewell to Andromache (right pair), Paris to Helen. After mid-6th c. BC. H. 45.7cm. (Würzburg L160)

**103.** Detail of a Chalcidian amphora by the Inscription Painter. At Troy, Diomedes slays Rhesos and his sleeping companions. Other views, *EGVP* fig. 475. After mid-6th c. BC. (Malibu 96.AE.1)

104. 'Pontic' amphora. Centaurs. Mid-6th c. BC. H. 39cm. (Würzburg L778)

105. The 'Northampton amphora'. A merman; men riding cranes, a dog, hare and hedgehogs. About 525 BC. H. 32.5cm. (London, Niarchos Collection; once Castle Ashby)

The emigration of craftsmen from East Greece, harried by Lydians or Persians, or simply in search of a better life, had its effect in Athens, even in the black figure studios, in matters of some shapes and styles of decoration (the palmette spirals are an obvious example), and there will be cause to reflect on this further when we consider red figure.[66] They travelled farther west too, to the colonial lands of opportunity and their rich neighbours, by now heavily hellenized in their arts. The Etruscan cemeteries proved to be so replete with fine Greek decorated vases that when first found they were all thought to be Etruscan until closer study, especially of their inscriptions, proved otherwise. It is still possible to find the old description lingering, such has been the allure of the very word 'Etruscan'.[67]

There is only one major black figure school which was located in a western Greek colony, the 'Chalcidian', which perhaps worked at Rhegion. It was successful enough to corner part of the Etruscan market despite competition from Athens, and was well distributed in the south. The style has quality both of execution and in originality of subject matter [102, 103]. There seems a blend of Athenian, Ionian and even Corinthian in the work,

whether a shrewd bid for the market, or more likely a reflection of the background (perhaps in Euboea) of its founding potters.[68] With other Greek work in the west to which we now turn, it comes almost as a breath of fresh air after the humid Attic styles which, with all their quality, were smothering all Greek markets.

By as early as 600 BC a Wild Goat Style artist seems to be working in Etruria (the Swallow Painter).[69] Most of the decorated pottery made in Etruria at that time was heavily influenced by Corinth, a little by the orient, in a prolific Etrusco-corinthian style. The local ware was a black bucchero, sometimes with relief decoration. We have seen how some Athenian potters targeted the market in Etruria, and an enterprising potter, probably from East Greece, started a workshop ('Pontic') for vases similar to the Attic Tyrrhenian but yet more colourful [104], and this developed into a flourishing Etruscan ware, losing something of its Ionian flavour on the way, but persisting to the end of the century and giving rise to other purely Etruscan black figure schools.[70] Another artist, a black figure miniaturist of the greatest ability, came from north Ionia to make vases of the Northampton Group, amphorae [105], giving rise to some related hydriai and dinoi (cauldrons [106]), made in Etruria, but this whole phenomenon lasted barely a generation.[71] After these, one, perhaps two painters, arrived in Caere to make some of the very finest of all Greek decorated vases, the Caeretan hydriae, full of colour, verve and considerable narrative ingenuity [107, 108].[72] They worked through the last quarter of the century, but where did they come

**106.** A 'Campana dinos'. Satyrs accompany the return of Hephaistos (left) to Olympus. Other view, *EGVP* fig. 491. About 525 BC. (Würzburg H5352)

**107.** Caeretan hydria by the Eagle Painter. The crippled Hephaistos on a mule returning to Olympus, with Dionysos, a satyr and a maenad. Other views, *EGVP* fig. 495. Late 6th c. BC. H. 41.5cm. (Vienna 3577)

**108.** Detail of a Caeretan hydria by the Eagle Painter. A sea monster (*ketos*) faced by a hero with a sickle, with marine life. Late 6th c. BC. (Paris, Niarchos Collection)

**109.** Corinthian ('Wide Group')
cup. Artemis with bow, torch and
dog, approaches an altar.
Mid-5th c. BC. Diam. 9.2cm.
(London 1969.12–15.2)

**110.** Boeotian Cabirion cup.
Odysseus blown along on his raft
of amphorae by the North Wind
(Boreas). Early 4th c. BC.
H. 15.4cm. (Oxford V262)

from? Their style is unmistakably Ionian but the only close parallel to their work in the east appears on a wooden plaque found in
Egypt.[73] This may give the clue: the painter(s) had trained as panel
or wall painters and transferred their skills in the west to pottery.
At home such decoration was nowhere near as popular on ceramics as in the Greek homeland, while there was a distinguished
tradition in Anatolia of wall painting with figures.

None of these non-Athenian wares survived much into the
fifth century, and to most Greeks or Greek customers figure-decorated pottery in the Greek style simply came to mean Athenian red
figure. The plainer wares of Corinth were still made and exported,
and in the mid-fifth century there is a small group of miniature
cups and boxes decorated with outline-drawn figures, mainly for
local use as votives or entertainment, it would seem (the Wide
Group)[*109*].[74] In Boeotia, the later fifth and fourth centuries see
many roughly drawn black figure and outline vases, mainly cups
(skyphoi), in what is called the Cabirion style, since many seem
designed for the sanctuary of the Cabiri near Thebes. Some of
their subjects are quite deliberately, and successfully, comic, sometimes parodying myth [*110, 231*] in the spirit of much theatre of
the classical period – in Athens, satyr plays and the comedies of
Aristophanes.[75] Elsewhere a potter will encourage his painter
from time to time to experiment with the black figure technique,
or more often the new red figure.[76] The most important of the new
derivative studios are in Italy and Sicily, and we shall come to them
once we have looked more closely at the phenomenon of red figure
in Athens, the style which *par excellence* we rightly associate with
the best of Greek vase painting.

*Attic Red Figure*

Around or soon after 525 BC, a date assigned from stylistic similarities with low relief sculpture at Delphi (the Siphnian Treasury) which can be closely dated, some painters in Athens began decorating vases in a new technique.[77] The motivation was mainly aesthetic, no doubt, but it also represented a new line for the growing export market, and the response was more immediate in Athens and Italy (Greek and Etruscan) than in the rest of Greece.

The figures were drawn in outline, with line for all interior detail of anatomy and dress, and the background painted black. At first there was a very little incision, for details of hair and the like, but it was soon abandoned, as was any added colour detail on dress. The brush had taken over from the graver, and superficially the result looks like a reversal of black figure. In detail it is just that, and many early figures retain much of the black figure patterning of dress and a degree of added colour, but the change was more profound. The overall appearance of the figured scenes brought them closer to the appearance, not of wall painting, for which a pale background was preferred, but of relief sculpture, in which the pale or coloured figures were set against a dark red or blue background, which might at any rate be much in shadow. But this cannot be the whole reason for the change, and the aesthetic and technical one, of the greater freedom allowed by a brush for linear work, especially in the hand of an artist used to it, must have counted for much. Contour was important, and was more emphatic with a dark background than it could have been (and was to prove to be) with a thin line only. We see the results very soon. Different degrees of intensity of line were possible: standard, dilute, and the so-called relief line which was crisp and dark, standing proud of the surface of the vase to catch reflected light, and often used to outline figures, rather as incision had been used by some black figure painters to mark contours off from the reddish background.

The pictures look far more 'black and white' now, or rather black and red, and there is more of the line-painter than engraver in the style. By using the different grades of black line the painter became far more expressive of patterns of anatomy and dress, and the change parallels, or almost precedes, the new attention being paid by sculptors to patterns of anatomy that more truly copy live forms. They have not yet reached a positive attempt to mirror life but they are well on the way, in both sculpture and vase painting, and the new suppleness allowed bolder and more expressive poses,

111.1,2. Attic bilingual amphora details, by the Lysippides and Andokides Painters, from Vulci. Both sides show Heracles at a solitary feast attended by Athena, clutching his kantharos and well supplied with food, in the shade of a vine; the black figure side (*top*) adds Hermes and a cup-boy, with the hero's quiver and sword hanging on the vine. About 525 BC. (Munich 2301)

112. Detail of an Attic amphora by the Andokides Painter, from Vulci. Details of hair are still incised, as in black figure, and there is much dress ornament and added red. Heracles seizes Apollo's tripod. About 525 BC. (Berlin 2159)

even twisting and three-quarter views. They were still some way off being able to express the roundness or fullness of figures, though in the early fifth century there are some rather feeble attempts to show the convexity of shields by shading, without yet proper observation of the fall of light on round objects. This, indeed, is never quite effectively achieved in this medium, which remains resolutely linear to the end, though it sometimes admitted wash and, later, colour masses. Simple line is not, however, a bar to expression of volume. Much of the effect depends on new techniques which I discuss in Chapter 9, with some problems which they posed. Some of the early painters made 'bilingual' vases, the old and new techniques on either side, and there are problems of identity since distinguishing features look rather different when attempted with a brush rather than a point. Later, though black figure quality declined after about 500 BC, both techniques, old and new, were practised in the same workshops.[78]

The Andokides Painter has generally been thought to be the earliest of the innovators, but he may not be; relative dating is not an adequately precise art, but his work has some revealing experimental passages [*111, 112*]. He has interesting links with both the

113. Attic 'eye cup' by Oltos, from Vulci. A Nereid holding dolphins. About 520–510 BC. W. 32cm. (Once Castle Ashby)

114. Attic plate by Epiktetos, from Vulci. About 520–510 BC. W. 18.7cm. (London E137)

great black figure painter Exekias and with East Greece, as we shall see. He decorated some bilinguals, on which the black figure sides are taken to be the work of another, the Lysippides Painter [219–221].[79] This is probably true, though I imagine he was certainly capable of painting black figure and surely did, sometimes. Exekias had links with the work of both artists, in technique with the former, in subjects with the latter. Was the Andokides Painter an immigrant from East Greece? It is possible, and some very distinctive head profiles by him and other early red figure painters are best matched in Ionian art. Or was he busy in another painterly craft, or even relief sculpture? He was followed, before the end of the century, by highly accomplished painters, among them Psiax, Oltos and Epiktetos [*113, 114, 239, 242*].[80]

The new technique seemed to encourage a degree of specialization by painters; most would work on any shape or size, but a distinction began to emerge between 'pot painter' and 'cup painter' and the signatures of both painters and potters indicate some movement of artists between workshops. The family craft begins to take on the aspect of an industry with a mobile labour force. Early red figure was for the élite of Athens, and enough was exported to ensure a good market for the new vases in Etruria, but it took some time before the rest of Greece was persuaded, or perhaps the merchants simply knew where the greater profit lay, and many painters were reluctant to change technique.

In the last years of the sixth and early fifth centuries the prime black figure was being made by the Leagros Group artists, named for the boy Leagros who was praised as beautiful (*kalos*) on some of the vases. The same boy is praised on a group of the new red figure vases, which are free with inscriptions and signatures, and include many cross-references. The painters have been called the Pioneers, which is rather misleading because they were not the first, but they do seem to represent a real artistic coterie.[81] This is a new phenomenon for ancient crafts, and in the Pioneers' apparently conscious pride and even rivalry we perhaps for the first time come close to a recognition by the painters that what they practise can be more than a craft. We shall look at them as individuals more closely in Chapter 3, and the apparent challenge of one to another – 'as never Euphronios' [*115*]. Whether the challenge refers to painterly skill (which is the more probable in the context) or party-going (which need not have been monopolized by vase painters), it was still an internal reference within the potters' quarter to be appreciated by the painters as well as customers.

**116.** Attic calyx crater by Euphronios, from Capua. Athletes: one ties up his foreskin to prevent erection during exercise and keep it tidy; a trainer directs a discus-thrower; a youth folds his dress. The figures are named, the boy at the left simply called 'the boy' (*ho pais*). Late 6th c. BC. W. 44.4cm. (Berlin 2180)

**117.1,2.** Details of an Attic cup by Phintias. A satyr seizes a boy's lyre; on the other side a girl rebuffs a randy satyr. Mortals confronted by 'immortals'. Late 6th c. BC. (Karlsruhe 63.104)

**118.1,2.** Attic hydria by Phintias, from Vulci. On the shoulder a ladies' drinking party, holding cups as for the *kottabos* game, and one saying 'this for you, Euthymides', which is the name of the seated youth at the music lesson below. Late 6th c. BC. H. 51.5cm. (Munich 2421)

**119.** Attic amphora by Smikros. A warlike satyr with a light shield (pelta) and a wiggly spear. He helps Dionysos against the giants. Late 6th c. BC. (Berlin 1966.19)

The concept of Art and The Artist is relatively modern, though a degree of Art for Art's Sake appeared with early Rome in the collecting mania for Greek works, which Greek artists then started to supply. None of the Muses of Greece had responsibility for the visual arts, which were left to Athena and Hephaistos, more concerned with domestic skills and advanced technology (magic). In the red figure vases the painters are still offering a product of a very sophisticated social type, not quite as élitist as the metal-worker whose raw material was more valuable, but with consider-able potential and greater freedom of expression. On the best vases we detect the same conscientious attention to quality that is apparent in the best sculpture of the classical period.

Of the Pioneers Euphronios, who later turned to potting only, to judge from signatures, and Euthymides, are but the best known among many fine painters, mainly of larger vases. These carry bold scenes devoted to myth, athletics [116] or to the pleasures of the table.[82] The symposion, for which many of the vases were made, provided a subject for their decoration too, and the new technique allowed the artist to dwell on details of behaviour as never before [117, 118]. But the myth scenes are the more compel-ling, their intensity and sometimes pathos never spoiled by the finesse of drawing [120].

In the early fifth century the Kleophrades Painter and the Berlin Painter continue the Pioneer tradition, mainly on large

**120.** Detail of an Attic calyx crater by Euphronios. Heracles strikes down Kyknos, while Athena storms past him to confront Kyknos' father, the god Ares. Late 6th c. BC. (New York, Leon Levy and Shelby White Collection)

vases.[83] Both are artists identified by techniques of attribution to be discussed in Chapter 2. They are contemporaries, yet there is a world of difference in their approaches. The former has heavy, sometimes forbidding figures, and is something of an intellectual to judge from his themes, many of which are his own and not derived from or even copied by his fellows. I figure the scene on one of his best known vases [*121*]. It shows the Sack of Troy by presenting, side by side, five different episodes which express several different aspects of such a disaster: sacrilegious murder, rape, the courage of a mother, the compassion of a son and of grandchildren, hope and despair. They deserve to be looked at closely. This is drama as carefully composed as a Greek poem or play, not idle story-telling, but there are relatively few other vases which approach this standard of invention, some of them his [*201, 205, 241, 252*].[84] He also painted a robust black figure, the last to do so of the great red figure artists, except for some who painted Panathenaic amphorae.[85] The Berlin Painter is a more self-conscious artist, more conventional in subject matter but a superb draughtsman, and adept at displaying single figure subjects, even

121. Drawing of the shoulder scene on a hydria by the Kleophrades Painter, from Nola. The Sack of Troy. From the left: Aeneas carries his father Anchises, with his son Askanios, from the doomed city; the Lesser Ajax advances on the naked Cassandra who has taken refuge at a statue of Athena beside a suffering palm tree; Neoptolemos slays Priam, seated on an altar with the bloodied body of his grandson Astyanax on his lap; Andromache, Hector's widow, fights back; the Athenian sons of Theseus, Demophon and Akamas, rescue their grandmother Aithra, who had been taken to Troy with Helen. Photos, *ARFH* I, fig. 135. Early 5th c. BC. (Naples 2422)

without a ground line, as it were spotlit against the glossy black ground so that the contour is emphasized ([*122*]; compare the earlier, Pioneer [*119*]). His figures are like statues where his colleague's are more like actors.

The late archaic red figure style of Athens, with the patterns of anatomy and glorious displays of splaying dress folds with zigzag hems, often revealing body contours beneath, ran on through the first quarter of the fifth century. It is a close match to the sculpture in the round and in relief of the day – the Acropolis statues and Athenian gravestones. The potters' careers must have been interrupted by the Persian occupation of Athens in 480 and 479 BC and they no doubt had to rebuild their businesses on return from refuge, but we notice none of this except, it may be, in the choice of some subjects (such as the Sack of Troy, another great city). The cup painters are no less remarkable than the painters of larger pots, and many of their works have survived since they were popular in the export market to Italy. They start by retailing the

**122.** Detail of an amphora by the Berlin Painter. Heracles proffers his cup; Athena stands with a jug on the other side of the vase (*ARFH* I, fig. 146). Early 5th c. BC. H. of figure about 37cm. (Basel BS456)

essence of the Pioneers, who also decorated some cups. Notable and early among them is Onesimos, followed by painters for the potter Brygos – the Brygos Painter [*123, 199, 268, 277*] and others, Douris [*124, 234, 238, 244, 273*], Makron.[86] For some as many as three hundred vases can be assigned, not an insignificant fraction of their output and permitting us to discern phases in their careers. Such apparent productivity for some painters is probably more a result of the generous exploration of places which bought their vases (mainly in Italy), than a reflection on the idleness of their fellows, especially the less talented whose products, we know, travelled in their hundreds.

It is easy to see how this identification of painters enables us not only to chart the development of the craft in Athens but also to

123.1,2. Attic cup by the Brygos Painter, from Capua. On one side Dionysos watches his satyrs assault Iris who is trying to take off with some sacrificial meat from his altar; on the other, the satyrs contemplate an assault on Hera – Hermes tries to negotiate, Heracles prefers force. About 490–480 BC. W. 27.5cm. (London E65)

124. Attic cup by Douris, from Caere. The dragon disgorges Jason before Athena; no part of the usual story of the Argonauts. W. 30cm. About 475 BC. (Vatican)

distinguish personalities and the preferences of some of the artists. I devote the next chapter to how this has been done, but the name of John Beazley should be mentioned here as a pioneer in such studies, who succeeded in turning an archaeological exercise in classification into a tool for study of society and the role of its crafts. Few of the painters have left us their own names in signatures, but those that have are revealing. A significant number, working in both black and red figure, have non-Athenian names. Immigrants seem to have played an important role in crafts in Greece, supplying skills that the citizens perhaps could not, or attracted by a market that did more than supply local needs. Some in Athens have ethnic names which suggest arrival even from outside the Greek world (Thrace, Scythia, Sicily, Anatolia), but this may reflect only their family background or patronage and their work is pure 'Athenian', whatever of their own experience they may have contributed.[87]

The potter/painter's craft in the archaic period runs in step with that of other arts. In the Early Classical period, down to around the mid-century, the monumental arts in desolate, but rich and victorious Athens, took a back seat, and we look rather to the sculpture on the Temple of Zeus at Olympia and the occasional surviving bronze (the Artemisium Zeus, the Riace bronze pair).[88] In Athens we read of major wall paintings, including some depicting recent events (the Battle of Marathon in the Painted Stoa), which is a considerable innovation, not followed in other arts for a while. Vase painting flourished still with a barely abated export trade. Styles adjust to the new 'severe' mode, but there is a hint too of the effect of the major paintings. We find more big figure friezes, sometimes on varied ground lines, and for the first time on a vase a composition in which the figures are placed up and down the field [125, 300].[89] Many of these scenes are of epic subjects which are thematically associated with the Persian Wars, such as Amazonomachies [126, 131, 132]. They give us virtually our only insight into the myth and image-making attitudes of the new democracy which had found itself a leader of that part of the Greek world still threatened by Persia. The novel compositions surely imitate those of the wall paintings, but need not have copied them closely; there will be more to say about this shortly. This break from the regime of the simple frieze, where the figures seem to parade in file before a black curtain, had important implications later in the century.[90]

The 'black and white' aspect of most vase painting was avoided in one technique which provided a white ground for the painting, making it more like panel- or wall-painting. The white ground had been used for some later black figure, provoking some problems in distinguishing the added white used for female flesh, which was commonly then abandoned, and leaving some sex-identity problems, just as there can be with the un-coloured red figure. In most black figure male flesh had been left unnaturally black, with an occasional red face and chest in early Attic, while female flesh was painted white over the black, and so rather easily rubbed off but always leaving a 'ghost' (as do the inscriptions in red figure, in white or red). There was a period of experiment too with glossy 'coral red' as an alternative to the black for areas of paint.

The white ground was used early in the century by red figure painters for some cups [127] and a number of other shapes which seem not for general use, but votive.[91] Soon a degree of polychromy brightens the appearance of the vases and ought to have led to experiments in drawing, such as we presume were being made in panel-painting; but it did not. The white ground was hardly even used for compositions which seem to copy wall-painting styles, like the multi-level. Instead, we see the best of the red figure outline styles, with colour areas included. The white does not always survive very well. It came to be used almost exclusively, until late in the century, for oil vases (lekythoi). The first of these with the white ground were black figure, some still sixth-century, then with outline/coloured figures and with the usual

125. Drawing of one side of an Attic calyx crater by the Niobid Painter, from Orvieto. Name vase. Artemis and Apollo shoot down the children of Niobe (Niobids) for her mother's boast of being more fecund than their mother Leto. The other side [300]. About 460 BC. (Paris, Louvre G431)

126. Drawing of a cup by the Penthesileia Painter, from Vulci. Name vase. Greeks slay Amazons. The most famous duels were either with Theseus (usually beardless) or of Achilles with Penthesileia, which is thought to be shown here. Many have decided that the moment of his falling in love with her is shown by the way their eyes meet – but they do not meet. Pre-mid-5th c. BC. W. 43cm. (Munich 2688)

**127.** Attic white ground cup, from Delphi. Apollo pours a libation; his raven watches. Early 5th c. BC. Diam. 17.8cm. (Delphi)

range of subjects. Then the technique was used exclusively for offerings at and in Athenian graves, and with funeral scenes upon them, often of attendance at the tomb [128], of farewell [129], or domestic scenes of the dead (normally women) as in life, or Charon with his boat receiving the dead for their passage of the River Styx [254]. This means that, since they were for local funerary practice, few were exported, and very soon the white ground becomes almost exclusively associated with funeral use. The few exceptions are found outside Greece, and it may be that their appearance in some way enhanced their value, seemingly imitative of silver or stone. The colours are matte for the funeral lekythoi of the second half of the fifth century, added after firing, which does not make for survival.[92] The amount of oil put in the vase could remain small, in a separate clay container set out of sight within the neck; this was really just a matter of over-dressing in the manner of many modern perfume bottles.

Another response to market forces was the growing specialization of both potters and painters. One workshop (of the Penthesileia Painter), of around and before the mid-century, is found to have employed a production line, with pots being passed from hand to hand to complete the decoration,[93] and there was probably always some use of apprentices to draw subsidiary decoration, and to fill in the black backgrounds. The backs of larger pots begin to attract stock and summary 'mantle figures' or athletes, in twos and threes, whose only function is to fill the space.

*94*

**128.1,2.** Attic white ground lekythos by the Inscription Painter. A woman with a box containing lekythoi, loaves and ribbons, and a man, at a grave. H. 37cm. (Boston 1970.428 Harriet Otis Cruft Fund)

**129.** Detail of Attic white ground lekythos by the Achilles Painter, from Eretria. The warrior's farewell. After mid-5th c. BC. (Athens 1818)

The middle years of the fifth century, while the Parthenon was being planned and built, offer more vases with a touch of monumentality in their design and painting – by the Achilles Painter and followers, also masters of white ground for lekythoi [*129, 253*]. The archaic style had been worked out, except in the products of a small group of so-called Mannerists, mainly dull artists but for their leader (but not founder), the Pan Painter, who had flair [*130*].[94] Dress and anatomy is sketchier now, more accurate in terms of real forms, the obvious example being the way in which the human eye in a profile view no longer glares frontally at the viewer but is properly observed, while dress falls naturally and not in mannered pleats. In figures, the delineation of both relaxed and action poses in simple line is totally assured, as it was by now in the round for sculpture; a first for the history of art. There is less and less detail, almost no added colour (except on a white ground) or serious distinction in the thickness of lines, where before there had been much play between the so-called relief line and the paler, often honey-coloured dilute paint, for minor linear detail and occasionally even for tentative shading.

**130.** Attic bell crater by the Pan Painter, from Cumae. Name vase. Pan pursues a shepherd boy past a Priapic herm on a rock. About 470 BC. H. 37cm. (Boston 10.185)

It is with the white ground technique, which came to be monopolized by the makers of funeral lekythoi, that we find real polychromy, and have a glimpse of the appearance of the larger painting of the day on wall or panel. The effect on composition in red figure has been mentioned already, with the new multi-level scenes in different registers. This did not, as one might have supposed, introduce a sense of depth or anything like perspective; the figures are all the same size and the uppermost are not the most remote, but often the most important – gods. Moreover, the figures are set against an uncompromising black ground. Early examples, by around 460 BC, simply had variable ground lines with more overlapping of figures [*131*], not as easy to read on the black background of a red figure vase as they would have been on a white wall or panel. But these new compositions were exceptional and not even always the work of the best painters.

In the third quarter of the century the Parthenon was completed, the canon for idealized realism in treatment of the human

**131.** Drawing of Attic volute crater by the Painter of the Woolly Satyrs, from Numana. Greeks fight Amazons. Notice the moribund Amazon part concealed behind the ground line at the right. Mid-5th c. BC. (New York 07.286.84)

**132.** Volute crater by the Painter of Bologna 279. Greeks fight Amazons; notice the Amazons' breast-corselets. On the neck, a symposion. Another view, *ARFH* II, fig.16. Mid-5th c. BC. H. 73cm. (Basel BS486)

figure was established in sculpture by Pheidias in Athens and Polyclitus in Argos, and the High Classical was born. Athens was, under Pericles, at the height of her power in Greece, not over the other major cities such as Corinth or Sparta, but over most of the islands and East Greece, which paid a form of tribute to her to help keep off the Persians. The access of metal wealth, not that well distributed, did nothing to discourage or diminish the output and quality of Athens' clay vases. Democracies have never been very good at dissolving the gap between the very rich and the rest. Vase painters responded to the way in which major artists treated the heroic themes of the period, for example in the Parthenon sculptures, with subjects and styles which were very similar – many a fight of Greeks and Amazons which mimicked the unsuccessful Persian assault on Greece and Athens of earlier in the century and featured the Athenian democratic hero, Theseus. Several of these are presented in the new multi-level manner [*132*].

**133.** Group of vases from an offering ditch at a grave in Athens. Including a white ground lekythos, two lebetes gamikoi, squat lekythoi, a lekanis and boxes. Late 5th c. BC. (Kerameikos)

It all ended in tears. In 404 BC Athens was dismantling its city walls after more than twenty years of war with the other major powers of Greece, having faced periods of annual invasion in Attica, and a plague which scourged the population crammed within its walls. The potters went on potting, however [*133*]. Markets had dwindled in the west in the face of local competition, yet many Attic vases still travelled to central Italy and elsewhere. The heroic flavour of the High Classical lingered strongly but a new painting tradition was developing which manifested itself in both style and subject.[95] It began by the 420s, but the prime artist was the Meidias Painter, of nearer 400 BC. The style was a delicate one of fine linear detail which, on bodies and dress, succeeded in suggesting rotundity, even voluptuousness, in the same terms as the best sculpture of the day [*134, 303, 304*]. There were no problems by now in showing foreshortening for figures and features, though still no real shading of volume, which depended rather on the contouring effect of the finely set lines, and there was much more patterning of dress. This is a period in which major panel painting was beginning to be of considerable importance in Greece, having moved on from the multi-level, early classical historical paintings of Polygnotus and others, either developing the old linear tradition which was closely matched on the vases, but with the enhancement of realistic shading, or depending more on mass and graduated colour, which was to be the way forward into the Hellenistic and Roman periods. It is at this point that the

**134.** Decoration of an Attic hydria by the Meidias Painter. Above, the Dioskouroi carry off the daughters of Leukippos, watched by their friends, by Aphrodite (at the altar) and Zeus (at the left). Below, a youthful Heracles (second right) has persuaded the Hesperides to pick for him the apples guarded by the serpent. The hero's companions Klytios and Iolaos stand in the wings; the girls have nice names: Health, Star Face, Golden Law, Shining. Photos, *ARFH* II, fig. 287. Late 5th c. BC. H. 52.1cm (London E224)

vase-painter's drawing techniques began to part company from the work of other painters and draughtsmen, and from now on develops only within an idiom which was bound before long to be found unsatisfying. But it had another century to run and was to find a new artistic vitality among Greeks far to the west.

The subject matter of the vases of war-torn Athens was either heroic still, as I have noted, or had relaxed into near-fantasies of paradise gardens, peopled by goddesses, usually Aphrodite, nymphs, and smooth-limbed youths who seem never to have gone to war or wanted to. Discreet gilding and added colour, if only white, adds to the gorgeous effect, but this is not merely copying metal vases (there are none attested for Athens with this degree of finish in these years) but seem to be the vase-painter's contribution to an attempt to produce a morale-raising and optimistic, peaceful effect for the beleaguered town; perhaps no more than a

**135.** Attic lebes gamikos by the Marsyas Painter, from Panticapaeum (Kerch, Crimea). Preparations for a wedding. Other sides, *ARFH* II, fig. 388. Mid-4th c. BC. (St Petersburg 15592)

form of escapism little related to reality or cult, but with no little thought for the market overseas.[96]

This is also about the time when there is a more general change in the balance of subject interest on the vases. It moves away from the party-going, and from the heroic, mainly military, in which some artists had caught the spirit of the day even by stressing the dire mythical crimes of women as freely as those of men (adultery, seduction, homicide, infanticide, etc.). Instead we find more scenes in which women at home play a major part. These may be mythical but are often simply of the toilette of a bride, where, with the presence of an Eros, the mortal and divine mingle [*135*].[97] The reason for the change is not easy to explain, apart from whatever war may have prompted. It could be that this

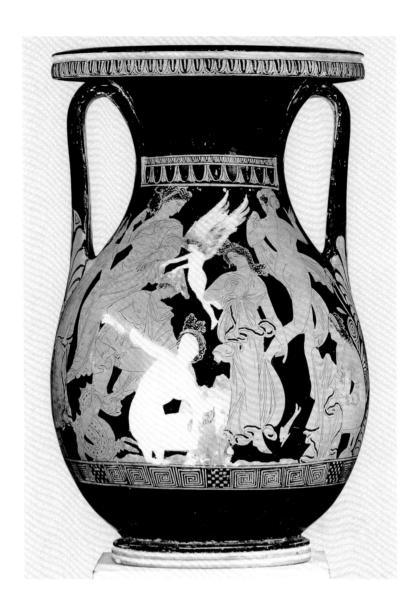

**136.** Attic pelike by the Marsyas Painter, from Camirus (Rhodes). Peleus grapples with Thetis, caught at her bath; her familiar, a sea monster (*ketos*), wraps itself around his leg. See also [*305*]. Mid-4th c. BC. H. 42.5cm. (London E424)

simply mirrors the spirit of the age – of Euripides and Aristophanes rather than Aeschylus and Sophocles – or reflects the fact that Athenian women are beginning to form a greater proportion of the market for the vases. There are certainly more shapes that seem appropriate to womens' life: what are taken to be jewellery boxes and the like. Throughout the history of Athenian vase painting everyday life was not ignored as a subject, but was never given any prominence in the painters' repertoire until now, while official civic aspects of the life of Athens' democracy were shunned altogether: we never see Athenian democracy in action. On these matters the comment was more subtle and less direct, as we shall see in Chapter 6, not as forthright as it could be on the stage. We have no contemporary 'portraits' on vases whatever.

Fourth-century Greece was much involved with inter-state leagues, soon overshadowed by attitudes to the new power in the Balkans, the Macedonians, culminating in Philip II's virtual take-over of power through all Greece, and his son Alexander's carriage of Greek arms and culture through Persia to Central Asia and India. Once the decorated pottery of Athens could reflect on contemporary politics and power, albeit at some remove, but such days were long past, and the craft continued to serve its community in less ambitious, more parochial ways. So we find many more scenes of the life of women, some interest in local religious practices, a more restricted range of myth, some of which may have been in part generated by new markets in the Black Sea. The trade to the Greek areas of Sicily and South Italy, as also to Etruria, declined as local, rival production of red figure grew, though not much more rapidly than overall production, to judge from finds in Athens. There was still a good market in Greece itself, however, and the houses of a north Greek city, Olynthos, show how very much Athenian red figure vases remained part of the Greek domestic scene.

The shape range seems narrower and some functions must have been taken over by plain vases or metal. The principal large shapes now are the hydria, the bell crater which has supplanted most other forms of crater, and the big pelike, a bulbous oil container. Cups are on the whole smaller, and there are many 'stemlesses', the nicest of which have a colour floral within the rim.[98] But there is a fair range of what seem almost toilet vases, boxes and oil vases, some of which are appropriately pretty. The tall lekythos gives place to the squat. There is a tendency to the more ornate in subsidiary decoration, and a more curvaceous profile for vase bodies and handles – not much to our taste.

The style of decoration is a logical development of what went before and can include some very fine linear drawing, especially in work by and around the Marsyas Painter in the mid-fourth century [135, 136]; he is one of the last fine painters also to decorate Panathenaics.[99] It is easy to be distracted by the rather gaudier appearance of many vases and overlook the very high quality of draughtsmanship, sometimes better appreciated in fragments! But for the most part the work is less careful. Before 400 BC the use of added white for female flesh, some areas of dress and other features, had begun, and it continued with varying degrees of precision through the fourth century [137] and could abet an illusion of transparency in dress. On the finer vases a relief effect was achieved by added clay for some features, such as wings or

**137.** Attic hydria. The court of Dionysos. Early 4th c. BC. (Cape Town)

**138.** Attic squat lekythos in red figure and relief by Xenophantos, from Panticapaeum (Kerch, Crimea). In a mixture of red figure (man at top left) and painted, moulded relief. Persians hunting, both real and monstrous (the griffin) creatures. Their names can be associated with historical figures of the late 5th century. Other views, *ARFH* II, fig. 340. (St Petersburg St 1790)

**139.** Detail of an Attic hydria, from Pella. Athena (off left) fights Poseidon for the land of Attica. He wields his trident; Athena's olive tree and Zeus' thunderbolt, dividing the combatants, are between them. Below, Victory (Nike) supports Athena, and sea creatures Poseidon. Yellowish paint for Poseidon's armour. Echoing the subject and composition of the central group in the west pediment of the Parthenon (*GSCP* fig. 77). Early 4th c. BC. (Pella 80.514)

**140.** Attic hydria in red figure and relief, from Panticapaeum (Kerch, Crimea), The subject as the last, with differences in composition – no thunderbolt, and Athena's snake at her tree. The main figures in high (Poseidon) and low (Athena) relief, the others painted, with relief detail. Mid-4th c. BC. (St Petersburg KAB6a; P 1872.130)

jewellery, and these may be gilded. Eventually, broader washes of colour are used, harking back to styles on white ground a century before, and no doubt in emulation of wall or panel painting, but these are few.[100] There had always been some potters who offered vases whose main figure work was in relief, the rest in red figure: Xenophantos was one, with vases that depict a Persian hunt, introducing the new world power that swayed Greek fortunes for nearly two centuries [*138*].[101] There are some splendidly ambitious pieces both in the usual red figure, and later with large relief figures, reflecting at some remove sculptural monuments of Athens, in these examples [*139, 140*] a Parthenon pediment.[102]

By the time the new great Greek city of Alexandria was founded in 331 BC the course of Athenian red figure had been run, and it is barely represented there. The last generation of the decorated vases is characterized by some gaudiness, and a lot of weak drawing for a dwindling export trade. The reasons for the demise are not all that clear. Export markets had declined, but not disastrously, and there remained a lively market, it seems, in Spain, in north Italy (at Spina at the mouth of the River Po), in the east (much traders' stock at Al Mina in Syria), and in the Black Sea (the site at Kerch in the east Crimea giving its name to one of the fourth-century styles). In the hierarchy of artisans the vase painter must have fallen fairly low but he surely would not have given up if there was still a living to be made, and it is clear that pottery production as such was still a lucrative profession. In a free market 'taste' can influence production more quickly than it can in an environment, as that of the ancient non-Greek empires, where it was dictated by a royal court, and conservatism in the arts was recognized as a positive force for confidence in survival. In the archaic and classical periods, to the end of the fifth century, the customers' taste must have been at least in part responsible for the rapid changes in decorative style in this most conservative of crafts. In the fourth century the general demotion of the status of the decorators, and a general growth in wealth which probably made metal vessels far commoner than hitherto, with new Macedonian courts now beginning to dictate taste, may have hastened the decision to abandon painted figure decoration, and to leave the market for any form of decorated vases in the hands of those making plainer wares without figures, except in relief.

The record of the rest of Greece outside Athens in this craft, apart from the plain vases, cannot be ignored but was of strictly local interest since the main markets for decorated vases were dominated by Athenian wares. The principal non-Attic schools are in the west and will be considered shortly. Various local sources for red figure vases can be detected, none very prolific or distinguished, and producing work mainly for local markets, no doubt far cheaper than Athenian imports of comparable or better quality. Many are being produced at a time when war may have made Athenian products less readily accessible. These sources have been identified in Boeotia, Corinth, Laconia, Crete, Elis and north Greece.[103] Their products are inspired by Athens' success with the technique but there were some local shape and subject specialities as one might expect, such as the Boeotian kantharoi. One Athenian is thought to have moved to Corinth to paint,[104] so it was not all a matter of copying. There was even some resurgence of older techniques, like outline drawing and black figure.

### Plain and Patterned Wares

It is natural to treat Greek vases of the sixth to fourth centuries BC mainly in terms of their figure decoration. There was, however, limited production of decorated vases without figures, and vigorous production of vases with no decoration at all. To these we now turn. Vases carefully decorated only with patterns were a commonplace of the earlier archaic period, but there are examples also from the workshops of black and red figure, mainly in Athens: the quality of subsidiary pattern on the figured vases is high and occasionally was allowed to replace figures altogether. Thus, plump stamnoi may be decorated with fine red scrolls and palmettes only.[105] 'Pattern Lekythoi' and alabastra, not always too carefully painted, but there are many exceptions, very often appear with pattern only, at best with scrolls.[106] Finer is the Group of the Floral Nolans, of around the second quarter of the fifth century, which has elaborate red figure scrolls and friezes [*141*]. The 'Nolan' amphora is a high-necked type of the period, and shares this decoration with a number of red figure lekythoi.[107] 'St Valentin' cups are another fifth-century phenomenon, copied also

**141.** Floral Nolan amphora. Early 5th c. BC. H. 33cm. (Birmingham 1616.85)

**142.1,2.** Attic black gloss cup with stamped decoration, from Italy. The scene, between sphinxes on columns, has Athena greeting Hermes, and Perseus who is fleeing from two gorgons. Behind them is the decapitated sister, Medusa, who has given birth to Pegasos and Chrysaor. About 450 BC. H. 11.7cm. (Boston 01.8023)

in South Italy; they include a degree of extra colour, especially on panels of a scale/feather pattern.[108] Here too might be mentioned several vases from late archaic on, where a major part is left black (or even coral red) and the figure decoration confined to a single zone, usually the neck. Plain black can be seen to be a design feature too, which leads us to the all-black vases.

Plain black vases, attractive mainly for the fine black gloss produced by careful Greek potting and firing techniques, had been made from the later sixth century on in Athens, and in increasing volume. They can be as well potted as the decorated vases and although they tend to reproduce the same shapes, there are some which are peculiar to the technique. Among these are some classical cups which seem particularly influenced by contemporary Greek metal shapes (bolsals), betrayed by the concentric cushion-like treatment of the underfoot, copying the turning patterns of vessels in either wood or metal. These and others carry stamped patterns, sometimes even of figures, which are their only form of decoration [*142*].[109] Other shapes are small, designed for the table, such as those called by us salt-cellars. Many of the cups are very fine-walled, but they were cheap, and modern taste for them may exaggerate their value in antiquity, since for us austerity has come to lend an element of 'class'.[110] The black gloss has in the past been called glaze, which is misleading since there is no glass-like fusing of the surface involved, simply fine preparation of the slip,

**143.** Attic 'West Slope' amphora, from Athens. 2nd c. BC. H. 23.6cm. (Athens Agora P599)

**144.** South Italian black gloss cup. Decorated with a roulette (the rows of dashes), and punches for palmettes and circles. The centrepiece is the cast of a silver coin of Syracuse. Late 4th c. BC. H. 5.2cm. (Chicago 1905.341)

which will fire a glossy black. The austere appearance was not long tolerated, especially for the larger vases, and they attract minor friezes of floral and other patterns in white, yellow and gilding, often applied in added clay, in relief, making them look like the metal vases that inspired some of them [*143*].¹¹¹ This is a mode of decoration for the plainer, painted clay vases that continues through the Hellenistic period (late fourth to first centuries BC) in all Greek lands; for though we know our 'black glaze' best from Athens, the black vases were being made in other parts of Greece, including the western colonies, usually following Athens' lead so far as can be judged. I show one made in South Italy which exhibits the rouletting and stamps, and a centrepiece which is a cast of a fourth-century silver coin of Syracuse [*144*].¹¹²

*South Italian and Sicilian Red Figure*

We turn now to South Italy and Sicily to observe the last major production area for Greek figure-decorated, red figure vases. For all the South Italian wares Dale Trendall has provided the service of comprehensive attribution to painters and groups that Beazley did for the Athenian.[113] Well over twenty thousand decorated vases spanning less than a century and a half are known, so this was no mean output, and at its best the qualities of potting and painting match the Athenian. Five main centres are identified. Athenians had settled at Thurii in Lucania (the underfoot of Italy) in 443 BC, and this must have something to do with the first appearance of local red figure in the area shortly afterwards. A main production centre may have been Metapontum. The Greek cities of Apulia to the east were not slow to take up the challenge of providing a local alternative to imported Athenian vases, and the Apulian provide both the most exciting and the most banal products of the new schools. The major centres for production seem to have been Tarentum and Ruvo. To the north west, Paestum was a smaller but distinctive centre, and farther north, approaching Rome, cities in the old Greek colonizing area of Campania also made vases in an individual style. Then there is Sicilian red figure, which may have been the inspiration for the Campanian and Paestan schools, and began around 400 BC, its pupils starting a generation later.

The market for the vases was principally local and Greek though they spread generally, as had the Greeks, through South Italy, seldom much beyond. Shapes are as expected but there are signs of observation of local, native shapes, either because they had some functional convenience or to encourage sale to non-Greeks. The best example is the 'nestoris' of Lucania and Apulia [145],[114] which copies a local Messapian form, and is named for its knobbiness which recalls Homer's description of Nestor's famous cup. The proliferation of handles and knobs on this shape reflects another trait in the potting of this area – a fondness for the more ornate. The big volute craters of Apulia copy the veriest detail of the relief and other decoration of their metal counterparts, with lids, bases, moulded figure handles, and then add some, notably the figure decoration on the body. But this is perhaps less a reflection of western taste than of the relative austerity of contemporary Athenian potting, in a patently declining industry. While we may assume a comparable usage for most of the vessel shapes in the west there are some important local preferences. The Apulian craters seem mainly destined for the grave, a specialization abandoned by this time in Greece. And they are so large, up to 1.5m, that a special compartment could be constructed for them at the end of the grave, where they and other offerings were deposited.[115] A number of them have open bases, deliberate, and this is a feature shared by some other shapes, even relatively small ones such as

**145.** Lucanian nestoris by the
Amykos Painter. Warriors depart;
youths and women. Late
5th c. BC. H. 44.5cm. (Paris,
Louvre K539)

oinochoai. It indicates clearly that they are not meant for everyday use, also that a wider range of vases than the craters was made for the grave.[116]

Some other Greek shapes take on a new lease of life – plates, and especially the fish plates which are perhaps the most engaging of the western products to modern eyes [282]. There is a rich series of animal-head cups, imitating metal [313].[117] In general, shape preferences are divided roughly between the symposiac (cups and craters), the toilet, and the tomb; and with appropriate decoration.

The first potters and painters probably came from Athens and there are close stylistic correspondences with the work of the homeland to be observed, but new styles of drawing soon emerge.[118] Athens could still look forward to some fine displays of line drawing on her vases, but the Lucanian painters developed big-figure subjects executed with both delicacy and considerable success in the depiction of personality and mood. This is some of the finest drawing anywhere in Greece [146].[119] Even in lesser work the slight sketchiness seems less a matter of haste or incompetence, than of good control in delineation of figure and pose [147]. It is very difficult to define what, by around 400 BC, makes the best South Italian painting look different from Athens, apart from the lack of interest in the full Meidian style. Only with lesser works do problems of identity of source arise, where shapes and subjects and clay colour help but little.

*112*

**147.** Detail from a Lucanian calyx crater by the Cyclops Painter. Name vase. Odysseus and his companions prepare to blind the Cyclops Polyphemos. More of the scene, *RVSIS* fig. 9. Late 5th c. BC. (London 1947.7–14.18)

In Apulia the figures are rendered rather as in Athens with lavish use of added white, red, yellow and gilding, also more by way of pale yellowish washes. Far more attention is paid to subsidiary ornament, and there are some fine floral fantasies based on styles which had been developed in wall painting and mosaic, but ignored in Athens' potteries [*148, 149*]. Flowers, leaves and wreaths, with other less definable objects (windows, writing tablets?) fill the background and can lend a rather fussy air, especially to the more vapid compositions of effeminate youths and Erotes with women, holding big platters and boxes. In some ways these are the most characteristic styles for the area through the fourth century and certainly easy to distinguish from Attic. A single woman's head is a very common subject for plates and bowls, with or without lids; they are ubiquitous [*149*]. Experts

148. Apulian pelike by the Painter of the Siren Citharist. Eros in a floral fantasy. Mid-4th c. BC. H. 29.2cm. (London market)

149. Detail from the neck of an Apulian volute crater by the Ganymede Painter. Mid-4th c. BC. H. of frieze 14.5cm. (Basel S24)

150. Campanian hydria by the Whiteface Painter. Kadmos attacks the dragon by a fountain house. After mid-4th c. BC. H. 49cm. (Boston 69.1142 Helen and Alica Colburn Fund)

151. Paestan amphora by the Painter of the Boston Orestes. Name vase. Orestes and his companion Pylades meet his sister Electra at the tomb of their father Agamemnon. Furies (Erinyes) with snakes await the outcome in the upper corners. On the neck, an elegant siren. After mid-4th c. BC. (Boston 99.540)

distinguish a Plain Style, which is not only these latish vases with heads but also simpler figure scenes, mainly on bell craters and pelikai;[120] the Ornate Style has much more to offer.

Campania (at Cumae and Capua) and Paestum started producing red figure by around 350 BC, with more lavish use of white on the figures [*150, 151, 213, 229, 230*].[121] Principles of attribution, which have placed so many Athenian vases that we can study development through the style and relationships of individual painters, work just as well in South Italy; possibly even better because there are plenty of vases and they were not so dispersed by trade as the Athenian, so that very prolific painters can be detected and workshops identified.

The subject matter of the vases has a very broad mythical range compared with fourth-century Attic. We do not find strictly local subjects, though non-Greek figures and armour may appear on some vases (Campanian with Samnite warriors).[122] All schools,

**152.** Detail from an Apulian bell crater. The stage is seen in profile. The elderly Chiron is helped up on to the stage; the audience top right is also in stage costume, but not the youth at the right, perhaps the stage manager. Before mid-4th c. BC. (London F 151)

but especially the Paestan, depict stage scenes, apparently of Attic Old and New Comedy (as of Aristophanes to Menander), with all the trappings of costume, stage set and stage [*152, 228, 229*], though more rustic than performances in the marble theatres of the Greek (including western Greek) world. There is some lively wit and imagination here – the painter Asteas is a prime executant and a fine draughtsman [*153*]. The main series of these are known

**153.** Fragment of a Paestan calyx crater signed by Asteas, from Buccino. A less than heroic Ajax takes refuge from rape by a harridan Cassandra at a statue of Athena; a priestess, holding a temple key, is alarmed at this reversal of the usual event (as on [*121*]). Mid-4th c. BC. (Rome, Villa Giulia 50279)

**154.** Detail from an Apulian askos by the Felton Painter. A dancing hag. About 375 BC. (Ruvo, Jatta 140)

**155.** Detail from an Apulian volute crater. The punishment of Theseus and Peirithoos in Hades, being bound by Furies, watched by Persephone at the left. About 375 BC. (Ruvo, Jatta 1094)

as *phlyax* vases after actors of western farce who can in fact have nothing to do with the scenes; there will be more to say about them in Chapter 6.[123]

Many of the big Apulian vases survive intact and their, to modern eyes, rather unpleasing shapes, and the crowding of figures, too readily disguise the extremely high quality of draughtsmanship. The better painters (the Darius Painter and the Underworld Painter) are totally competent with all renderings of human and animal action, but also in delineation of mood and emotion.[124] Here only does Greek vase painting come very close to the virtually modernistic effects achieved in major painting, on panel or wall, which we see in Macedonian graves. We are already being presented with a command of pictorial expression [*154, 155*] which must have become commonplace in the Hellenistic period and which we can glimpse in the best work made by Greeks for early Rome.

The multi-level scenes of myth on the craters have been thought by many to be inspired by the theatre (tragedy), although none shows the stage details and costumes and masks as do the comic scenes, and any connection with staged performances may at best be indirect. Vase necks are often filled with florals and heads. On the body several have a central building (*naiskos*)

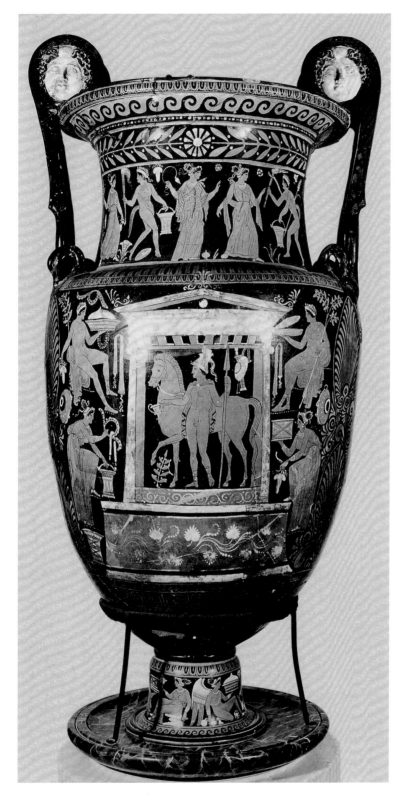

**156.** Apulian volute crater by the Baltimore Painter. The dead as a heroized youth with his horse in a naiskos, with attendants. This is the reverse of a vase with the killing of the Niobids on the front. About 325 BC. (Ruvo, Jatta 424)

**157.** Apulian volute crater by the Underworld Painter, from Canosa. On the neck Greeks fight Amazons. The body: the building is the palace of King Creon of Corinth who is trying to succour his daughter, poisoned by a crown which her brother tries to remove. She is the victim of her rival, the eastern witch Medea who is seen below preparing to kill one of her children, while another escapes, left, and her lover, Jason, Creon's intended son-in-law, arrives too late from the right. At the centre is the serpent car driven by a mad Fury (Oistros), in which Medea will escape. At the right is the ghost (inscribed *eidolon*) of Medea's father, King Aietes, whose curse is being fulfilled. Above, Heracles, Athena and the Dioskouroi attend, representatives of the Argonaut expedition where the story of Jason and Medea began. About 325 BC. (Munich 3296)

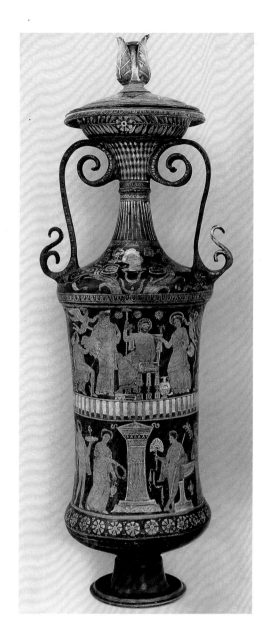

**158.** Apulian loutrophoros by the Darius Painter. Persephone and Aphrodite appeal to Zeus over the fate of Adonis, seated left; below, men and women at a grave stele. After mid-4th c. BC. (New York 11.210.3)

containing an heroic figure, often with a horse, reflecting on the status of the dead [*156*]. Is this the hall of Hades? There is some concern in South Italy with Pythagoreanism and Orphism, doctrines which reassure Everyman that the afterlife need not be something to fear, and the vases with a jovial Hades welcoming the heroic dead are in this spirit.[125] In other scenes the central building may serve as palace or temple, a focus for the display of a mythical occasion enacted by groups of figures set at either side and below, with the top register commonly reserved for the appropriate deities. Inscriptions are not uncommon, and these scenes are a richer source for the detail of Greek myth than most Athenian

**159.** Drawing from a volute crater by the Darius Painter, from Canosa. Name vase. Centre, the Persian King Darius (III, the one defeated by Alexander) listens to a messenger from his western empire haranguing him. The latter stands on a base labelled 'Persai' (= Persepolis, Darius' capital). Either side noblemen, Persian and Greek (with some Persian dress, so subjects). Below left, a Greek accountant in the royal treasury counts resources; below right, Persians supplicate the King for relief. At the top, from left, Artemis and Apollo; Zeus, with Victory (Nike) at his knee, receives the personification of Greece (Hellas) introduced by Athena; a Fury, Deceit (Apata), leads a personification of Persia's western empire (Asia) away from sanctuary at a herm of Aphrodite (?) – a divine commentary on the outcome of the discussion below. About 325 BC. (Naples 3253[81947])

vases and many contemporary texts. As pots and paintings they are *tours de force*, and their rather over-elaborated settings should not detract from their extreme value to us as far more than documents of the potter's craft. I show a crater by the Underworld Painter [157],[126] one of the most prolific and informative of these 'scenic' artists, beside the Darius Painter. The mythical cast is enormous, acting episodes of a story which are broadly synchronous and certainly closely linked in narrative; and there is a walk-on cast of nurses, old men, spear-bearers and relatives. Few other large vases, like the loutrophoros [158], are as well endowed with populous mythology.

It is on the Apulian vases too that we see some scenes which Athens abjured, since they seem to relate to specific contemporary events, and might in this respect be influenced by wall painting which also now turned often to the depiction of the contemporary, notably battles. There are some scenes of a Greek horseman attacking a Persian in a chariot which closely resemble the scheme used in the famous Alexander Mosaic (which copies a painting), probably showing Alexander the Great fighting Darius III at the Battle of Issus. More remarkable is the Darius Painter's name vase

[159] where the Persian king is in court at Persepolis (Persai, to the Greeks), his Greek accountant receiving tribute below, listening to a western subject warning him, it may be, of Alexander's continuing advance. In the upper register Greek gods and personifications of Victory and Deceit provide a commentary on the destiny of the Persian Empire.[127]

All red figure decoration for South Italian vases seems to have expired by the beginning of the third century BC, gradually overtaken by plainer products, with the range of added and colourful trimmings that we observed also in homeland Greece.

### The Hellenistic Wares

The Hellenistic period, east and west, was a very busy one for the ancient potter, but less rewarding for the modern viewer, and less well articulated to answer the questions of historians and archaeologists. The plain black vases became somewhat less plain, sometimes quite large and gaudy with added decorative elements in relief or paint, their bodies often fluted to imitate the common decoration of metal prototypes.

One characteristic is for groups of Hellenistic vases to be called by misleading names. The plain black vases with colourful floral and other additions, remarked already [143], are known as West Slope Ware in Greece, but were not made to be found only on the west slope of the Acropolis of Athens;[128] and in the west the corresponding Gnathia Ware was not made only in a town of Apulia where much was found, but over much of South Italy and in Etruria. Here more was also admitted by way of figure vignettes in added colour – white, yellow, red, orange, pink, green [160, 232].[129] A few versions of the technique, made in third-century Etruria, are executed with as good an understanding of shading and highlight as could be desired at this scale in such a medium. Only here does the vase painter truly attempt to emulate the panel painter in the realistic rendering of figures.[130]

Moulded hemispherical cups with the simplest floral and figure patterns in relief were not made only in Megara (near Corinth) yet most are still called Megarian bowls [161]. This is roughly the eastern shape we have remarked already, which also attracted the flat feet and little loop handles, usually called skyphoi. Some more elaborate relief cups with inscribed figure scenes of myth moulded upon them are understandably called Homeric Bowls [162].[131] All these relief wares are inspired by metal prototypes and some of their patterns may even have been moulded from them. They are particularly conspicuous on some

160. Gnathian squat lekythos. A woman, possibly Leda, with a swan. Her dress is orange brown with a red border. After mid-4th c. BC. H. 19cm (New York, Callimanopoulos Collection; once Castle Ashby)

161. Megarian relief bowl, from Megara. Heracles attacking Auge, the group repeated four times, with a figure of Pan, with animal skin and throwing stick, placed between. 3rd c. BC. H. 13.8cm. (London G103)

162. The decoration of a 'Homeric' relief bowl, from Amphipolis. Above, Hecuba (Hekabe) mourns in Troy (Ilion). Below left Achilles, backed by Athena, fights her son Hector, and at the right dead Hector is dragged round Troy behind Achilles' chariot. The events of Homer's Iliad Book XXII. 3rd c. BC. (Mannheim, Reiss-Museum Cg 349)

163. Calene black relief phiale. A Dionysiac feast. 3rd/2nd c. BC. (St Petersburg)

**164.** A lagynos, from Benghazi. 2nd c. BC. H. 15.9cm. (London F513)

**165.** A 'Hadra' hydria from Egypt. Inscribed after firing with the name of the dead whose ashes are within. About 200 BC. (Oxford 1920.250)

smaller shapes in black gloss, a notable class being made in Campania – the Calene – with moulded figure groups decorating cups, lamps and bowls [*163, 288*], a practice that survived strongly into the Roman period.[132]

There is plain painted Hellenistic pottery too, usually decorated with florals on a pale, sometimes glossy slip. A new jug shape is the lagynos with high thin neck and broad low body [*164*]. Hydriai also attract this decoration. Hadra Ware is named for the appearance of its hydriai as ash urns in an Alexandrian cemetery, but they were made in Crete, and there are many other towns in the Greek world in which this was an acceptable mode of painted decoration [*165*]. The Hadra type in Alexandria was later also produced locally, then with names and dates inscribed on the vase. There is indeed an uninterrupted succession, from the archaic period on, of such simple, floral-decorated and striped vessels.[133] For something more elaborate, in the west especially, there are some elaborate funerary vases with colourful decoration applied after firing and often by way of moulded or modelled additives, from Canosa in Apulia and Centuripe in Sicily [*166*]. Egypt had long been used to the production of real glazed vessels, their bodies not clay but a vitreous 'frit' miscalled 'faience'; the

166. Sicilian lidded bowl, from Centuripe. Polychrome painting on the lid of women performing a wedding ritual. 3rd c. BC. H. 61cm. (New York 30.11.4)

**167.** 'Faience' flask in the form of Eros riding a goose, from Tanagra. 3rd c. BC. H. 17.8cm. (London K1; 1875.11–10.2)

technique now acquires Hellenistic Greek decoration on vessels for the Alexandrian Greek market. My example is a more exotic version in the technique [*167*].[134]

On any Hellenistic site decorated pottery, painted or in relief, is a minority find beside the traditional plain table wares or those serving carriage and storage, notaby the conoid amphorae and a range of domestic shapes, including cooking ware, which had always formed part of the potter's stock in trade. Metal, even glass, had come to replace many of the more admired painted shapes, and set the standard. Perfumed oil was certainly in demand, no longer in elaborate clay vessels but in metal or even semi-precious stone or glass. In clay there are only the ubiquitous plain, thin and handleless flasks ('fusiform', like a spindle, or globular like the older alabastra) for the mass market [*168*].[135]

These plain clay flasks seem an appropriate finale to this summary history of the potter's craft in Greece. In the seventh century BC their purpose was served by the finest potting and painting [*31*], but now only by far more precious materials, or the humblest forms in clay. As a major craft attracting and displaying the work of accomplished potters and decorators, Greek pottery can be seen to have both declined and significantly changed, in keeping with the spirit of the times and expectations of its customers, no longer quite the measure of social and civic life that it had been in earlier centuries, though still a major factor in production and trade, and an essential marker for the archaeologist and historian.

The following chapters dwell mainly on the pre-Hellenistic record because this is where there is more scope for speculation about the significance of both shape and decoration, and there is much more to occupy the eye and imagination. Hellenistic pottery is more the preserve of the archaeologist, but no less rewarding for some areas of study, notably trade. For the heyday of painted decoration, especially the sixth to fourth centuries, we have seen that archaeological skills in pottery classification have refined our knowledge of the craft to the point at which we may often be able to identify the hands and careers of individuals in the potters' studios. There can hardly be any more closely defining criterion for an ancient artefact, and it alone renders a higher potential to the other more obvious information that the vases offer. This is why the procedure employed for such identification occupies pride of place, in the next chapter, before any more obvious historical, social, technical or archaeological matters; the more so since it has become fashionable in some quarters to distrust or decry it.

**168.** Hellenistic clay unguentaria from tombs in Athens. (Kerameikos)

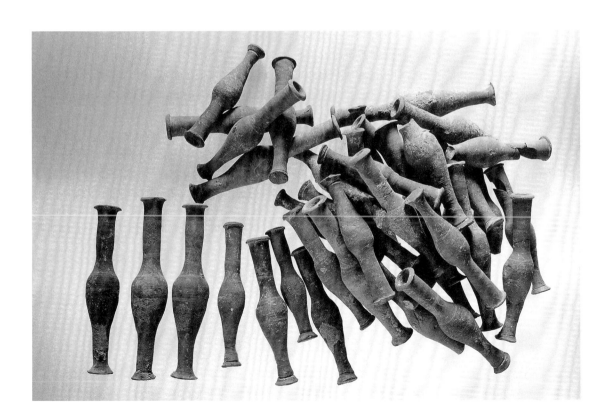

# Chapter 2: Connoisseurship

In Greek vase studies, as in many other areas of art history, the word 'connoisseurship' has acquired a meaning narrower than 'expert judgement' and is applied especially to expertise in attributing works to individual artists or schools. This has, in the last hundred years, become a major study, and is often taken to be an end in its own right: which of course it is, since we assign especial qualities of originality and style to those artists whom we can recognize, whether or not we can name them, and judge the history of artists to be an essential part of the history of art along with many other considerations of a social, aesthetic and iconographic character. I shall revert to the value of the study later in this chapter and elsewhere, after considering the techniques.

In our subject the techniques were most readily applicable to the range of Athenian decorated vases since they were plentiful, generally regarded as being 'the best', and had the added advantage of offering some artists' signatures. These signatures were very few. Of the nearly nine hundred artists recognized through connoisseurship, and accounting for probably barely half the surviving figured vases, only some forty have left us their real names. And very much less than one per cent of the vases known have any signatures at all, since the practice was not spread thinly through the whole population of artists, but many signers made a habit of it, mainly in the late archaic period, while in the fourth century virtually none did, and a majority of the better artists did not sign at all in any period.

The signatures take the form *X egrapsen* – 'X drew [me]'. This is quite explicit, using the word for painting or drawing. There are other signatures in the form *X epoiesen* – 'X made [me]'. Sometimes these are manifestly potters' signatures, especially where we find an *egrapsen* and *epoiesen* on the same vase, differentiating the tasks, and sometimes even the same name 'X drew and made me', while close study of shapes can often confirm the association. From signatures on late sixth-century Athenian vases we can see that some thirty per cent of those naming painters admit the same artist as potter. The only possible alternative meaning for *epoiesen* arises from allowing the word to imply overall control of the making, that is, the role of the workshop owner, and this has become a popular view. But elsewhere in Greek art the use of the word clearly implies active involvement in production and it must have been normal for the owner to be a potter.[1] I am not aware of any instances where its use cannot mean 'potted', even with such a busy signer as Nikosthenes. But *epoiesen* on its own might also or alternatively mean 'painted', as is shown by instances where the painter's hand (from an *egrapsen*) is assured. And there might always be cases where the name may be borrowed or, as it were, licensed, within a workshop for particular occasions. It is doubtful whether this can be called forgery since that implies that the signature counted for something, and if that were true we should have far more of them, especially of the better painters of the grander vases. There is only one clear instance.[2] That fashion had a lot to do with it is shown by the red figure Pioneers (late sixth century) who sign a lot and even refer to each other. It is certainly nothing to do with advertisement in the modern sense, with the solitary possible exception of Nikosthenes, who signs his vases freely, having probably potted and painted most or all himself, and was aiming at the Etruscan market.

At all events, early in the study of the vases it became clear that the inscriptions gave important clues, though it took a while to determine that *epoiesen* might mean potter only. Various scholars of the end of the nineteenth century collected these names and made further attributions to their hands, notably Paul Hartwig, who studied especially the red figure cups, and Adolf Furtwängler, who was probably the greatest classical archaeologist of all time. In the light of later work we can see that many of their attributions were correct, but this does not mean that they employed the techniques which are now recognized as the most effective, and which were introduced by John Beazley in 1908/9. His predecessors followed signatures, then seem to have gone by the 'look' of the vase, composition and figures, and any close similarities of treatment, but they virtually never defined what these were in detail, or ever used them as prime sources. Their technique was much like that we practice ourselves when we reckon that we can recognize the difference between a Tiepolo and a Veronese, without having to explain in detail just why.

The new lead came from the study of artists of early Italian and Renaissance painting. In the late nineteenth century Giovanni Morelli practised attribution by attending to the way painters treated detail in their work – the handling of dress or especially anatomy – which might be judged peculiar to each artist and not taught or necessarily determined by a model. I illustrate his

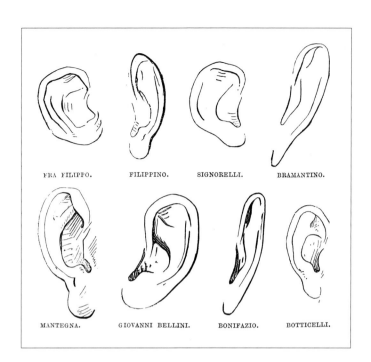

**169.** Morelli's drawings of typical ears

comparative drawings of typical ears [*169*].³ The technique was taken up especially by Bernard Berenson, and the result was broad agreement about individual styles and the possibility of attribution to artists even when they had no names. Their names had to be devised for them, and Beazley followed suit. In effect Renaissance painting was not the best subject for such study since there was too much variety, and there was in time a positive search for realism, when the influence of the appearance of the model might determine how some otherwise potentially significant features were treated. On the whole it is easier to apply pre-Raphael than post-. As a result the technique has met with some heavy criticism over the years, though it is still practised in all its essentials. Kenneth Clark, as often, saw the main point: 'The so-called Morellian method, when seen at a distance, amounts to little more than the sensible observation that those parts of a figure which an artist draws unconsciously, in particular such physiological details as earlobes and finger nails, are the parts of his work in which he is most likely to reveal his identity'.⁴

Greek vase painting is a far more promising field. Everything was linear. Drawing from life was probably quite exceptional. There was no great variety in the figure work. Dress was as simple as it could be and therefore similar forms were constantly repeated but in ways which might reveal individual treatment. And anatomy was much in evidence. This was important, as Morelli had realized, since all artists had a common model – life – which the connoisseur knows as much about as the artists did and can use as the point of reference.

Starting from an article published in 1910 John Beazley devoted most of his long scholarly career to the connoisseurship of Athenian vases. Having demonstrated the technique in early articles he went on to produce magisterial lists of painters and attributions, having looked at and placed the majority of examples available for inspection in museums and publications. Some have complained that he did not explain his technique, but his early articles do just that, and only the image-blind or lazy might not follow the lines of reasoning. He was not infallible, and often corrected himself, but his authority is generally recognized and the method accepted.[5] Recent revisionist attempts have failed, and some criticisms are mainly the result of ignorance of what the technique was, even thinking it was somehow involved with Freud and the subconscious, rather than handwriting and the unconscious.[6]

How did Beazley come to the method? It had already been practised in Classical art history by Furtwängler, but on sculpture, not vase painting. There it was a matter of trying to deduce what were the favoured renderings of individual sculptors whose work could only be recognised from copies identified from literary sources, not signatures or style.[7] It was not a question of using similarities in observed renderings to determine authorship. Beazley knew Furtwängler's work, of course. This is a case where, as often, non-academic factors in a scholar's life may influence his work, and the possibilities are worth pursuing.

Morellianism was much in the air early in the century, but not much in Classical or Greek art circles and certainly not in the area of vase painting, or Furtwängler would have used it. I venture to suggest the path that led Beazley to the technique. After graduation at Oxford Beazley settled quickly into the security of Oxford life which left plenty of time and opportunity for research without overdue demands of teaching and administration, which was at any rate being ably handled in those days by the professor, Percy Gardner. Beazley was an aesthete. He had travelled in Europe and came of a craftsman family, but was averse to any Arts and Crafts attitudes, indeed techniques of potting and painting were never of major interest in his writing about Greek vases. His attitude to 'his' artists was that of a Bernard Berenson, not a William Morris.[8]

He was much involved with the poet James Elroy Flecker, one year his senior, whom he met in 1904. They jointly edited an undergraduate magazine, *The Best Man* (1906), and Flecker dedicated his first volume of poetry (*The Bridge of Fire*) to him in 1907 and encouraged Beazley to write poetry too, which he did, dismally. They lounged around Oxford and dressed up,[9] no doubt emulating the divine Oscar who had shown Oxford what aestheticism was about (he had died in 1900); T.E. Lawrence ('of Arabia') was of the same circle. Beazley could even seem to some 'idle and irresponsible' (1910); but he was a brilliant classical scholar. He had been taught Greek art by Percy Gardner, and was himself teaching Greek vases for the new Diploma in Classical Archaeology. His first vase article, in 1908, was all about iconography and literature with not a word about attribution or connoisseurship. In 1908 Flecker gave up school-teaching to go to Cambridge where he studied oriental languages and in 1909 proposed to a young woman, before setting off to the east in 1910 in the consular service. In 1909 Andrew Gow graduated in Cambridge, having read Classics with archaeology, and must have met Beazley. In the following year they were exploring the dealers together and bought jointly a picture they had attributed to Simone Martini; and Beazley published his first connoisseurship article.[10] They were in Paris together, with Flecker, looking at Greek vases. It was, I believe, Gow's influence or at least companionship that led Beazley to take Morellianism seriously for both pictures and pots, and Gow who led their interest in Simone Martini, whose hand they must have determined in a Morellian fashion. Their scholarly association, Gow in Cambridge (until his death in 1986), Beazley in Oxford (until his death in 1970), persisted throughout their working lives, with Gow providing a wealth of knowledge about the offbeat subjects that the more fastidious Beazley seems to have shunned; Gow's main subject for research was more traditionally literary – a fine edition of the poet Theocritus. When Beazley published his catalogue of the Lewes House gems in 1920 it was dedicated to Gow. But it was Gow, I am sure, who wrote the anonymous review of it in the same year which made the first association in print of Morelli's name with Beazley's technique with vases, throwing in a reference to a painting by Simone Martini for good measure.[11] Gow collected paintings, remained strongly committed to painting studies and served as trustee to both the Fitzwilliam Museum and the National Gallery, to both of which he bequeathed important works. The painting he and Beazley had bought is no longer thought to be by their painter: Beazley alone did better with Greek pots.

Beazley's use of photographs, not published drawings, or better, his reliance on personal inspection backed by photographs and drawings made himself from the vase, was crucial. Beazley significantly did not start with painters who had left some signatures; indeed he ignored the signatures as a guide to hand, and was quite prepared to believe them misleading on occasion, and to prefer his method to what he might read on the vase. Furtwängler had already realized the difference between potter and painter signatures, and that Euphronios the painter did not decorate the vases that Euphronios (in older age) potted.

Beazley's 1910 article[12] was on Kleophrades, which was in fact the name of a potter, and the sobriquet 'Kleophrades Painter' had to be coined for the artist who painted at least one of the potter's vases. Another of the potter's works had been signed by a different painter, Douris. Other scholars had assembled works under the name Kleophrades. Beazley, augmenting their lists, soon reveals his criteria in the course of his description: 'the full nostril strongly marked by a rounded black line with the lower side doubled', and so on, hair, whiskers, eyeballs, lips, cheek, ankles, fingers: 'The ears vary. The painter has not yet formulated his rendering'. This shows that he had already determined to his own satisfaction the various criteria on which attribution might be based. Not all need apply always and they might change with time, but comparison with similar criteria for contemporary painters, of which Beazley makes a point, shows that where the vast majority of criteria coincide and are not shared by others an individual hand can be determined. To dismiss the technique as relying simply on comparing ears is to betray sad ignorance of the whole process, which is best evaluated by practising it for oneself.[13] At any rate, ears are not to be despised (see Morelli's [169]), since we characterize faces by eyes, nose and mouth, not ears, which may therefore be treated in a summary but personal and revealing manner. Many vases remain unattributed, of course, but of those that are I would guess that far less than one per cent of Beazley's attributions are in any sense controversial, which are better odds than most in archaeology.

The technique can, in fact, be 'proved' by appeal to the recurrence of the basic criteria on batches of *signed* vases by different contemporary artists. A simple demonstration of just one or two criteria in the signed works of Euphronios and Euthymides is given in [170]. Ears are slightly different, nostrils are Cs on one, recurved on the other, anklebones are defined by a single line on one, double on the other, and Euthymides uses dilute paint, not black, for these details. In general he uses dilute more, for dress details and especially for anatomy (except for the *linea alba* below the navel), where Euphronios uses fine black. These are two

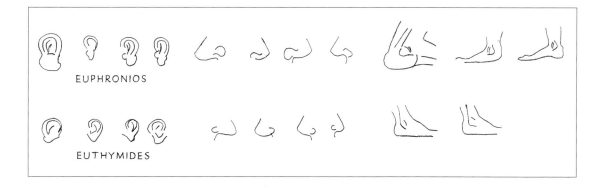

EUPHRONIOS

EUTHYMIDES

170. Anatomical details taken from signed vases by Euphronios and Euthymides

171.1,2. Prints by Japanese artists: *1*. Toshusai Sharaku (AD 1794) an actor as a money-lender; *2*. Kitagawa Utamaro (AD 1792/3) three famous beauties. H. 37cm, 39cm. (Tokyo, Riccar Art Museum)

172. Ears, as drawn by a selection of Japanese print masters of the 18th and 19th centuries

contemporary painters whose styles are close enough for 'at a glance' attributions to be hazardous. The criteria mentioned, and others involving appearance of dress, as well as Euphronios' obsession with the anatomical detail of fingers, eyelashes and knee caps, recur, in discrete groups, on several other vases which can therefore be attributed safely to each artist. And they are markedly different from the modes of other contemporaries, with or without names. For Beazley, the fact that the few signatures supported his attribution of a larger group of vases to one hand was a secondary consideration. Through his career Beazley was incidentally demonstrating the strength of his method, notably in attributing fragments in different museums (six in one case) which were found to join; the initial sorting was by style, then subject, then shape of fragments.

It can also be 'proved' outside Greek art. At its simplest, by observation of the details of drawing by favourite cartoonists, who are not hampered by observation of live models. And at a higher level, in Japanese prints where the linear techniques are quite close to Greek red figure. For many of these the subjects are not helpful – landscapes, etc. – but there are many of heads or busts alone, or whole single figures, generally of women or actors, and of more detailed whole figures [*171*].[14] The obvious, indeed only, criterion for us is the ear, since eyes and mouths are minute, the dress variegated, and the undress too embarrassing to analyse in detail (and at any rate too consciously rendered). The artists drew their subjects (not from life) onto paper which was then placed over a block for the block-cutter to follow, line by line, like producing a carbon copy. Artist and, sometimes, cutter sign. Quite cursory examination of the signed work of a few great names readily reveals the Morellian criteria for attribution, even with only one feature to study, rendered in very few lines. See [*172*], chosen rather at random (this is not my subject), from works of artists of the eighteenth to early nineteenth centuries. An ear offers few possibilities

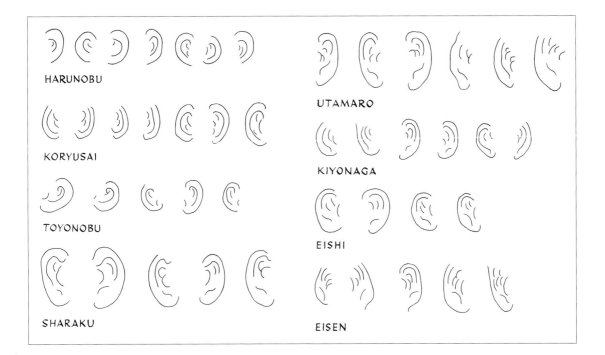

HARUNOBU

KORYUSAI

TOYONOBU

SHARAKU

UTAMARO

KIYONAGA

EISHI

EISEN

for variety yet it can be seen that each artist keeps mainly to one form and that it is often quite different from that of a contemporary. But there is possibility of confusion between some painters, and here the signatures are the decisive factor, though there is also in the observation a means of detecting forgery.[15]

A different modern analogy comes to mind after observing two pot-painters at Vietri sul Mare (Salerno) decorating plates with very simple floral and animal patterns, each hardly more than a half-dozen strokes of the brush. It was impossible to distinguish their hands without, perhaps, close analysis of pressure on brush or the like; but they were deliberately attempting to create completely uniform products for the tourist trade, a very different matter from the aims of the Greek vase painter. They even, unfailingly, placed exactly the same number (thirty-four, I think) of dashes around the rim, by eye.

It becomes clear that each artist can be betrayed by his drawing, just as we may be by our handwriting even to the satisfaction of the law and our banks. The common factor for the artists was life, the real shape of an ear or ankle, or the way it was remembered, or how dress falls; just as for us there was a common model in the way we were all taught to shape our letters at school. The way the painters drew such details, and the way we write, are not totally unconscious since they were based on 'real' forms, but they rapidly become so. Thus, a young painter may have consciously copied the way his teacher drew an ear or hand, but soon adjusted to his own 'style', unconsciously. This can be observed from study of painters in a single workshop, which becomes possible in fifth-century Athens. But this is also an area in which the question may arise whether 'a painter's' work should be divided, or whether two should be conflated, in the light of changes in drawing over what might be a long working life.

There is more to it than this, of course.[16] Painters reveal themselves also through their choice of subjects, the compositions and poses they employ, the shapes they decorate, determined by themselves or their potter employers. The nexus of criteria is thus considerably increased, and a majority can convince, so that we are able to identify an uncharacteristic subject or composition by an otherwise predictable artist which may have been specially commissioned. This is but one of the bonuses a scholar can enjoy from the technique. Another is the possibility of explaining a problematic scene by appeal to others from the same hand which might offer a clue to a particular approach or treatment, a process scholars seem slow to learn. Thus a history of style for the art can be built up. For the individual artist a career can sometimes be charted, with the help of criteria which have played no part in determining his identity, but by observation of development of vase shape, subsidiary decoration, changes in subject matter, employer, even development of writing.[17] And yet we find the mindless assertion: 'Beazley's artists prove to be shadowy figures. We cannot know where they were born, their social status, their level of education, their relationship with each other or how and where they were trained. We cannot be sure how long they practised their craft, how many pots they painted or how far their output and their manner of painting changed over the length of their careers.'[18] We cannot *know* many things about antiquity but it has become easier, thanks to connoisseurship, to answer such questions about the painters than for most 'historical' figures of antiquity. These are no shadowy figures. One is bound to suspect that the motivation for the complaint quoted went beyond ignorance.

There can be no better place at which to start an enquiry into Athenian vases in particular, their role in society and what they meant to their public, than with their painters; and these are now revealed as individuals who can be placed in relationship with each other and with their customers.

The increasingly close approximation to live forms, translated into two-dimensional line, which is displayed in the development of Athenian black and red figure painting, was an ideal basis for the application of these techniques of attribution. It has worked as well with the other comparably large body of material offered by the schools of South Italian red figure vases, which have been studied especially by Dale Trendall, pioneered by Beazley.[19] In earlier periods, where recollection of live forms was less important – that is, for the other black figure and earlier archaic styles back to Geometric – we deal to some degree with the same type of criteria, but also more with treatment of individual details, sometimes of realia, and to a large extent with composition and subsidiary decoration.[20] The results are no less easily obtained but in some of the more prolific schools, such as Corinthian black figure, the lack of the very individual features which are so much help in Athenian red figure, means that there is more room for doubt in some instances, and not all scholars' lists of painters correspond in the way that Beazley's, however much augmented, continue to satisfy critical students of the later period. For this rather more mechanical application of Morellianism there is also proof available in a different sphere. Michael Roaf observed such detail differences in the repetitive figures on the Apadana reliefs at Persepolis (fifth century BC); mathematical analysis reduced them to clusters suggesting the work of individual teams and artists; and the proof appeared when the discreet corresponding masons' marks were observed on the slabs themselves.[21]

Readers will have noticed that, for naming vase painters who have withheld their real names, recourse is made to using the source, location, identity or subject of one of their better known works, a *kalos* name they use, their favourite potter, or quirks of style (Elbows Out; or, for potters, Club Foot). There are also many nuances of relationships which Beazley distinguished and tried to define.[22]

To extend the same process to the study of potters is not quite so easy, yet the hand of the potter might be revealed through shape or the treatment of detail. This has been achieved in some areas of the study, and the *epoiesen* signatures help, but are too few.[23] Most of these are painted but several potters have left their signatures in the form of neat graffiti, pre-firing, which suggests perhaps a more personal interest in claiming credit than the painted inscription, perhaps put on by the decorator.[24] Experiment has proved enlightening. With the aim of determining how readily pot shapes might be copied free-hand, without drawings or templates, a simple form was offered to three potters for copying. All produced copies that would satisfy most eyes and hands, but it was still possible to determine through close analysis and measurement the work of the different potters, even when each was intent on producing the same result.[25]

Scholarship of the last hundred years has transformed the study of thousands of Athenian and other Greek decorated vases, valued mainly for their decoration and a few inscriptions, to a closely knit nexus of individual artists' careers through which the history of the whole craft can be read. The study is an end in itself, but equally a means to many other ends as the following chapters will show. The human element is vital, and in the next chapter we look more closely at the people who made and painted the pots, their lives and fortunes.

# Chapter 3:    Potters and Painters

Making pots was a dirty, messy business. It called for clay, water, fire and, especially for the right conditions for the firing of the black gloss paint, lots of deliberate smoke. This would be one reason for keeping it away from a town centre today, but at any rate it also needed room for kilns, clay washing and fuel, as well as access to clay beds and sources of fuel. If these were perforce distant, a good road or coastal or river link was desirable. Kilns have been found in various places in Greece, but complete potters' establishments in major centres are potentially more informative. That for archaic Corinth lay well outside the urban centre, 1.5km from the Agora (market place), but just within the city wall. It was in use from the eighth to fourth centuries BC. It is assumed that there were other potters' quarters in the town, but this is by no means certain or necessary for this period. Marketing would have been done in town, even on the quayside which was some 5km away, but what has been found are only the living and working quarters, not the kilns. It seems that this was a specialist community, even with its own parish church not far distant, for the god Poseidon and his consort Amphitrite, higher on the slopes of Acrocorinth and near the clay beds. Here the craftsmen dedicated small clay plaques, some decorated by fine and named artists, others by less professional hands, but all in the trade, since so many show scenes of work in hand, from the clay pit to the kiln: precious testimony to the more personal aspects of the craft and the life of the potters' quarter [*173*].[1]

In Athens the potters concentrated in a district and deme which took its name from their craft – Kerameikos (*keramos* = clay): the deme Kerameis. This lay on either side of the city limits in the area of what was to be the Dipylon Gate, and was from early days one of the prime cemeteries of Athens. The tombs ranged along the road leading away to Eleusis; the potters along a road of some 1.5km towards the Academy – the dead would not complain though professors might. In town they were adjacent to the classical Agora, but in early days this was occupied at least in part by potters, while the market place and assembly area were on the far side of the Acropolis, and the port, at Piraeus, was 10km away, with no useful access by river. The Agora as we know it was first laid out

173.1–3. Corinthian votive clay plaques dedicated at a sanctuary of Poseidon and Amphitrite at Penteskoupha, near Corinth's potters' quarter: *1.* work in the clay pit, with refreshment being offered; *2.* a potter runs to adjust the chimney which is flaring dangerously; *3.* a cross section of a kiln, the stoking channel to the right below the pierced floor, the chimney above. 6th c. BC. H. 10.4, 9, 9.8cm. (Berlin F871, F616, F892)

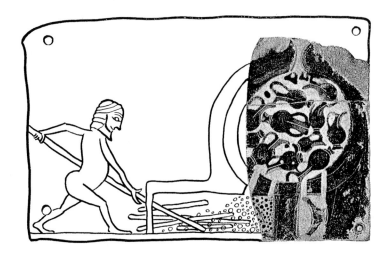

under the sixth-century tyrants, but the western part of Athens seems to have been much devoted to the exercise of various crafts.[2] However, since this is the only urban area we know well from excavation, we cannot rule out the possibility that there were other manufacturing areas. There is evidence for fourth-century potting south of the classical Agora, kilns have in fact been found also outside the north gate of the city, towards Acharnai, and we might expect them at the east nearer the modern clay beds and potteries of Amaroussi. The only dedications of Athenian potters that we know are grander than the Corinthian clay plaques we have noticed. They were made on the Acropolis itself: some marble monuments and vases which, from their decoration and inscriptions, seem to have been made especially as dedications from, as it were, a tithe of profits.[3]

There have been many finds of kilns around Greece, all of much the same pattern, well matched by the representations on the archaic Corinthian plaques.[4] On the north Aegean island of Thasos there is a site well away from the main town, but close to clay beds and a harbour, which was busy in the late archaic period, and areas where the clay was worked can be made out.[5] Far later, in the second century BC, a potters' quarter has been located at the palatial site of Pella in Macedonia. It was dedicated to the production of clay vessels and figures made from moulds and stamps rather than on the wheel: a measure of the different interests of the Hellenistic pot-buying public.[6] Itinerant potters have also to be considered, though it is likely that such would have been specialists, making kilns for special commissions for tiles, architectural terracottas or big pithoi.[7]

Crafts tend to run in families, the more so those requiring more than one pair of hands. Athenian vase painters who have signed their work seem to name their fathers when they are in the same profession, so we can make out some family careers, but also a painter whose father was a sculptor, and who painted a clay plaque dedication for his father to offer (Euthymides and Pollias).[8] In the fourth century and later there was a potter family bearing the names Bachhios and Kittos, whose members signed extant vases (Panathenaic amphorae), received a decent burial in Athens, were hailed as competition winners, and were rewarded with citizenship at Ephesus for unrecorded services to the community.[9]

In small businesses in villages the potting was probably not a full-time profession and the family surely had to work its own land like other folk. In the city this was less likely to be true once the industry had expanded through the export trade. Some vase

**174.** Scenes in a pottery from an Attic hydria. From the left: appraising an amphora, fashioning a large pot on a wheel turned by a boy, carrying pots, the owner or customer, carrying clay?, raking out a kiln decorated with a satyr mask for good luck. Late 6th c. BC. (Munich 1717)

**175.** Drawing from an Attic black figure skyphos showing the preparation of clay in large vats or baskets, with pots being finished (below the handles) and at the right of each side a sacral herm, one being attended (to right). About 500 BC. Drawing by Helen Wilson Kolb. (Harvard 1960.321)

scenes show potters at work and suggest a staff of six or more [*174–178*], but it may be that the numbers on the vases are dictated by the field available to show them. At the very least, a potter might need some help to turn the wheel [*176*] and could do all the rest himself.[10] There are plenty of one-man potteries in the Greek countryside today, but their wheels are power-driven or managed with a treadle, and their kilns are fired by gas or electricity. I feel sure that even a Euphronios sometimes carried the wood and skimmed the clay. But there was always work for the younger members of the family, apprentices, and no doubt periods when special activities occupied all their time – building a new kiln, collecting clay and fuel, packing for the trade.

From the numbers of painters identified and the evidence of their surviving output an attempt has been made to calculate how

many hands were at work in the industry in classical Athens. The sums, not wholly futile we hope, suggest at least a hundred painters at any one time, so perhaps up to five hundred in all involved in all the processes, especially if we consider that there were more undecorated vases made than decorated; a tidy proportion for a town the size of Athens, and occupying no little land.[11]

This is not a subject in which ancient texts are of much value to us in terms of understanding the potters as people and citizens, rather than occasionally tycoons (Kittos and Bacchios, it seems, see above). Aristophanes mentions two rather wretched potters who were also noisy politicians: the hyperbolic Hyperbolos who was eventually ostracized, and Kephalos who was decree-crazy and 'makes poor cups but a good politician'.[12] A fourth-century Corinthian potter, Therikles, made very fine cups, which took his

name, from precious metals and wood as well as clay.[13] Agathokles, king of Syracuse, started as a potter and when he fell on hard times, returned to the craft and laboured to make a clay cup as fine as the golden ones he once held.[14] Pottery could, it seems, be taken as a serious and noble profession by some, and an Athenian fifth-century poet, listing the most notable products of various Greek and non-Greek peoples, praises an Athens which 'invented the potter's wheel and the child of clay and the oven, noblest pottery, useful in house-keeping'.[15] Plato observes that a fine clay vase can be 'very beautiful'; though ugly when set beside maidens![16] You have to take a very jaundiced view of Greek pottery and life to disagree with either proposition. Several otherwise barely decorated vases, finely potted, carry their potter's names, not without some measure of pride, I should imagine: Chian Nikesermos, Athenian Teisias.[17] Inscriptions sometimes comment on the quality of the ware in a self-conscious way – 'I am a good cup', 'Exekias made me well'.[18] And it may be easy to overdo the distinction between a citizen-élite and the banausic craftsmen, since many a noble family owed its position to the market place. 'Where there's muck, there's brass.'[19]

The personnel of a pottery might be full citizens, but most of them are anonymous and unknown beyond identities that can be won from connoisseurship, and only a few have left signatures. A painter(?), Lydos, in the later sixth century in Athens signs as a slave (*do[u]los*).[20] From the signatures on vases it has been observed that many of those employed in the Athenian potters' quarter bore non-Athenian names: some might be slaves, many might be metics – immigrants with limited rights who seem to have been especially active in the crafts in Greece; or rather, craftsmen who were ready to travel where their special skills were best employed. We may contrast the painter who calls himself 'the Lydian' with the Lydos who says he is a slave. Some could certainly be treated very harshly [*177*]. Other inscribed names with ethnic or topographical connotations are non-committal about status – Skythes, Sikelos, Thrax, Kolchos, Mys. The Athenians used sometimes to name slaves for the area from which they came.[21] Ionia was probably an important source, to judge from various features of painting, shapes and technique introduced in the mid-sixth century and later.[22] The inscriptions sometimes reveal a hand practised in scripts other than Athenian – in Rhodes Argive, in Athens Samian, Keian or Doric, in Corinth Sicyonian and other.[23] But it is perhaps possible to make too much of this phenomenon. For example, a Laconian vase found in Cyrene is inscribed with a painted name in the local, not the Spartan script. Does this mean that the artist in Sparta had learned his letters in Cyrene? Or, since it is so far his only inscription from many vases, was it bespoke and copied for a man going to Cyrene to dedicate it there?[24] We shall see that style and shape may be better clues to the wandering artisan.

From the mercantile graffiti on the Athenian vases it has also been observed that some of the merchants wrote in an Ionic rather than pure Athenian script, so may not have been Athenian but East Greek by upbringing. The two observations could well suggest that the same people were involved in each activity and that the potters or members of their family/workshop could be their own merchants. However, the painters' inscriptions on the vases are mainly Athenian in style.[25]

If, however, some potters were of more mixed origin, and did some trading, this would explain how some were able to observe their market at first hand and learn to adapt to it. It is potter-work that betrays respect for a distant market, as in Etruria, in a way that the painters' work does not, and the potter must always have been the senior partner. The fact that the potter Nikosthenes' black figure imitations of an Etruscan shape [187] almost all went to one Etruscan town, Caere, proves very close potter-trader collusion. Not all potters would have traded, of course, nor would potters have been the only traders in their wares; the cargoes could have been shared and selective. But it is noticeable that merchant marks tend to go with the production of individual painters, and therefore workshops, [26] which suggests no slight link between trade and production. While Lydos ('the Lydian', not the slave just mentioned) was painting and signing vases in Athens there were merchants using a type of personal trademark peculiar to Lydia, not the usual Greek letter or monogram ([181] right).[27]

At any rate, there need never have been an off-season for making pots, as there was for sailing. After all, pots do not deteriorate with time, and the argument that in the wet season the clay would not dry out so well falls in the face of the lack of any wet season in central Greece: there is minimal change in barometric pressure through the year (about 5mb), no month without some rainfall, at worst (November) less than 7cm average.

Even if all this is only partly true it goes far to explain what the potters might have been doing all year, and it logically binds more closely production and marketing, which is what we might expect. This has been an unpopular view recently among scholars who wish to divorce pottery source from trade and use, mainly to discredit Greek involvement in non-Greek areas: an attitude that I deal with elsewhere.[28] Sostratos of Aegina has been recruited to support such a view, since he was recorded by Herodotus as a busy trader from an island that made no vases for export except some cooking pots.[29] But we have then to believe (as I have; such is the allure of coincidence) that the many Athenian pots with the trade-mark *SO* of his period (around 500 BC) were carried on his ships. This could well be true, but the *Lexicon of Greek Personal Names* II (Attica) lists over 150 names beginning with *So* . . . (male and female, each with several owners, but over a long period), and Sostratos was itself a busy name.[30]

And women? Pots are domestic furniture, until trade makes them of no less importance for commerce, either as containers or *per se*. In many early cultures women are the potters. On Geometric vases many patterns seem inspired by woven patterns, traditionally a craft for women, and the common border pattern for red figure is a textile pattern of squares. That women might have played a part in early vase decoration is possible, but hardly in potting once really heavy vases were in production. One should also be wary of gender stereotypes since later history has shown a significant male role also in potting and weaving (and cooking). Among Greek vase scenes of potters at work only one has a woman doing something to the handle of a large crater – the 'Caputi hydria' [*178*].[31] All named potters and painters are male. 'Douris' could be female, but his treatment of sex scenes is very much that of the male,[32] and one might have expected female participation in painting to have become more apparent in choice or treatment. We can have no reason to think that they played any significant role in those aspects of the craft that concern us most, except as customers affecting the product, assuming that they held the purse-strings.

We seem to be well at home with the potters and painters of Athens and we know them by their names, or more often by names invented for them. They did not attract the sort of attention that might have secured them a record in texts – but neither generally did those employed in the senior crafts of sculpture or architecture until the advanced classical period. There is, however, one period, the first generation of the new democracy at the end of the sixth century, when we seem to come close to being able to observe, and in some detail, a coterie of painters – the so-called Pioneers of red figure whom we have met briefly in Chapter 1. They were not in fact the inventors of the technique, but the first practitioners to exploit it to its full potential in terms of draughtsmanship,

**178.** Attic hydria, the 'Caputi hydria', by the Leningrad Painter, showing a pottery attended by Athena herself and two Victories crowning workers. The finishing touches are being put to two volute craters (at the right, by a woman), a big kantharos and a calyx crater. Athena, as 'Ergane', was patron of craftsmen. About 475 BC. (Milan, private collection)

composition, subject matter, potting. Many of them were particularly literate, and their vases record more than the names of the protagonists in their scenes.

On one vase Euthymides writes 'As never Euphronios' [*115*]. The latter must, in the circumstances, be the painter known to us. Whether Euthymides' friendly gibe relates to Euphronios' painting or some other behaviour, perhaps that depicted on the vase (drinking, dancing), we cannot know, but the reasonable assumption is that it is a reflection of their rivalry as painters rather than party-goers, and at a time when drawing skills were being consciously refined; and this had been the general view of scholars until scepticism became a virtue in all such judgements.[33]

A messy and muddy craft hardly creates the setting for a Montmartre atmosphere of artistic endeavour and self-criticism. Yet potting was a more public affair than most – contrast the jeweller alone at his bench – and there were the equivalent of coffee shops in Athens, the exercise grounds for youths (*palaistrai*), as well as evening parties (*symposia*), both being popular subjects for the Pioneers' vases. About a dozen Pioneer painters can be identified and there were surely more whose works cannot be closely placed. One interesting feature is that, but for the two already named, very few of their vases have been found, and most of them in Italy which was the best market for early red figure. It might be that they were vase painters part-time, since it is about now that panel-painting seems to have become important, or perhaps they were also sculptors, since relief work of the period is very close indeed to vase painting and the two arts were never closer. Euthymides, son of a sculptor, is himself named on vases by others, once being toasted by naked courtesans at their own party, while he is shown on the same vase, in a different scene, at a music lesson [*118*]. Smikros names himself at a party on one of his own vases. There are many other cross-references. It is difficult to believe that all or any of these references to themselves or their companions are simply wish-fulfilment on the part of despised artisans. Smikros = 'Tiny', perhaps because he was tall, I had thought; but the name, and various others that have seemed nicknames, can be found well established later as citizen names, including Epiktetos, 'Acquired', which might seem a slave name, or Onesimos, 'Profitable'. We must not over-romanticize.

Another aspect of the inscriptions on the Pioneers' vases is best introduced here but will recur – the *kalos* names. The years from around 520 to 470 BC see the main proliferation of inscriptions on vases naming handsome boys, and there is no shortage of scenes depicting homosexual activity, mainly of a strictly paidophiliac character, with the object of affection a child of about ten to fifteen years; a decidedly different phenomenon from the continuing homoerotic activity of Greek youths and men of more mature years, which is less often depicted. The inscriptions are either in the form *Leagros kalos*, naming the boy, or simply *ho pais kalos*, and a *pais* is no older than fourteen or fifteen, and is so shown in many rather explicit vase scenes of the period, where the activity is a matter of fondling rather than intercourse. All this tends to be thought of as upperclass behaviour, which sits uneasily with the fact that it is best recorded in the first two generations of the new democracy (which was, however, hardly at all non-upperclass). The inscriptions, like modern graffiti, bear no relationship to their context, and appear in vase scenes where the subject is as likely to be heroic as everyday. Many of the names can be related to later careers, and clearly no shame was attached to this childish vulnerability. Their prevalence might suggest an easy familiarity with the upperclass as well as with paidophilia among the painters, and sometimes the boys are also named for real (as labels, without the *kalos*) in scenes of party-going or athletic exercises. Some seem

**179.** Detail from an Attic psykter by Smikros(?). Among various courting scenes is this couple – Euphronios soliciting young Leagros (both named, but not easily read in the photograph). Late 5th c. BC. (Malibu 82.AE.53)

general favourites, named by several painters; others seem almost exclusive to just one. On one vase it is Euphronios who seems to be importuning the child Leagros, the most popular toast at this level of Athenian society in the years around 500 BC [*179*].[34] This is likely to be the Leagros who figures later in public life and became a general; the dates fit, and had been used to date the pots, but there is much more corroborative evidence for dates, as we shall see, and we return to this, and Leagros, in Chapter 10. Euphronios himself, as we can judge from attributed and signed vases, spent the end of his career potting, not painting, perhaps through failing sight.[35] The very few women praised for their beauty were probably courtesans.

Not all the Pioneers' works were devoted to the good life, and there are many monumental compositions of myth which display both their drawing virtuosity and a strong sense of drama [*120, 308*]. They were versatile too, not specialists in either cups or larger pots, though preferring the latter.

Other professional relationships can be discerned. That of potter and painter does not always have to be attested by signatures, but we can see from them that painters were generally loyal to a potter, though there are distinguished exceptions, especially in the late archaic period at Athens. In Chapter 1 we noted the mid-fifth-century Penthesilea Painter's workshop, which seems to have managed a form of production line with separate painters contributing to the decoration of different parts of the vases – generally rather repetitive and unoriginal works. What the effect of such relationships was on the craft is more difficult to judge but, with the painters, schools can sometimes be identified, often working for the same potter and dominated by a painter whose choice of subject matter, and sometimes traits of drawing, seem to have been influential. The existence of such groups, determined by observation of style, is to some degree confirmed by the way their vases were often marketed by the same merchants.[36]

I have mentioned the Bacchios and Kittos who moved to Ephesus. Were other potters or painters migrant? In the eighth century the Naxian Cesnola Painter [25] seems to have moved to the Euboean Straits where his style was influential.[37] In Boeotia in the first half of the sixth century it is possible to identify painters who had moved from Athens, probably the better to serve a profitable market. Their hands can be detected both in Athens, on Athenian shapes, and in Boeotia where the shapes owe more to Corinthian example, and the clay is different.[38] There may be Corinthian potters and painters in Athens too about this time, to account for a spate of new shapes, though Corinth had always been a good supplier and imports could have served as models. But there are drawing styles and subjects too being copied, and there may be something in the report that the Athenian lawgiver Solon encouraged the immigration of craftsmen.[39] The red figure schools of South Italy were surely started by emigrants, and we saw that an Athenian (the Suessula Painter) moved to Corinth in the later fifth century.[40] All these examples are dependent on painter-attribution and are yet further demonstrations of what such studies can teach us of the history of the craft, but we have found possible examples also by studying the way some painters write and their declaration of origin (above).

Ionian artists had probably been set on the move with their families first by Lydians by around 600 BC, then, in the mid-sixth century, by Persians. In Athens their influence was on pottery shapes and elements of decoration, and yet more obviously on sculpture. It is not impossible to detect some immigrant artists, or at least artists from immigrant families, whose views on vase decoration had been partly conditioned by their former homes. Amasis is an interesting case: he has a hellenized Egyptian name which does not make him Egyptian, but perhaps in some way connected with Ionian enterprise in Naucratis, where Greeks also made

**180.** Attic alabastron of Egyptian shape by the Amasis Painter (potter). Its lip is missing. Mid-6th c. BC. H. 9.2cm. (Agora P12628)

pots.[41] He made the earliest known Athenian example of a copy of the Egyptian alabastron shape [*180*]. He seems to have been both potter and painter but in this case, and as with the near-contemporary who signed himself 'the Lydian' (Lydos), their work is in no way alien, since whatever they contributed helped form the relatively homogeneous 'Attic' style of their day. Anything really foreign would have found no market.

In the colonial world, in early days, immigrants must have started the few local potteries that we can recognize, but they also had an effect on others. From the eighth century on there are vases made in Campania and Etruria, of local or Greek shapes, and clearly, to judge from their decoration, from Greek hands, which must have been made by folk from the nearby Greek colonies – Euboeans from Ischia or Cumae, an Ionian, an Argive?[*44*], Corinthians. In the sixth century immigrants set up potteries which soon developed individual styles that we easily recognize as becoming Etruscan after a generation or less (the Pontic vases [*104*]), while more direct immigration from Ionia brought a potter who made the splendid Caeretan Hydriae [*107, 108*]. The exact origin of their work in the east is not recognized and they may not have started their careers as pot painters – a profession of less interest in these years in Ionia, it seems; we found one of the group painting on wood, to judge from something he made in Egypt. This whole phenomenon is as readily charted in the sculpture of the day, and especially from the effect that Ionian sculptors had on the development of Attic sculpture from the mid-sixth century on.

An artist working away from home, on commission (as most sculptors did), was tempted to record his home with his signature. In our subject, the Athenian Teisias making cups in Boeotia calls himself Athenian; the painter of a wooden plaque for dedication in Sicyon, calls himself a Corinthian;[42] and when Xenophantos 'the Athenian' made two exceptional relief/red figure vases for a Black Sea client it is probably because they were bespoke for a foreign market (as most exports were not); but they are exceptional, the larger one bearing a detailed study of a Persian princely hunt [138].

Our potters and painters are not shadowy figures, and their recapture by archaeological and art-historical techniques is no mean feat of classical archaeology, with lessons for other periods and places. We know them well because they were busy and their work was in demand far from home, so the trade, our next subject, is a major source of evidence too.

# Chapter 4:  The Trade

Our potter has completed a successful firing, the kiln has cooled and the vases, extracted, stand in the yard. They have been checked for faults and lids fitted where required. What next? The village potter would probably wait for customers to come to him as need arose, but might have made a batch of containers for a local farmer for his wine or oil, bespoke. He might wait for customers who knew there had been a new firing, or have a stall in whatever local market there was, or take his wares to neighbouring villages, by road or boat. We can only make plausible guesses, and may be too easily misled by modern practices. By the classical period he may well have been going out of business in the face of distribution from major potteries with organized production and distribution methods, and reduced to part-time potting at best, or specialist work making tiles for a new building.

The Athenian potter of the sixth to fourth centuries had a somewhat different problem and one that bears heavily on our understanding of his craft and products. Ignoring for a moment the shapes and decoration chosen for the pots, we may assume that he already has a clear idea of his market. The market has, after all, already broadly determined for him what shapes and decoration he should provide. He has many close neighbours doing much the same thing, and though customers might come to him, he could well look for a more immediate retail outlet in the market place or where his pots might answer a need – near a sanctuary for dedication, perhaps even near a cemetery (easy in Athens if he was in the Kerameikos). In Athens the potters' quarter was close to the market place and on a thoroughfare, so it was easy for potential customers to inspect products in the workshops (*ergasteria*).[1] 'Hello, buy me!', say some cups. Again, we can only guess. But a significant proportion of his work was to go outside the city, often far outside to distant parts of the Greek world and even beyond it. I shall discuss later what notice he may have taken of such a potential market in his choice of shapes and decoration – it will prove to be precious little. Here we have to turn to a complicated nexus of archaeological evidence – distribution maps, price and mercantile graffiti – where the interpretation is difficult and multiple answers are commonplace. Alan Johnston has done as much to elucidate all this in his careful archaeological/historical studies as Beazley did to distinguish painters. I do not repeat the evidence and arguments here, but simply attempt to offer what I regard as a plausible account of what happened after the firing, based on Johnston's assessment of the evidence.[2] It is, so far as I can judge, as near the truth as we are likely to get until more or different evidence becomes available.

The potter almost certainly had an arrangement with a merchant. He might indeed be his own merchant or share the job with other potters. But it seems to have been in the potter's yard that marks were made on the pots to identify their eventual carrier, some of them even painted before firing. Corinthians and Rhodians had done this long before, using painted letters or locally acceptable symbols for identification.[3] The practice may even go back to around 700 BC when the same Cypriot graffito was used on Greek pots found, one on a north Greek site, the other on a south Italian one.[4] We can well believe that such usage was one of the first calls made on the newly learnt alphabet – a matter of personal identification. In Athens the marks are commonly letters or monograms of two or more letters, sometimes simpler symbols [181], and we have remarked already a very few of Anatolian origin. Similar marks cluster around the products of individual potters (that is, their painters, who can be more readily identified) and their workshops, so there seem to have been some regular arrangements for such trade, and the potter seems to have been as much a prime mover as the carrier. He was bound to be since he supplied the surplus for export.

181. Examples of merchant marks on Attic pottery

Most of these merchant marks are seen on vases of around 570 to 450 BC, the period of busiest Athenian export to Italy, and the marks seem almost confined to vases intended for the trade west. Many have letter forms which are Ionic and not of the type in common use in Athens at the time. This need not exclude the potter's own hand, as we have seen, but the probability is that many or most were professional merchants who were gathering stock which they would accompany, as *emporoi*, to their market. Some might be shipowners themselves, like the Sostratos we have met already, but his arrangements for the pots were made with the

*154*

potters, if the *SO* graffiti indeed refer to his merchant fleet. Ionians were busy professional traders and had managed ports or entre-pôts for trade in Syria (Al Mina, seventh century), Egypt (Naucratis, seventh century on) and Etruria (Graviscae, Pyrgi, sixth century). There is an interesting echo of the same Ionian merchant names on dedications found as far apart as Naucratis and Graviscae,[5] while at the latter site the Aeginetan Sostratos dedicated a stone anchor.[6]

For Attica the port of Piraeus was the exit point; was it also ever the collection point, with a wholesale market that merchants might visit? This might apply for unmarked wares or plainer wares of later periods, and then we might suppose some middle-man, or the potter himself, taking them down to the harbour with or without specific expectations. A large find in the Piraeus mainly of red figure bell craters of the later fifth century, and mainly from one potter and painter (so not secondhand), might be a consign-ment of some sort, or the stock of a hardware wholesaler.[7]

Phoenician ships could later carry Athenian vases, but the evi-dence we have, from a text and a wreck, show that they were in Phoenician waters (the Atlantic coast beyond Gibraltar, and off Spain) and we do not know that they were picked up in Athens,[8] though there seems to have been a Phoenician quarter in Piraeus in the later classical period. In fifth-century Egypt Phoenician wine arrives in Phoenician ships, Ionian in Ionian ships.[9] It seems, however, that the best customers, in Etruria, themselves took no part in the trade and were at the mercy of Greek decisions about what they might purchase.[10] Where there seems to be a concentra-tion of direct trade with a source, as of Selinus in Sicily with Corinth, the traders are likely to be Corinthians.[11] The Mediterranean can be a tricky sea for sailors but the risks were not inordinate, and a merchant could finance a trip on loans (bot-tomry), at least in the later classical period. In earlier days the mechanics of overseas trade must have been far more varied and even haphazard, and could not have been wholly in the hands of professionals (except the sailors, that is). It is likely that the trade in pottery, as that in foodstuffs and raw materials, was a source of wealth for some who were not of the established land-owning classes.

And was there a secondhand trade, in singletons or sets?[12] This is certain for the Panathenaic amphorae which were made to be filled with Athena's sacred oil as prize vases for victors in the Panathenaic Games, as the inscriptions on them proclaim [73, 74]. It is said that oil, especially stale oil, may corrode interiors, and not all the Panathenaics were painted within. Some in the export market with clean insides have been thought 'empties' for trade, which complicates the picture.[13] There could well have been a secondhand trade in other vases too. This would help explain the apparent indifference to any but Athenian subjects in choice of decoration. It has been suggested that complete symposion sets were made for special occasions, then sold on, and one can imagine other possible sources for the better vases, but decidedly not for the majority.

It would not have been easy to purchase from individual potters 'sets' of different shapes for single occasions, or types of occasion, such as symposia, once there was specialization among the potters. Who would have made up the sets? Not the potter; just possibly the merchant, who would have found it easier to pack similar shapes together but could put little vessels inside big ones; most likely the purchaser, and it has been observed how in Etruscan tombs the imported and local vases may combine to make a proper table service.[14] But one graffito listing a batch of vessels names only five types of probably oil and vinegar vases, the small packed in the big, no doubt, and this was probably written in the pottery [182].[15] Another [183] packs two types of small condiment vase into six craters.[16] The Panathenaics generally have no merchant marks on them, other than some of the sort that appear on plain amphorae, and the secondhand trade in these and any other commissioned sets was not a matter for the potter, yet there must have been some collection and sale point for them, somewhere.

Yet another source for the Athenian customer might be admitted. An anecdote of about 300 BC reveals something that we might not easily have guessed, that there were potters who hired out crockery for specific occasions, the *keramos misthosimos*. If this applied to table as well as kitchen ware it makes good sense, since the finer pots were not so cheap that ordinary families might keep a whole symposion service for exceptional use, or even that richer ones were always equipped with enough table and kitchen ware for a large party. This is a consideration that might bear on a second-hand trade. (One Chairephon used to consult the pot-hirer about where there was to be a party needing more crockery, and then gatecrash it.)[17]

The village potter was serving his community with his skills and might expect no more than a living for himself and his family from his sales, probably with whatever his agricultural efforts might provide, and no doubt much being managed by payment 'in

**182.** Graffito on an Attic red figure pelike by the Nikias Painter(?) 'Stamnoi 3; price 3 drachmae, 3 obols. Oxides 11; 1 1/3 obols. Lekythoi, small 50; 3 obols. Lekythoi, normal 6; price 3 obols. Oxybapha 13; 1 obol.' For the vase, Scheibler, fig. 128. (Naples 151600)

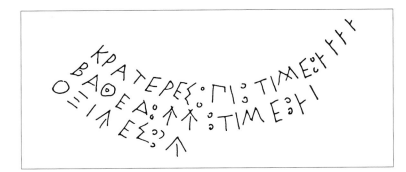

**183.** Graffito on the base of an Attic red figure bell crater by the Kadmos Painter. 'Craters 6; price 4 drachmae. Bathea 20; price 1 drachma, 1 obol. Oxides 12.' For the vase, Scheibler, fig. 126. (Vienna 869)

kind'. The commercial potter, and as such we must judge most in the big archaic and classical potteries of Greece, in Corinth, then Athens and South Italy, might expect more. A very few graffiti on pots indicate prices, for the pot itself or batches, as [*182, 183*]. From them we can see that a decent but not exceptional five-figure Attic vase of the mid-fifth century might cost as much as three drachmae. This must be but a fraction of the cost of the big multi-figure vases from the élite potteries, while simpler vessels cost less, often much less than a drachma. An owner writes on his cup that if anyone breaks it, it will cost him a drachma.[18] Plain black vases are around half the price of the simpler decorated ones, and often only a fraction of an obol (six to a drachma) for the smallest, virtually mass-produced. In the classical period a drachma was an average day's wage, nowadays, say, at least £50 or $100. The returns were not therefore substantial, but they were not meagre either for the producer. The prices are 'for the trade' and the pots would have had a considerable 'mark-up' by the time they reached a customer in Italy or Africa, possibly more than once if more than one merchant was involved in the carriage, or more than one retailer before the point of sale. The potters were perhaps even rather better off than many craftsmen of their social level. They would hardly have set about making such a massive surplus for trade if it had not proved to be worth their while, and some could afford rich dedications on the Acropolis at Athens, the only craftsmen in this category.

'Decorated Greek vases were very cheap' (implying cheap and nasty), is the cry of a very few scholars whose motives are not altogether altruistic since their condemnation is extended to those who collect and study them and includes the strange notion that monetary value in antiquity should determine our estimate of what antiquity has left us. Their mathematics are also interesting.[19] In the home market the vases were certainly not particularly expensive, though slightly more than ordinary decorated vases are today; an average teapot, for example, need not today cost a day's wage. By the time the ancient vase reached a distant customer they were probably quite, if not very, expensive; rather like the early eastern porcelain which reached Europe and commanded prices comparable with silver vases, until Europe started making its own porcelain, and even then remained expensive, though cheaply mass-produced in the east. When it first appeared in Europe eastern porcelain could be mounted in silver and gold, it was so esteemed. In Central Europe plain black Greek cups were given Celtic gold attachments.[20] To much of the ancient world, even parts of Greece, the best black and red figure vases were probably no less exotic in appearance than was the first porcelain, which is why local potter/painters sometimes tried to copy them for profit.

That pottery could ever form a serious element in state trade is difficult to gauge, and only conceivable for limited periods in Corinth and Athens, which had other commodities and manufactured goods to export too. Export/import taxes were imposed, and in times of trouble could be tough. In around 400 BC in Athens there was an import/export tax of only two per cent.[21] The profit to the state was not negligible in years when a sizeable proportion of the annual output was for export. There was in the fifth century a higher import tax to Egypt being charged on 'Ionian' goods (about twenty per cent), which would have affected the final price. The Phoenician imports attracted only ten per cent tax.[22] I am sure Phoenicians and Etruscans did not let Greek pots in free.

Apart from the livelihood of their family and probably payment to painters, the potters had few serious expenses: no land tax, clay probably free and simply to be transported, though there is some evidence that clay for special purposes could travel and would therefore incur expense. Fine Corinthian clay was preferred for architectural terracotta revetments and taken where it was needed. If your kilns had no local source, because you were working far from home, you had to import. Nile clay is mainly mud and the Chian potters who made votives for the local sanctuaries in Naucratis must have imported; it might travel as ballast, and we hear of a Phoenician ship bringing clay to Egypt in the fifth century, while the Greeks brought empty vases as well as wine.[23] It might seem easy to have acquired wood for the kilns but there must have been brisk competition in the neighbourhood of Athens for its many uses, including domestic. A recorded price of one drachma for 80lb (36kg) of firewood is not exactly cheap.[24]

Packing for transport must have been a problem. The fired pots were relatively robust though handles and stemmed feet were vulnerable. In some periods really thin-walled vases must have been especially difficult to pack and carry – I think of the Chian chalices [94] and some of the finer Athenian Little Master cups [71, 72] of the sixth century. Later the firing seems harder and the black cups are about as tough as good, though often thinner, porcelain. Shapes were determined by use and made no concessions to packing problems; quite the reverse, though some chunky fourth-century black cups (Castulo cups [184]) stacked well and seem to have been picked out for the export market (to Spain), though not exclusively so.[25] Oriental porcelain was packed in flat wooden boxes, but wood may have been too valuable for such use in Greece and soft wicker baskets are more probable containers and offer the possibility of padding round the sides. They would also be handier for travel overland. Wooden containers for various things do seem to have been used, however, to judge from what was reported from shipwrecks.[26] The packing was rubbish: we cannot easily translate the word *phorutos* used in one text (what the wind blows along?),[27] but it probably includes shavings and straw, and I doubt whether there was as much rubbish about in antiquity as there is today.[28] The porcelain boxes were stowed low in the ships from the east because their contents would suffer less from any intrusive sea

**184.** 'Castulo cup', from Nola. W. 15.7cm. (Paris, Louvre N 1841)

water than the silks and tea stored above them. We do not know where the decorated pottery went in antiquity, but the plain sealed amphorae of oil or wine were heavy; they could and did go low. Pottery is heavy (lift a stack of dinner plates!), even unfilled, and could have been stored anywhere, not thereby being any more of a 'space-filler' than any other cargo in a ship which was not a specialist conveyor of, for instance, grain. It has been remarked by an expert on ancient wrecks that tableware was generally placed 'either above or at one end of bulkier cargoes'.[29]

| Values for commodities weighing 40 kg (88 lb) | |
| --- | --- |
| | drachmae |
| Decorated vases | 30–17 |
| Oil: 9.1 choes | 13.5 |
| Wine: 9 choes | 9 |
| Wheat: 1 medimnos | 6 |
| Barley: 1.25 medimnoi | 6 |

| Values for commodities occupying 144,000 cu cm (5.1 cu ft; 144 litres) | |
| --- | --- |
| | drachmae |
| Decorated vases (large) | 24–15 |
| Oil: 2 x 7–choes amphorae | 21 |
| Wheat: 2.75 medimnoi | 16 |
| Barley: 2.75 medimnoi | 14 |
| Wine: 2 x 7–choes amphorae | 14 |
| Decorated vases (small) | 12–8 |

185. Comparative values by volume and weight

Comparisons in terms of weight and volume with other cargoes suggest that pottery could earn its place on ships, in terms of wholesale value, with most of the usual items of trade (oil, wine, corn) [185]; while in terms of its probable cost to the ultimate and often distant customer it probably compared very favourably indeed.[30] It is noticeable that what we would regard as the highest quality pieces tended to go to the richer and more discriminating markets – Etruria or the east, and to some rich colonial areas. Farther off, the pots purchased most cheaply in Athens must have secured a good enough profit in a market where they would appear exotic whatever the quality. So we find fairly poor red figure in quantity from a wreck en route to Spain, and there is a concentration of a particular group of very late black figure cups (Lancut Group);[31] they were clearly not made only for such remote trade but were an obvious choice for the clever merchant, who as a result stimulated the production.

160

**186.** Holes drilled for mending with rivets and clamps of lead or bronze in an Attic black figure amphora by the Antimenes Painter, from Rhodes. (New York 06.1021.51)

The ship has docked, the merchant has taken his load of pottery ashore. If the skipper is the merchant he probably hands on specialist cargoes to a local merchant. And if a merchant has accompanied his cargo as *emporos* he too might have to negotiate sale to a local merchant rather than himself attempt to retail. The only exception could be in ports such as the Etruscan where a market was, as it were, on the doorstep. It is possible that there was in such towns a showplace for imported goods to be bargained for by local traders, like the Deigma which served this purpose in the port of Athens.[32] Where the market was more remote middlemen were certainly involved, which meant a further mark-up of the price. Gordion, the old Phrygian capital in Asia Minor, imported good Athenian black and red figure in quantity. Its nearest port was 325km away and the problems of conveying the vases over-land could hardly have been negligible or without effect on price.[33]

Breakages must have been common. Many vases have been found mended for continued use after breaking, even liquid containers like cups, though we can hardly imagine that they were still wholly leak-proof. Lead and bronze clamps and pins were used, fastened through pairs of holes drilled in the walls of the vase [*186*], or a bronze rivet to fasten a foot back on.[34] Sometimes one vase was patched by a fragment from another. The need for mending might arise even in the potter's yard, but surely only for a major piece with elaborate decoration. Mends are more apparent in the Attic pottery exhibited in Italian museums than in Greek ones, so most of the breaking probably happened en route or after arrival, by which time the vase was too expensive to discard. One of the very finest Chalcidian black figure cups, which travelled to Etruria from south Italy, has drill holes for mends of two different sizes, so perhaps it was twice mended.[35] Vases which had been dented before firing were often let by, also those that had stood too close to others in the kiln and taken part of their decoration, like a transfer – 'ghosts'.[36]

The volume of production and trade is not easily assessed in absolute numbers. Various calculations have suggested that perhaps one to three per cent of the original production has survived. This is likely to be a gross overestimate, and a fraction of one per cent is far likelier.[37] A recent count of archaic sites in Italy on which Athenian decorated pottery has been found yielded a list of over 350.[38] Some of these sites have been busily excavated, but none of them completely, and generally only tombs and a very few sanctuaries, not houses. The cemeteries of Vulci in Etruria have proved a major source since the eighteenth century; and they are still, it seems, a major source for the illicit market. Finds at other sites often amount to no more than one or two pieces from a very few tombs that have been discovered, often by chance, without any further excavation of tombs, sanctuaries or houses, where, if the tomb finds mean anything, the numbers might well reach hundreds at least. Yet more revealing is the contents of a wreck of around 515 BC off Marseilles (Pointe Lequin IA), which was found to have more than 800 Attic black figure cups on board, with many other Attic shapes. And since the main pottery cargo was some 1600 Ionian cups and most of the amphorae are from Miletus, the Attic was likely to have been picked up on a voyage from farther east.[39] Such a very large cargo in one shipment to what was hardly the richest potential market argues an enormous export trade from Athens overall.[40]

Clearly, even the most prolific sources of Attic pottery can have yielded so far only a tiny fraction of what was exported. Vases carried to remote corners of the Mediterranean in such numbers must have soon ceased to serve as status symbols except in the lower reaches of society, though they were probably relatively expensive locally, to justify the bother of carrying them. I would guess that the annual production of figure-decorated pottery in Athens of the archaic and early classical periods, which were the most productive, was well over 50,000, a figure supported by other estimates of personal production and percentage of survival. This puts the total production of Athenian black and red figure into the

187. Attic 'Nikosthenic amphora' potted by Nikosthenes. On the shoulder a heroic battle; below, dancers. The handles are broad and flat, decorated with florals. About 525 BC. H. 31cm. (Rome, Villa Giulia 50558)

*162*

**188.** Attic black figure kyathos.
Dionysos. Late 6th c. BC.
H. 16cm.(Amsterdam 8193)

millions, and of the plain black vases several times as much, at least
in the home market.

The question of the extent to which potters or carriers targeted overseas markets is a complicated one. Chapter 6 will consider whether any of the vase scenes were deliberately chosen for
export, with a mainly negative conclusion; what there are appear
mainly on shapes of the type to be mentioned here. There have
been thoughts that the Corinthian column craters were domi-
nantly export models; they were certainly well received in the
west, but travelled east too.[41] The earliest apparent specialist production for a foreign market is of the Attic Tyrrhenian amphorae
[58], for Etruria, where the corinthianizing scheme of decoration
seems to have been judged attractive to a customer better used
hitherto to Corinthian vases, and this is supported by the fact that
all known Tyrrhenian amphorae went to Etruria. A successor,
perhaps in the same workshop, Nikosthenes, made black figure
copies of an Etruscan bucchero amphora shape and sent them all
to Caere [187]. Another Etruscan shape he copied is the kyathos
[188], a low-footed, one-handled kantharos, like a dipper (whence
its Greek name); also the splaying foot for some cups which had

189. Attic black figure mastoid cup. Lyre player wearing a turban. The 'song' is nonsense. Late 6th c. BC. H. 12.4cm. (Madison, Elvehjem Mus. 1979.122)

been pioneered by the western Chalcidian potters.[42] The latter themselves picked up one or two Etruscan shapes since Etruria was their 'foreign' market.[43] A later potter of Attic black figure made larger one-handled kantharoi on high feet, another Etruscan shape,[44] and 'mastoid cups' are yet another Etruscan shape, for a while made and decorated in Athens for export to Etruria [189].[45] These shapes form a very small proportion of all exports.

Multiple cups were an East Greek affectation; an Athenian made one which went east to Samos.[46] In the mid-fifth century Sotades made versions of eastern horn cups which were well received in the Persian empire, from Susa to the Sudan. They are given bases, in the Greek mode, composed of figure groups which seem also suited to their market: pygmy and crane [190], negro boy and crocodile [191], a Persian and camel. Several carry scenes of Greeks fighting Persians (or their alter egos, Amazons) and not winning.[47] But not all such pieces went to the Persian world or any foreigner. A Thracian cup shape was also copied in red figure, and one sent to Thrace has Thracians painted on it [192].[48] As a riposte, perhaps, to the new South Italian red figure production, Attic potters made a very few examples of shapes popular in South Italy [193],[49] like the nestorides [145]. All were of course then sent to South Italy; most would have looked far too odd in Athens.[50]

Fired clay pots survive more successfully than any other arte-facts of antiquity, and they naturally therefore attract the attention of archaeologists concerned to discover something about ancient trade. The evidence they offer for trade in *pottery* is total but it is

**190.** Attic red figure horn-shaped figure vase from Sotades' workshop. Satyr and maenad on the lip. The body is moulded as a pygmy carrying a dead crane over his shoulder. Mid-5th c. BC. H. 29.7cm. (Bonn 545)

**191.** Attic red figure horn-shaped figure vase from Sotades' workshop, from Italy. A Thracian figure on the lip. The body is moulded as a negro boy caught by a crocodile. Mid-5th c. BC. H. 26cm. (Munich 6203)

well to be wary about assuming that the same pattern can be deduced for other items. However, few ships probably carried pottery only, so it is evidence for trade in other, perishable materials. Pots were expensive enough and travelled in sufficient numbers to have been taken seriously by merchants. And although the 'nationality', in so far as this means anything, of the carriers may not be known, the way the trade can be seen to have been conducted from Athens' potters' quarter suggests that the closest links existed between maker and carrier, and the latter should be judged a 'fellow-countryman' or at least a 'regular customer' unless there is good reason to believe otherwise.

192. Attic red figure jug (foot missing) of Thracian shape (its local model beside it), by the Eretria Painter, from Apollonia Pontica (Bulgaria). Thracians wearing fox-skin caps (*alopekides*), patterned cloaks (*zeirai*) and boots, carrying light shields (*peltai*). About 425 BC. H. 12cm. (Sozopol 261)

193. Attic red figure standed volute crater by the Meleager Painter. The shape imitates the Apulian version of the shape, and it was exported to South Italy. A symposion on the neck; on the foot hunting, and satyrs with maenads (Dionysos on the other side of both neck and foot). Early 4th c. BC. H. 76.9cm. (Malibu 87.AE.93)

# Chapter 5: Pictures and People I

It was the pictures on the vases that first attracted both popular and scholarly attention, as they still do. Study of their content and meaning has always been a busy subject. 'Iconography' is the word for it; or 'iconology', a word recommended by Erwin Panofsky for later European studies which had become obsessed with authorship and tended to ignore social, historical and literary contexts. This had never been a problem for classical archaeology which was firmly based in texts from the beginning, and only subsequently had to learn how to look at pictures.

A very high proportion of the figure scenes on Greek vases deals with subjects of myth. The few that present everyday life, increasingly in the late archaic and classical periods, often give it also a heroic flavour. This is especially obvious in scenes of weddings and fights, less so in the very popular scenes of party-going and the symposion. Specific contemporary events are avoided, and only the generic such as sacrifices and processions, weddings and funerals, and some craftsmen, are admitted. So we have no identifiable contemporary portraits of people or battles, although Greeks fighting Persians became an acceptable subject at the time of the Persian wars [*194*],[1] and subsequently, as their successes were heroized. Identifiable mortals may appear, but only local minor celebrities in generic scenes, or only after they were long dead and to some degree heroized (Croesus [*246*], Sappho and Alcaeus [*277*]). Even in the major arts such subjects are barely evident in the fifth century (a wall painting of the Battle of Marathon, a generation after the event, since it too had acquired heroic status), and they, with true portraiture, only begin to become common in the fourth century.

This is an unusual situation but one easily explained in terms of the Greeks' own view of their past and its relevance to their present; it may indeed lie close to the core of the reason for the unique character of the Greeks' culture and art, and their dedication to representations of the human figure. The non-myth scenes unwittingly define for us important modes and stereotypes in Athenian life and thought. Whether they did the same for any ancient viewer, rather than simply record the comforting and familiar, is an altogether different matter. Social and political

**194.** Attic red figure cup by the Triptolemos Painter, from Italy. Duel between a Persian and a Greek, of about the period of the Persian Wars. Both wield sabres (*machairai*, as used in sacrifices; see [*121*]). The Persian has Scythian dress, bow, and bowcase. The 'Persians' on such vases often have the dress of Persian subjects. About 480 BC. W. 29.5cm. (Edinburgh 1887.213)

image-propaganda, of the sort we are subjected to today, cannot lightly be imposed on our record of antiquity, however much the prospect may seduce the historian of ancient society. Too many other predictable 'social stereotypes' are simply ignored in the repertory of vase iconography, not least any direct reference to political life in an Athens which must have been seething with political comment. The only politicians to be mentioned on pots are either when they were popular as little boys, or on broken fragments (*ostraka*) used as voting slips for banishment (thus, 'ostracism'). The painters are neither individually nor in sum a Hogarth delineating critically the social scene. To treat them as though they were can only distort the view of antiquity they offer, and deny us the opportunity to share some moments of its innocence and spontaneity.

To understand the strong myth content in Greek art we have first to realize that for Greeks what we call their mythology was regarded as part of their history. Families could trace descent from gods and heroes, and although the remoter past might be thought of as in some way special, when men and gods could converse, when heroes exercised real though magic powers, and there had been numinous entities such as Chaos and Night, still there was an uninterrupted progression to the present, rather than the whole-sale reversals typical of the cosmogonies of other ancient peoples. In general the Greek artist avoided trying to represent or personify vague primitive forces, even though they had names and were made in Greek myth to behave like humans. Monsters serve only to be defeated by heroes and gods, many of them such as the centaur are remarkably plausible, and the more terrifying demons of folklore were not represented, however much the ordinary Greek may have been troubled by them. The Greeks had their stories of the Creation, and of the decline of Man from an Age of Gold through Silver to Iron and Brass, but this was essentially of foreign inspiration and made no impact on popular thought and art, only on literature, and little enough there.

It is natural to seek parallels and solutions to present problems through reference to the past problems and solutions in a family or society, and whether or not you believe that history repeats itself, it at least admonishes. If your 'past' included stories which we would regard as myth, the same comparisons were invited. This 'myth' was a compound of folk tales of a type current in much of the world, views of the world order and of the role of the gods whom they had invented, which the Greeks shared with the civilizations of the near east, and heroic rewriting of 'real' history – in this case their Bronze Age past, its kings and their exploits, such as the Trojan War, whether or not such an event ever took place in anything like the manner in which it was later sung. In many different periods and places epic mythical accounts are found to conceal, sometimes with almost total success, some historical truths. From the earliest Greek literature it is clear that appeal to the past was a regular part of any attempt to explain new situations or resolve dilemmas. Myth is parable. This may take the form of invoking the achievements of ancestors, and thereby coming to admit a degree of assimilation of the present and its leaders to their mythological or even divine paradigms. The process was one which gathered momentum in the western world, assisted by the deification of rulers, through Macedonian kings, Roman emperors, even to Napoleon, presented in literature and art as divinities. Only in early Greece does this seem to have been the exclusive process in literature and art, until 'history' in our sense was invented in the fifth century.

Knowledge of these stories was gained in antiquity mainly in an informal fashion, at mother's knee and from raconteurs or improvisers at street corners, which meant that there was no positive canon for any story, although one might easily be established if a version, such as an epic poem, was written down and regularly recited. But even Homer could be ignored by writers and artists. There are several snatches of song or poem put in the mouths of figures on vases, or shown in scrolls [244]; none is from Homer. The process allowed infinite freedom to the artist to vary the content and even the outcome and personnel of his stories, to suit his audience or the situation on which his story might try to comment. This meant that Greek myth was always on the move, and new versions could be created for a purpose, or even accidentally through misunderstanding, poor memory, or the exigences of the medium employed. With no boundary between myth and history this freedom of invention, of both detail and whole stories for special circumstances, readily overlapped into the writing of what we call 'history', presenting problems for the modern student of ancient history that do not concern us here.

The stock of myth was not learned and preserved only from poetic recital, although poetry is a good support of memory. Nor were there any problems of copyright, or need to follow an established pattern for a story except in such general outline as would ensure recognition. Texts were rarities and few Greeks were literate. There were recitals at festivals, the Homeric poems perhaps having been edited for this purpose in sixth-century Athens.[2] With the fifth century a more sophisticated rendering of the traditional tales was presented on the stage, but play-going in classical Athens was a very different matter from practice today. The major festival in Athens, the Great Dionysia, was a matter of four days viewing, with up to five plays a day and no following 'run' at the town theatre, or necessarily in the 'provinces'. This is not an easy way to disseminate new ideas about old tales, except to other literati. But the use of myth was the same, and Athenian playwrights used the stories to comment on the more puzzling aspects of their society, as well as and sometimes even rather than, simply narrating particular episodes – the problems of the conflict of family and state, or state and religion, of personal responsibility and the will of the gods. They are the familiar problems of all ages, and appear in roughly similar guise in Homer. This has made for their survival, but in this form they were probably not very close to the conscious responses of the ordinary viewer. We should not pretend that they are much easier for us, although the continuity of classical thought and manners in western civilization makes the classical stage somewhat more accessible to the modern western audience than, say, a Japanese Kabuki play. In such a society, and even today, pictures can play an essential subsidiary role in making stories familiar, together with whatever messages they may have in the context in which they are recounted or depicted. This is an area of study in which art and literature can be seen to follow parallel courses, interacting yet independent, and the understandable old view that art could only follow literature is easily set aside.[3] This brings us back to the vases.

Here we are bound to become Atheno-centric, since Athens' potters and painters offer us the fullest possible range of material. Much the same results might be detected in other parts of Greece, especially where figure-decorated pottery was prolific, as in early Corinth, but it is more difficult to trace, and we have seen that even in the Geometric period the Athenian artist took a view of his role somewhat different from that of other Greeks, and that the Athenian customer in some way must have expected and approved it. Even when Athenian vases had won most markets for decorated wares they could never have been as numerous elsewhere as they were in Athens, and at any rate, so far as we can tell, the messages they bore were specific to Athenian society, though intelligible at a different level everywhere, even to non-Greeks. Probably not every family possessed even one figure-decorated vase, but many possessed several, and the medium would have been perfectly familiar to all outside their own homes, in public and private contexts. Our own visual experience is not confined to what we hang on our walls at home, though it may be conditioned by it to some degree. The only other pictorial displays in ancient Athens that we know of would have been in and on a minority of public buildings, mainly temples, and these were in their way permanent and unchanging, designed for different though often related purposes and messages. In the classical period there may have been many painted wooden panels too. The vases probably give us a far better idea of how the ordinary Greek visualized his own world, which he did not distinguish from his myth-historical past; this is why all myth stories were told 'in modern dress'. But since these stories, these pictures, were a regular means of comment on the present, they can reveal very much more.

This role of the vase scenes in society is clearly important, but it would be a mistake to think that it must have been deliberate, that state or individual propaganda was designed for painted vases in the way we are today instructed, even subliminally, in what our leaders, political or commercial, wish us to vote for or buy, through the press, television and internet. Far more probably they reflect the mood and attitudes of the day which, if it was a matter of the special application of a particular theme, figure or story, were first

172

expressed in other media – probably not visual, but in hymn or poem or speech by priest or politician in a civic assembly, even common gossip. Once such a message was promulgated any individual, including a vase painter, might be moved to express it in other ways for his fellows, and if he were a person of imagination he might also work into it his own interpretation or embellishment of the theme, just as we find the fifth-century playwrights doing with their subjects. But we must be wary of thinking that all the vase scenes were fraught with such messages; many were simply mindlessly repetitive of what might once have been pregnant subjects, many repeat the familiar narrative because this is what the mainly unthinking public was used to.

The vases, then, have a great potential for our understanding of Greek society, especially at a level of education and shared thought and experience lower than that of poets, priests, politicians and generals. Which is not to say that some vase painters could not be as thoughtful and innovative in their approaches as other artists, of the word or image. We are entitled to try to understand the messages in the terms in which they were devised by their artists and understood by their buyers or viewers. Much will of course depend on the content of the story, for which we may have other relevant evidence in surviving literature, though seldom of the same period. But we should remember that we know far more, from the vases, of the popular visual experience of narrative art, than we do of literary expressions, even of the same stories, at least for the period in which the vases are available and were being so used, from about the mid-sixth to mid-fourth centuries BC in Athens.

I shall revert to the question of the content of the stories by presenting some case histories in the next chapter. The rest of this chapter is devoted to trying to explain how we think we can understand this content, and thereby perhaps the purpose of the pictures that survive, usually without explanatory inscriptions, and in a two-dimensional medium whose handling ancient authors disdained to discuss for us. Knowledge of ancient Greek gives us immediate access to their literature, but narrative art has a language, vocabulary and syntax too, which need to be deduced from the physical evidence remaining. This we have to attempt with little help from texts, but with better understanding, often won from study of other periods of art, of how a human brain responds to an image, and of what is needed for us to share the response to visual stimuli of humans whom we can no longer interrogate. This narrative language is not one peculiar to vase painting, though it is

**195.1,2.** Attic red figure hydria by an Early Mannerist. The departure of the Seven against Thebes. At the left a youth looks for sympathy; the youth cutting his hair (to dedicate as a memorial) is the only one named – Parthenopaios; the charioteer is Amphiaraos. About 475 BC. (Private Collection, Toronto)

to some degree bound by the field and medium offered. It operates also in other arts, and of these it is sculpture that is the obvious and public alternative. As I have intimated, this is a source in which somewhat different intentions may have been influential in matters of choice and presentation, but the 'language' is the same. If we can learn how to read a vase scene it should help us to read the Parthenon frieze also, since we shall have learned to some degree to share the visual experience and expectations of the classical Athenian. We may even be able to judge whether some modern explanations, which are not motivated by visual considerations, are indeed in keeping with what our experience has taught us about how an ancient artist might present his theme or message.

Inscriptions on the vases are an obvious guide, but usually there is none. The problem is not so simple, however, since we are at a loss to explain why a painter may be helpful on one vase, silent on another; or, even more puzzling, why in a complicated scene he may label an obvious figure, like Athena or Heracles, but not the others, despite the fact that they clearly have identities and are involved in very specific actions whose nature may elude us. With major figures like those mentioned it may have been a matter of habit, of accentuating the obvious, but sometimes out of a band

of, for example, the seven heroes preparing for the Theban expedition, one only is named and the others not immediately distinguishable except through quite complicated (for us) iconographical comparisons, since they all look like warriors [195].[4] The ancient viewer would not have had to work so hard. The inscriptions normally just name figures; there are very few real legends (as in cartoon bubbles), virtually no captions to a whole scene, and a few remarks made by the painter to the viewer which are irrelevant to the scene and usually erotic. Occasionally a bespoke inscription names a donor or divine recipient, and we have already considered artist signatures. That inscriptions had a certain value of their own, either decorative or giving status to be appreciated by the illiterate or the foreigner, is shown by the number of nonsense inscriptions that are found, especially on archaic vases [189].

Attributes and dress are other obvious signals of identity: Heracles' lionskin, Athena's armour, Zeus' thunderbolt [196].[5] They are often carried even in incongruous situations and their presence, for example Poseidon's fish, is not to be regarded as crucial to the scene involved but just an identifying mark. But there are cases where they too can play a narrative role, as where Heracles' arms are ostentatiously put aside for his contest with the

196. Attic black figure hydria.
The Gods. Heracles faces Athena,
a common pair; Zeus with
thunderbolt and Hera face
Demeter(?); Hermes faces Ares.
After mid-6th c. BC. H. 43cm.
(Basel BS499)

197. Attic black figure hydria
shoulder. Athena watches
Heracles fight the lion. His club
and cloak are set aside above
him, his quiver and shield
behind the lion. Iolaos runs up.
Late 6th c. BC. (Charlecote Park)

198. Fragment of a black figure
plaque from a funeral monument,
by Exekias. Mourning women.
About 525 BC. H. 14cm. (Berlin
F1812b)

lion, in which weapons could play no part since the beast was invulnerable [*197*]. Sometimes too the choice of attribute can be significant, indicating identity of cult or action: Apollo with lyre rather than bow, for example. One might have expected shield devices to be equally informative but generally they are not and they reveal rather the habits and preferences of the painter, with very rare exceptions.

The action and apparent intention of individual figures are usually made clear. Here we must recall that the model was not life, or the stage, although life was indirectly the inspiration. Conventional gestures in life, such as are more apparent today with Mediterranean peoples than northern Europeans, can be repeated in art. But study of modern gesture has shown that the same gesture can mean different things in different places or periods, so modern analogy has to be used cautiously.[6] Hand to head clearly might indicate grief, tearing the hair or beating the brow [*198*];[7] it is so in Egyptian art, and in modern life, as recent distressing news scenes show. In Greek art it also indicated general dismay, but not always at ill fortune. It can be used thus for a warrior destined for death (as most of the Seven against Thebes [*195*]), and for a randy satyr, an archetypal Keatsian Bold Lover, overwhelmed by the prospect of a sleeping maenad to molest [*199*]. A raised hand, sometimes with two fingers extended,

**199.1,2,3.** Lip of an Attic red figure head cup by the Brygos Painter. Satyrs assault sleeping maenads. Early 5th c. BC. (Warsaw)

seems to indicate speech, but may on occasion imply warning [*159*]. A handshake implies equality of status, companionship, appropriate for welcome or farewell but not exclusive to such occasions. A trivial example – thumb and forefinger or little finger in a circle, nowadays either an approving or obscene gesture, appears very rarely on vases, but notably in the work of one black figure painter which might lead us to speculate on his origins in some area where the gesture was common.[8] A frontal face makes a direct and emotional appeal to the viewer, which I discuss in the next chapter.

Action figures are drawn in profile, arranged with minor overlapping and no indication of depth of composition until the fifth century, and then tentatively. Most ancient arts addicted to narrative present figures in this way (Egypt and Greece); others more concerned with demonstrating divine or heroic presence than narrative, value the frontal for face and figure (much in Mesopotamia and farther east). There are very few wholly frontal figures in Greek vase painting but they are naturally important in sculpture, for single figures and sometimes in groups where there may be a narrative implication but the dominating presence is emphasized (as the central group in the east pediment of the Temple of Zeus at Olympia, where there is a narrative content too). Action, especially victorious action, tends to move from left to right, which is the way our brains 'read' a picture.

Composition too can aid identity, and here we meet a phenomenon that is central to the study of iconography in Greek art of our period – the use of formulaic groups and figures. The relatively

marionettish figures of geometric and archaic art can be persuaded into expressive postures of no great subtlety. Groups are readily devised for stock scenes, as fighting, but also for myth scenes. Where identity may be a problem but we have groups identified by inscription, we have to ask whether we are entitled to attribute the same identity to similar uninscribed groups. This is bound up with another problem. Many myth occasions are relatively generic in type – arrivals, departures, duels – and only inscriptions can distinguish them from the everyday, even the everyday heroic, while the same formulaic conventions are observed in presentation. Are we to believe that a formula was devised for a generic scene, then used for a specific myth occasion, and that thereafter it should always be so interpreted? Or could the formulae for myth scenes be borrowed for generic situations, even when the setting is in its way heroic, with chariots or the like? It is of course not so easy to distinguish myth from life when all myth is enacted 'in modern dress'. It is probably safer to judge each case on its merits and not favour one or other of the procedures just described; neither seem absolute. Any single theoretical explanation is bound to be wrong for many instances.

The creation of stock groups and figures is not a peculiarly Greek procedure. We find much the same in Egypt, mainly for ritual scenes but also for some of action – the victorious Pharaoh and his victims. The Near East presents much the same record, with the addition of action scenes of myth or confrontation with the divine or monstrous, in a manner which prefigures the Greek, and is displayed best either in monumental relief or on cylinder seals. Farther afield, the same classical approach informs the development of narrative art in India, where scenes of the life of the Buddha are composed with the same formulae as a Greek or Roman might use for the Labours of Heracles.[9] In the instances named one might imagine that one culture borrows the treatment from another, and this is often demonstrable (the east to Greece; Greece to Rome and the East), but it seems an instinctive reaction by any artist to the demand for an intelligible narrative scene which has no recourse to inscriptions or captions to be understood, and is not prejudiced by any attempt at a 'still', as with a camera. The narrative and ritual scenes on the Moche pottery of north Peru of the early centuries AD, totally undisturbed by Old World manners, are managed in exactly the same way. Thus, in [200] we have three versions from different hands of the same scene, with the slightest variety of figures, poses, action and furniture, but observing the same formulae for each group and for the

200. Scenes from three different vases, from different hands, of the Moche culture of north Peru. Each treats the same scene in a succession of the same formulae, with minor variations. The subjects seem to involve both sex and cannibalism. 3rd-5th C. AD

**201.** Red figure hydria by the Kleophrades Painter. The Mission to persuade Achilles to return to battle. From the left, old Phoinix (Achilles' adviser), Odysseus, Achilles (still mourning the loss of Briseis), and a youth who might be Patroklos, who will wear Achilles' armour and be killed. Early 5th c. BC. (Munich 8770)

assembly of all groups, just as we might see in different versions of scenes of Heracles and the Lion in archaic Greek art.[10]

[201] is a good demonstration of a group that can be instantly recognised from other scenes where all or some of the figures are named, though knowledge of Homer would surely have led us to the answer. The outer figures may vary in age and dress, and so identity, not always in accord with Homer, but the central pair are unmistakable – Odysseus in an unusual relaxed cross-legged pose and the distraught Achilles. The latter is the silent figure of Aeschylus' near-contemporary account of the episode for the stage, not the noisier, indignant Achilles of Homer.[11]

A few case histories may show what problems remain in matters of identification, an investigation which is bound to include the iconography of other media. In late Geometric art there are groups of a warrior bearing the body of a dead comrade from the field, over his shoulders. Little over a hundred years later a bronze relief identifies the pair as Ajax carrying Aristodamos; and very shortly afterwards, on the Athenian François Vase, they are identified as Ajax and Achilles [202], a scene with a far stronger epic flavour. Where the scene appears with no names, are we to see Achilles still, or a generic heroic or even mortal group, and what was the identity of the geometric group? Achilles' armour survived with him and was not despoiled by the Trojans, since it has then to be fought over by Odysseus and Ajax, yet some

**202.** Handle of the François Vase [62]. Achilles' body, naked, carried by Ajax.

**203.** Attic black figure amphora by Exekias, from Vulci. Achilles' body, still in armour, carried by Ajax. About 525 BC. H. 42cm. (Munich 1470)

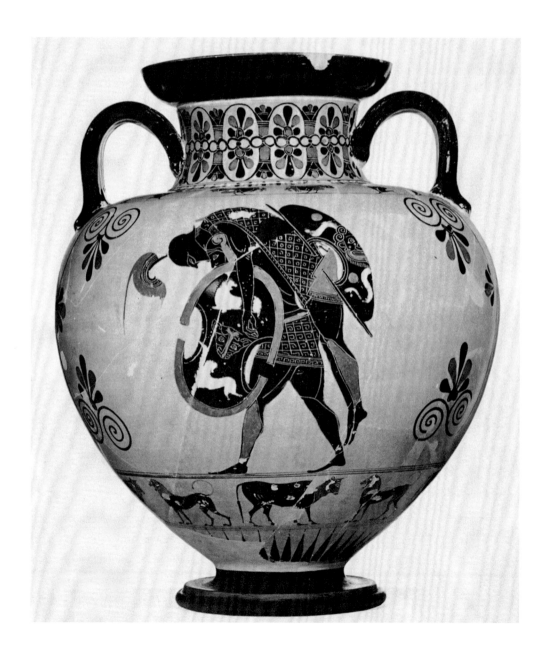

204. Corinthian column crater. The Departure of Amphiaraos. At the left Eriphyle, Amphiaraos' wife, clutching the amber necklace with which she has been bribed. Amphiaraos glares round at her, sword drawn, as he mounts his chariot. At the right a mourning seer. Various animal omens. Before mid-6th c. BC. (Once Berlin 1655)

of the identified Achilles corpses are naked, as on [202]. Here it seems that another formula intervenes, that the battlefield dead should be shown naked, as suits their pathetic condition, and not because they have been stripped of armour.[12] In some of the Achilles scenes the traditional formula for a pathetic death in battle outweighs the narrative interest in the armour; elsewhere the armour is ostentatiously still worn [203].[13]

The next case is of departure. In the seventh century, probably in Ionia where elaborate iconographic formulae were devised for metalwork rather than clay vases, a scheme for the depiction of the fateful departure of Amphiaraos for Thebes was created. We see it in full on Corinthian [204] and Athenian vases of the second quarter of the sixth century. The hero mounts his chariot, his sword drawn threateningly, not for the foe, but towards his wife Eriphyle who stands in the wings holding prominently the necklace with which she has been bribed to persuade her husband to join the fated expedition. He glares round at her while his son (who will later avenge him by killing his mother) begs him to stay. At the right a seer, who knows well enough what will happen, holds his head. After this, the 'warrior's departure' scene becomes quite popular on Athenian vases, without names but still heroic since no one went off to battle in a chariot in sixth-century Athens. But some of the supporting figures whose postures (the mourning seer) or whose attributes (the amber necklace) told the story, get deselected, or reduced to appear as unexceptional onlookers – wife holding child, household elder – and without the earlier inscribed vases we would not have known the origins of the group. Nor do we know now whether in the later scenes the viewer was intended to recognize a specific myth occasion, when the most important markers were missing.[14]

For an example of a complicated formula devised to show a god (1) encouraging a hero (2) to attack another hero (3), who is being succoured by his divine parent (4), him/herself under threat of attack by (2), but applied to two quite different stories, and on the same vase, which makes the point of the comparison, see [205], another exceptional work of the Kleophrades Painter.[15]

Sometimes too the formulae can be misleading if we ignore origins. In battle scenes where one figure attacks many, the victor

**205.1,2.** Attic red figure cup by the Kleophrades Painter, from Camirus. A – Athena (her legs only preserved) supports Heracles who has struck down Kyknos. The latter's father, Ares, tries to protect him. B – Athena supports Diomedes who has struck down Aineas with a boulder (as described by Homer, though both his hands are full). Aineas' mother Aphrodite drags him away from further harm. Early 5th c. BC. W. 32cm. (London E73)

**206.** Attic red figure amphora by Polygnotos. Theseus attacks an Amazon while the Amazon Antiope moves away to the left. Mid-5th c. BC. (Jerusalem, Israel Mus. 124/1)

usually acts from left to right, but may be placed not at the extreme left, in the wings, but nearer the centre. Behind there might be a companion, if appropriate to the story, but since the processional scheme imposed by the medium is meant to represent an action developed in depth, it was not uncommon for one or more of the opponents to be seen behind the victor, stealing away out of the picture. Remove most of the actors for a smaller field, leaving just the hero and one opponent; then, if a third figure is desired for a symmetrical composition, a second opponent may be included, retreating. On [206] the victor is Theseus striking at an Amazon, but the Amazon stealing away behind him, and deriving from the old more populous formula, is named Antiope. Friend or foe? At this date certainly foe, which is what the iconographic formula implies, though the reduced cast of actors makes the point less obvious. Indeed, Theseus raped Antiope and carried her off. Only much later sources have them as lovers and her supporting him against her sisters.[16] The fifth-century viewer would have known how to interpret the figures and we think we can too, but only after the formulaic treatment and its origins are understood.

The archaic figures may have been marionettish, but with the late archaic period comes such competence in realistic depiction of the human body that virtually any pose can be shown accurately and plausibly, and it is clear that artists were at some pains to understand the potential of this new-won skill. Even so, not all were of the first rank, indeed few were, and we know from other periods that artists will readily devise and then settle for a range of stock poses and features which will serve different occasions. The simplest modern analogy is the strip cartoon where it is easy to see that a very few standard body poses and expressions can serve a multitude of occasions. Even the artist working from a model can readily be tempted into standardized delineation of features like ears, eyes, the curve of a calf or belly – elements of a personal 'handwriting' which helped us understand connoisseurship in Chapter 2. On the fifth-century vases the drawing of a common pose, relaxed or in action, can be applied indiscriminately to figures in quite different situations or of quite different identities. These cliché figures change with time, from the stiff archaic to the realistic and fluent classical, and are shared between artists, but each has its point of conception, and usually in one artist. All this is another weapon in the armoury of the connoisseur.[17]

Finally, we should consider how the scenes are presented on the vase. Friezes and panels are the commonest fields for figure decoration, but some friezes are short and fan-shaped (the outsides of cups) and some panels are circular (insides of cups), while even the rectangles are mainly trapezoidal with curving sides. Framing patterns become less important with time and figures can sometimes overlap into them, seldom, I think, deliberately to make some sort of intrusion into the viewer's space, though this is alleged and is the way it appears. Occasionally pattern and figures can interact and the artist indulge his fantasy, as when a sphinx's tail grows into a handle palmette or the decorative detail serves as furniture.

The early border patterns are either geometric or floral orientalizing. From the later sixth century on in Athens the commonest ground line is of squares decorated in a manner that recalls tapestry patterns familiar years before in East Greece and Lydia. These are not patterns that appear much elsewhere as subsidiary ornament, except of course on dress (the marble *korai*), and it is odd to find them so common on the vases, unless the scene is thought of as in some manner resembling weaving, which was also a medium for figure work (recall Penelope and Athena's Panathenaic peplos).[18]

In the composition of scenes the painter was of course restricted by his field. In two dimensions, with no perspective, little overlapping (too readily misunderstood, especially in red figure), and only one ground line, except for the few up/down compositions inspired by wall painting, the painter instinctively posed his groups serially, unaware of the possibilities of representing three dimensions in two. We must not think of him labouring over the problems of reducing a group in depth to a simple frieze: this was the only idiom he knew and his subjects were construed by his imagination in the only possible way for him. It would be as wrong to try to re-dispose his figures realistically in depth as it would be with comparable figures in sculptural friezes (the Parthenon east frieze centre is a case in point). If there was no room for all the personnel of a scene it was a common practice to omit some, to the point that even a single figure or pair in a characteristic pose from a fuller scene could be presented. We should probably not treat these as simply excerpts, since for the viewer, then and now, the whole was readily called to mind, which must have been the intention, whether or not everything was on view. Sometimes such vignettes are chosen for depiction in their own right, even when space was available. There might, on the other hand, be too much room for the basic scene. In sixth-century black figure, where the available fields are always filled, the sides of a panel or frieze may be occupied by 'onlookers', unnamed mortals. They seem more than just a filling device though they can seldom pretend to have any role in the action. And by being, as it were, permanent viewers they enhance the status of the action they attend.

The backs of vases are often relatively neglected and the prime 'front' scene can usually be identified, although some good painters are equally careful with both sides, and sometimes the two sides complement each other in subject or composition. Where there is more than one figure scene on a vase there need be no linkage, or it is more often horizontal (front and back) than vertical.[19] On the big geometric and orientalizing vases the backs are usually given simpler, non-figure patterns, and at worst simply broadly brushed loops or flowers. In black figure the backs and other less conspicuous areas and friezes can be given animals, sometimes quite large ones to fill the space, as on Corinthian craters. In red figure it is not uncommon to find a meaningless or at least inactive group of athletes or 'mantle-figures' filling the back panels of vases. Cups, which do not have a front and back, do not discriminate, but the 'front' is generally taken to be the side which is visible with the orientation of the interior scene. From the placing of their handles we must judge that cups were hung with their inside to the wall. We can see too that generally the orientation of interior cup decoration is seldom quite horizontal, but dictated by its pose when balanced on a handle or held by the painter. On some of the finer cups it seems that the size of the foot was partly influenced by the area of the exterior cup decoration that it might obscure. Thus, the two arcs of decoration between the handles could be seen at either side of the underfoot (itself carefully finished and in rare examples decorated).[20]

We can see that potters and painters were not indifferent to how their vases would be viewed. In our museums they are as evenly lit as possible and photography tries for the same effect. But in the hand they can be shifted to reflect light from different angles, and the whole image gains life [*247.1*]. This is particularly effective when attempting to see and appreciate the sparkling relief lines of early red figure, or any other modest relief decoration, which is difficult to view in reflected light in display cases, and regularly deliberately flattened by professional photographers, who often succeed even in disguising the fact that the vases are three-dimensional, an effect then abetted by publishers who may cut out the background altogether.[21] Since colour is seldom an important ingredient in Greek vase decoration the continuing use of black and white photography of vases does not much detract from, and may even enhance, appreciation of skills of linear drawing, and need not diminish three-dimensional effects of both detail and the whole.

# Chapter 6:    Pictures and People II

'The image, to the Greeks, is something more than a simple representation; it is a social fact'.[1] Gestures and sound are probably the earliest forms of communication, visual and auditory, followed by speech. In earliest times images seem to be the expression of shared experience and shared hopes or fears, with a religious connotation, only later becoming also a medium for information or advice. Homo sapiens' choice of them seems to have been determined by his physical and intellectual condition and by his environment. This must be why there are considerable similarities in the images and patterns chosen for depiction by communities who have no contact with each other. I think of cave paintings worldwide, or the scrolling patterns on early pottery which seem also to occur worldwide and are not obviously determined by technique, nor from observation of the patterns natural to various crafts, such as the linear and weave patterns which often succeed them in pottery decoration. They were more likely inspired by the grandest of all images in the common sight of mankind everywhere – clouds – a motif which seems to have persisted longest in the imagery of the Chinese. Much depended on the way of life imposed by the environment, and response to it. Figure decoration by early man is generally of beasts crucial to survival, to eat or be eaten by, or 'self-portraits' as of hunters, or attempts to delineate those supernatural powers on whom survival was also thought to depend.

These simple principles often lurk still behind the choice of decoration for all manner of objects even in the urban civilizations of the temperate Old World, but by the period we are dealing with they have been heavily overlaid by tradition and by highly sophisticated means of conveying identity, action, even narrative. In some respects geometric Greece seems to start afresh in its craftsmen's search for modes of visual expression, but we cannot discount the earlier record in the country, much of it still visible above ground or from chance finds, and there is an overwhelming contribution from the arts of neighbouring cultures, to the east and south, where there had been no serious interruption in such expression, as there had been in the Greek world at the end of the Bronze Age.

We may think ourselves able to identify the sources of many decorative patterns, or in figure work distinguish what was intended to depict life, story, or the gods, but we are seldom vouchsafed any explicit indication. There is so much subtlety in Greek art and literature that complete understanding may always elude us, but it may also be easy to overestimate intentions and fail to take at face value what is offered. We should not assume that what seems obvious to us must always in some ways have been less obvious or quite different to an ancient viewer. This is why the last chapter was devoted as much to the language of Greek art as to its content.

Figurative Greek art was long viewed simply as an illustration of texts, which is patently absurd. Recently there has been a move to privilege the viewer over the object, a naive extension of the by now mainly discredited attitude of that mode of literary criticism which privileges the reader, and his incommunicable understanding, over both the text and the author. We are viewers too of ancient art, and it has proved too easy for some scholars to slip into the habit of interpreting it in terms of a twentieth-century understanding of 'the arts'; but this is a perception based on centuries of instruction, study and artistic production that has no relevance at all to what went before. There is no reason not to try to make Greek art accessible to the modern viewer, but this must be done in the terms in which it was made and understood in antiquity. We share with the ancient viewer the same retinal images when we view ancient art, but not the same understanding. What we *do* share was put there by the artist. That the ancient viewer saw and understood what the artist intended is no more than a reasonable assumption, in part based on the probability that the artist had no intention to mislead or be obscure, and that if he had, he would have had no career or following. That we might see and understand in the same manner as the artist and his ancient viewer can only come about from much research into ancient attitudes and life, into the conditions, rules and expectations of antiquity, and from a lot of imaginative empathy; but most of all from careful and detailed inspection of what remains, and understanding of that language of Greek art explored briefly in the last chapter. It is not beyond us, and it is not too difficult to proceed from the obvious to the obscure, especially when dealing with a relatively humble but prolific and varied source such as Greek vase painting.

In the rest of this chapter I explore what appear to have been the intentions latent in various sequences or groups of pottery decoration, in terms of their origins and the messages which they conveyed; we need not expect them all to be profound, but many are certainly more subtle than we might imagine, and they tell us much about how art works and how ancient Greeks thought. I start with the beginnings of figure and narrative art in the ninth to seventh centuries BC and the principles of depiction established in those years and long to remain valid; then the apparent use of the stories of heroes, Heracles and Theseus, to mirror the fortunes of a city, Athens, and even to be remodelled to this end; then the choice of scenes offered by the painters of South Italian red figure from the later fifth to the end of the fourth centuries, serving a readily definable and sophisticated society, not much affected by market forces, but often alleged to be much influenced by the theatrical – this record has to be compared with Athens; then consideration of the high life scenes that occupy many vases; finally, to review the various forces that determined choice of decoration, and the means by which the vase painter may have attempted to impart some emotional impact to his pictures beyond simple narrative and presentation of recognizable figures.

### Beginnings and Principles

Around the middle of the eighth century BC the Dipylon Painter in Athens created what were to be the standard geometricized figures for men and animals [13].[2] These were to be the norm, though seldom so sedulously executed, for painters for the rest of the century. Most painters retained the generalized stick figures which had preceded his work, and these are what we see in the geometric vase painting of other towns. Such figures had not been particularly prominent on earlier vases: a few appeared as vignettes in corners of a vase – a mourner, a horse; and there was an occasional action scene, usually a fight. Only in Crete do more figures appear, geometricized or already orientalized, but not creating a major new idiom.[3] The new big vases that were being made in Athens as grave-markers encouraged something better, to match the monumentality of their setting [13, 14].

Silhouette stick figures can be quite expressive but only of presence or of vigorous action. The figures look naked but women can be given skirts, men helmets, and it is easy to show basic instruments like shields and spears. There is nothing non-contemporary that we can detect, not even undeniable deities, yet there has been support for the idea that the funeral scenes show heroic burials, and that there are heroic features, like the chariot processions; these may imply funeral games, which we have no reason to deny rich eighth-century Athenians.[4] The fighting

207. Attic geometric crater. A file of warriors with the most stylized type of 'Dipylon shield'. Below, a sea battle, the dead 'in' the sea, shown above and below the warship. After mid-8th c. BC. (Athens and Brussels)

scenes do not go beyond what we might expect of contemporary experience, on land and sea [207]. There has been support too for the view that the big oval shields with side cut-outs, the so-called Dipylon shields (as on [209, 211]), reflect the figure-of-eight shields of the Bronze Age and indicate a heroic occasion, but they are just highly stylized renderings of the usual shields of hide stretched over a frame, which by around 700 BC were generally displaced by round shields. These will serve the new styles of hoplite fighting in Greece, and are seen defeating the old shield types on several Geometric vases.[5] It is difficult to uncover any true archaizing of equipment or dress in Greek art, at any period, or indeed any invention of plausible but long-lost gear; it is all 'in modern dress'. The shields may not be the only living relic of the Bronze Age since the funerary iconography (and behaviour) seems also to have originated centuries before in Greece, though it is not clear to what extent, in its turn, it was influenced by Egyptian art, while other figure and decorative elements seem prefigured in Greece's latest Bronze Age vase decoration.[6]

The new figure style does not drive out geometry, and the scenes are composed as geometric patterns which only resolve themselves into figures and furniture on close inspection. The laying-out of a body (*prothesis*) or its passage to the cemetery (*ekphora*) are presented with expressive but stock figures of mourners and family [13, 14]. If figures hold food or other offerings their intent is clear from the context [208];[7] hands to head denote grief; some sit, some stand, sometimes in two registers and at different scales, but this is to fill the space and there is no real attempt to suggest depth of composition rather than a strictly

*192*

208. Attic geometric crater details. The laying-out of a man, his shroud cut away to show two small figures beside him (one apparently feeding him!). From the right warriors approach with food offerings: one with a string of discs (eggs, shells?), then pairs with dead animals, fish, fowl, as well as two live waterfowl; at the right two stand side by side. After mid-8th c. BC. (New York 14.130.15)

209. Drawing from an Attic geometric oinochoe. A fight, with dead and prisoners; 'Dipylon shields' are carried. Late 8th c. BC. (Paris, Louvre CA2509)

symmetrical pattern, which is what Greek artists generally sought to achieve. The artist shows what he knows to be there – all heads, legs and tails of horse teams, often a charioteer perched on top of rather than in his chariot. It looks naive, but not to eyes which do not seek realism, but respond to the message of simple symbolic shapes which resemble life without copying it.

There is no room for story-telling here, and no one is identi-fied by any inscription (the Greeks had only just learned to write). So the scenes are generic but appropriate in context – a woman laid out on a vase intended for a woman's grave. On [209] there is a more complicated fighting scene than most, with some attempt to show encounters of different types, perhaps post-battle, but nothing that we can characterize as a true and identifiable narra-tive. It does, however, seem to be devising formulae – two roughly similar groups of seven and eight figures, with a fish to mark the end of the frieze.[8]

So when can we begin to look for a story rather than a general-ized picture of the everyday? There has been a false dawn for this for some scholars, since there are a few figures which look like Siamese twins, and obscure twin heroes mentioned in Homer are invoked. Why they should be so favoured for so long and all else ignored is an unanswered and unanswerable question, but the figures are better regarded as solutions to showing two men side by side, using the device employed for horse teams – one body, all heads, legs, arms – but less successfully since the bodies are

vertical, not horizontal (a pair at the right on [208]). Where there are two bodies we cannot be sure whether they are truly linked by more than an attempt to demonstrate comrades in arms. The figures disappear totally at just the time that the geometric art that created them declines, which suggests that they depend on the conventions of art and have no identity, but they manage to command lingering affection in some quarters, along with the 'heroic' Dipylon shields.[9]

The source which will stimulate real narrative was already apparent modestly on the Dipylon Painter's vases. Repetitive rows of animals, grazing, walking, recumbent, which derive in style but not always in detail of form from eastern metalwork, begin to fill narrow friezes formerly occupied by geometry [210]. But they are presented with quite a different purpose, to make an animate/abstract frieze, since at first glance the subject seems to be an intricate repetitive geometric pattern. This is not the impression given by the eastern objects that inspired them, where commonly the animals may vary their poses, identity, and the direction in which they face. This is, indeed, what contemporary orientalizing metalworkers in Greece copy in bronze or gold; but not the vase painter.[10]

The east also provided the first formulae which could be used for story-telling in the manner described in the last chapter. Not ordinary fights, but something specific, like a man fighting a lion, often copied without identity in eighth-century Greek metalwork, but eventually recognized as a mode for showing a Greek story, Heracles fighting the lion, on a Greek vase [211]. Here the vase has also the same lion and hero, but shouldering a sheep, recalling Heracles' role in the story, as saviour of the flocks of Nemea.[11] We should not, however, think the geometric artist completely incapable of at least implying identity without borrowing an eastern image; for example, the warrior carrying a dead comrade, examined in the last chapter, and very possibly referable to the most famous epic instance.

Some ordinary eastern fighting groups are copied but the monsters were more biddable. It took some time before identities were attached, however. Winged lions with human heads had been known in Greek Bronze Age art, and are soon popular again, but it is not until the end of the seventh century that they take on special Greek functions as death demons, and in the sixth that the female form is adopted for the Theban Sphinx, the monster of the riddles, faced by Oedipus (a later example [212]), and they acquire their Greek name. So too with human-headed birds, who may in early

**210.** Attic geometric amphora of the Dipylon workshop. Including geometricized friezes of grazing deer, recumbent goats, grazing geese. Mid-8th c. BC. H. 51cm. (Munich 6080)

194

211. Attic geometric tetrapod stand. On the lip warriors with 'Dipylon' and round (hoplite?) shields. On one leg a warrior (Heracles) fights a lion; on the other visible leg a similar confrontation, but here he carries an animal on his shoulders, to save it, no doubt. Late 8th c. BC. (Kerameikos 407)

212. Attic red figure cup by the Oedipus Painter, from Vulci. A regal sphinx on a column poses her riddle to a pensive Oedipus; before her mouth the words 'and three-footed' – part of her riddle – What goes on four feet, then two, then three? Answer: 'Man, as a crawling baby, an adult, an old man with a stick'. About 475 BC. (Vatican, Mus.Greg.Etr. 16541)

days be male, but by the sixth century are identified and named as the dire female Sirens who beset Odysseus (as on the later [213]), and also acquire a funerary role. So too with griffins, whose role in myth comes much later fighting Arimasps or serving a northern Apollo [261]; and with the chimaera [70], derived by the Greeks from a common Syrian monster, which was a winged lion with a human head at its chest, and a bird's-head-tipped tail: for the Greek chimaera the wing grows a goat head and the tail becomes a snake. In each case the eastern image and the Greek name were separate, only assimilated with time.[12]

A very special case was the Greek gorgon Medusa with her petrifying face. An Attic vase painter first devised for her a face that looked like a bronze cauldron with griffin heads [34], but a different eastern form, a facing lion head with gaping jaws and lolling tongue, was adopted in Corinth in about the mid-seventh century and mildly humanized with human eyes, ears, and locks (sometimes of snakes) for the mane, and was soon to be adopted all over Greece [214, 215].[13] By the classical period the face could become that of a beautiful, though no less deadly, woman, following the general Greek practice of de-mystifying the monstrous.

Citing these figures and illustrating them has incidentally introduced the other eastern feature which allowed better opportunities for narrative. Silhouette was abandoned for more realistic

**213.** Detail of a Paestan red figure bell crater by Python. Two sirens, provided with human arms to manage tambourine and lyre, beguile Odysseus, who is tied to his mast to hear them but not to be seduced, while his men's ears are closed with wax. Mid-4th c. BC. (Berlin 4532)

**214.** Gorgoneion painted on the base of a Corinthian figure vase. It has vestigial horns, lion's jaws, but no mane or hair. Mid-7th c. BC. (Syracuse)

**215.** Attic black figure cup. A two-bodied Gorgon holds a deer. The head is the type canonical in the archaic period in Corinth and Athens: human hair, eyes and ears, lion's jaws. Mid-6th c. BC. Diam. 29cm. (Copenhagen Ny Carlsberg I.N. 3383)

forms, in the eastern manner, and incised eastern bronzes and ivories showed how a brush or graver could introduce detail to a figure which enabled identification through dress and attribute. It had been suggested that this was why Greece adopted orientalizing manners of drawing, but the technique came long before its ready application to narrative.

All this explains appearances, but not content. There are several action scenes of myth in the seventh century. Other figure decoration is readily taken up with orientalizing animals whose message is not easily read, if indeed there was one beyond the decorative and energizing effect of such figures on a pot. It is difficult to attribute any deeper meaning to them, apotropaic or magic. If there had been such an intent I think it would have been made more explicit, with inscription if not wider usage in religious contexts; however, where the animal figures are large, heraldically composed, we do touch something of the eastern awe at such symbols of supernatural strength, whether threatening or not, especially when they are monsters like griffins or the lions, honorary monsters hardly met in the Greek countryside. Other figure subjects present inactive divinities or heroes, or epiphanies, like the chariot groups on many Cycladic vases [36]. The animals and monsters play their part now in attendance on a god or goddess whose power is demonstrated by controlling them. This is another eastern image adopted for some Greek gods, notably Artemis, who may also acquire wings but may have nothing more to control than geese [216]. The wings are an indication of exceptional divinity, accorded to few deities in Greece, and then generally only in the archaic period.

By around 600 BC, especially in Corinth, greater subtlety of composition and detail allow action and other scenes of quite complicated myth [54, 204]. These are mainly self-explanatory and can be admired in all the handbooks, so I dwell only on some principles of narrative composition which were observed on them from the beginning, but were barely perceptible on the earlier vases.

A simple story written or narrated moves from one episode to another, and is only hampered by being unable to backtrack and re-introduce people or events without interrupting the flow. A story presented in a single picture can present the full cast but cannot indicate progression of events without a sequence of pictures (like a strip cartoon or, the ideal, film), or unless sequential events are put into one frame – which is more common than one might imagine in the arts of both west and east. Greek art abjured the strip method, even in temple metopes where the row of rectangular fields rather invited it; nor did it allow repeats of figures in one field at different moments in the narrative. There are exceptions even in our period, and more commonly later, but they are very few indeed and quite unsophisticated. So the Greek artist, the vase painter in our case, does not attempt a 'still' from a narrative

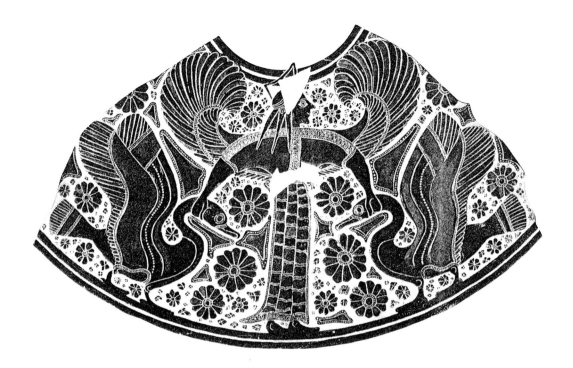

216. Drawing on a Corinthian alabastron by the Taucheira Painter, from Delos. Winged Artemis with two geese. Early 6th c. BC. (Delos 451)

sequence, indeed such a concept only becomes the expected treatment in western art after the invention of the camera.[14] The Greek did, however, have to decide on the most significant phase of a story, which might not always be the moment of maximum action, but its preparation, or sequel. For a few stories compositions were devised that deal with more than one phase, and they are not usually then put on the same vase. Different events on a common occasion, however, can be, such as the events at the Sack of Troy [121], or a sequence of separate events involving a single figure, like the labours of Heracles or events in the journey of Theseus to Athens [222]. This is commonly done without any dividers between the groups.

Recognition of the narrative thus depends on other factors. Foremost is the expectation and experience of the viewer once the scheme and figures are identified by whatever means. There are indeed some obscure subjects which even texts have not elucidated for us, but we may be sure that there must have been clues to identity in the mind of the contemporary viewer, or certainly of any customer for a bespoke vase and scene. Even the unexpected could be, and can be, understood by application of knowledge of the conventions for identity of figures and action. These then become crucial, and they make the study of iconography not a subject for the faint-hearted or those unwilling to look around long and hard. Every scene has to be judged in the context of the

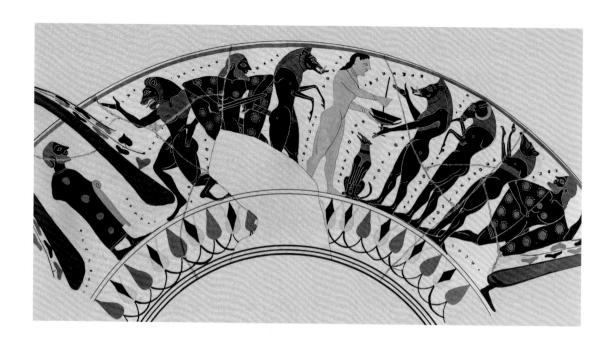

217. Drawing from an Attic black figure cup ('merrythought') by the Painter of the Boston Polyphemos. Naked Circe (white) mixes her potion for Odysseus' companions, already turned partly to animals. At right, one escapes to warn Odysseus, who himself appears from the left with drawn sword to threaten the witch. Mid-6th c. BC. (Boston 99.518)

whole range of media, of all other contemporary production, especially by the same artist if he can be identified. The role of a painter or any other artist composing a new scene or intending to embellish a standard one is to present figures in a way that characterizes their role in the story, rather than in any action immediately dictated by their companions or the setting. There is nothing particularly subtle about this. It is indeed limiting, yet we can see that it could present a rich range of scenes, while the archaic conventions are often easier to fathom than those in later classical art, which is more realistic and therefore less likely to rely on conventional gestures and properties. Drawn cartoons with minimal legends can tell stories very effectively: 'Photo-romans' rely wholly on their texts.

By presenting figures 'in character' in a single scene it becomes possible to allude to past and future. This was certainly not a deliberate act, but the product of the application of the principles I have just described. A favourite instance is a black figure scene of Odysseus' companions turned into animals by the witch Circe [217].[15] The scene has no time unity but expresses narrative, since Circe is shown as a witch with her poisoned cup, the companions already translated with animal heads, but one companion escaping right to warn Odysseus, who is already coming to the rescue from the left. There is no logic here but a sweet demonstration of narrative that needs no closer time/space unity. I feel less confident than before that 'synoptic' is a satisfactory term for

**218.1,2.** Attic black figure lekythos by the Sappho Painter. Heracles with sword and bow rushes up behind Athena who has already engaged the lion with her spear. Heracles' useless weapons hang on a tree. About 500 BC. H. 17.9cm. (Theodor Collection)

this process, which has been much more of a commonplace in western art than many realize and is a natural way to compose a pictorial narrative, not a sophisticated invention of archaic Greeks.

Sometimes it is not only figures 'in character' that contribute to this effect. On the lekythos [218] the tree at the right with bow and quiver in it might signify elsewhere only the presence of Heracles who has had to set aside his weapons to fight the lion (as [197]). But here the lion is faced by a Heracles brandishing weapons, and an Athena who is already attacking it (a very unusual action scene for her). The message is clear – not sword, bow (two of them!), nor even Athena's spear can prevail; it declares the lion's invulnerability and intimates how it will be overcome.[16]

It is mainly in other chapters that observations have been made about scenes specific to or determined by particular vase shapes, usually reflecting their use in society. In this chapter the shape connection is less apparent, but should not be forgotten.[17] I doubt whether Circe's magic cup on [217] need in any way allude to the properties of the cup on which it is painted! – yet its other side has Odysseus fighting Polyphemos, who will be defeated by drunkenness. It is perhaps easy to be too clever in finding such messages.

### Heracles and Theseus. Civic Messages?

I here explore the use of heroic or divine figures in what appears to be ordinary narrative, but which may also reflect civic identities and activities. The general principle is not contestable – from the use of appropriate images of gods or heroes to identify towns on their coinage, to that ready assimilation of rulers to heroes and gods which is made explicit in later times. If the associations mean anything, as they must, on coinage or in laudatory poems, addresses and portraits, they might be expected to emerge also in popular art, and so on vases. Athens has the most to offer over a long period, but the story does not begin with vases – or with coinage, not yet used in Athens when the story begins.

Athena as Athens' patron goddess was the obvious symbol and identifier of the town, although other towns too claimed her as a principal deity.[18] This sort of identifier is static, and power is expressed through dress and attributes – her weapons, armour and aegis. If her relationship to a specific civic event is sought some sort of activity is required, and myth offered little for her beyond her part in the war of the gods and giants, which was indeed well exploited, and was regularly woven on the peplos robe dedicated to her image on the Acropolis. It becomes an important subject for vases, several dedicated on the Acropolis, soon after the reorganization of the Panathenaic Games before the mid-sixth century.

Athena is always prominent in the Athenian gigantomachies, usually beside Zeus and Heracles. She had already in Homer been associated with the hero Heracles, Zeus' son by a mortal woman, who was to come to embody all human virtues of courage and piety, as well as most human vices, more than any other figure of Greek myth. There was nothing Athenian in his story, yet the

Athena-Heracles image was proportionately far more popular in archaic Athens than in any other part of Greece, including those areas where he was 'at home' – mainly Boeotia where he was born, and the Peloponnese, home of his descendants. This is not just a matter of more plentiful evidence from Attica, but of the proportion of scenes vis-à-vis other subjects, on vases and other objects made in Athens, against those from elsewhere.

Early in the sixth century it seems that a king of Sicyon, Kleisthenes, had used the Athena-Heracles image to signify Athenian participation in the so-called First Sacred War which he waged against Delphi, and the image was that of the older and appropriate story of Heracles wresting Apollo's Delphic tripod from him. In a sculpture group that he erected, and in subsequent Delphic imagery, the tripod scene is prominent, and Athena the helper. Megacles, son of the Athenian who had helped Kleisthenes, and Kleisthenes' own son-in-law, suggested to the Athenian would-be leader Peisistratos that a ruse to introduce him into Athens could exploit the association. So a country girl, Phye, was dressed up as Athena and brought Peisistratos by chariot into Athens, to the Acropolis, in a procession which must have echoed in the mind of any watcher that group of Athena conducting Heracles by chariot to immortality in Olympus, which was to be seen by then on vases. No text tells us of this reference to Heracles, but there was no other occupant of Athena's chariot at this period in Athenian art. There is other evidence that the tyrant family in fact made the Acropolis its home for a time. The mere fact of using a pretend-Athena is a declaration of her role as both the city's symbol and the patron of its ruler.

From this point on Heracles is everywhere in Athenian art. There are eight pedimental stone groups from buildings of the middle two quarters of the sixth century and, apart from two unidentified and one for Dionysos, all show Heracles, not even always with Athena. This is true especially on Athena's Acropolis, where Heracles was not even worshipped. He figures nowhere else in the architectural sculpture of Greece of these years except in some metope reliefs on a temple of Hera in central Italy and on the Siphnian Treasury at Delphi (the rape of the tripod, without Athena since this is not an 'Athenian' version). On the Athenian vases, by the thousand, he and Athena are everywhere, often in quiet situations which dwell on their association, almost like consorts, shaking hands, sharing a libation, or the hero being served in a solitary feast (not a symposion), like any eastern potentate [111]. There is a richer range of myth scenes too on these vases

219. Attic black figure amphora by the Lysippides Painter. Heracles mounts a platform (*bema*) to play the kithara before Athena. About 520 BC. (Munich 1575)

220. Attic black figure amphora by the Lysippides Painter. Heracles crouches to pat a docile Kerberos, at the entrance to Hades where Persephone stands, allowing him to collar the beast with the chain he holds. Behind him Hermes offers encouragement. About 520 BC. (Moscow, Pushkin II 1b 70)

221. Attic black figure eye cup in the manner of the Lysippides Painter. Heracles wrestles Triton. About 520 BC. Diam. 36.4cm. (Malibu 87.AE.22)

than anywhere else in Greece, including some novelties which are worth dwelling on since they may reveal their special message for Athenian viewers.

The tripod episode is naturally prominent, and the procession to deification on Olympus, a better fate than consignment to Hades which is what the basic Homeric version told. It was probably the invention of Athenian mythographers and editors of Homer. Heracles can even become a musician on Athenian vases, rivalling Apollo [*219*]. Where he removes the awful hound of Hades, Kerberos, from his home, we find a batch of scenes in which he does not have to fight for the monster but receives him from the underworld goddess Persephone, tamely [*220*]. She was a goddess of Eleusis, whose festivals had been taken over by Peisistratos and centred partly on Athens, one of the excuses being that Heracles had been purified of crimes in an associated festival in the city. Peisistratos also absorbed into the city the countryside worship of Artemis, and when Heracles seizes her stag in one of his labours shown on Athenian vases, she may be seen calmly handing the beast over. At one point, in Heracles' fight with the Old Man of the Sea, Nereus, the latter is changed from being a semi-monster to being wholly humanoid, while the old image is adopted by a Triton, fought by Heracles, but with no justification that can be found anywhere in literature [*221*]. One is

bound to suspect a special occasion promoting such a story and peculiar to Athens, possibly her amphibious adventures against Megara. And so on. The evidence is circumstantial but compelling. Objectors ignore the sculptural evidence, and contend that what is at stake is some sort of organized party-political propaganda via the vases, which is absurd, and they fail to see how much it is in keeping with Greek use of the past from Homer on. This is a view developed by the present author from early days, having noticed only stray parallels between art and politics before understanding the underlying pattern in sixth-century Athens.[19]

By 510 BC the rule of the dynasty of Peisistratos in Athens had been driven out and replaced by an incipient form of democracy and different 'ruling families'. This heralded the emergence of another Athenian hero, to be fêted on monuments and vases – Theseus. He had a better Athenian pedigree than Heracles, though not impeccable, and had not been ignored in earlier Athens, though barely visible in art beside Heracles' record. One of the first indications of his new role was the creation of a series of adventures which brought him from his childhood home of Troizen in the Peloponnese to Athens. These were presented on vases rather in the manner that a smaller choice of Heracles' labours had been. Several vases present the sequence of events side by side [222], never quite matched in depictions of Heracles' labours (except in sculpture). Theseus too is supported by Athena, but her favourite Heracles was not, could not be, forgotten, so some sort of reconciliation was required. Some of Theseus' deeds are modelled on Heracles' to the point of possible confusion in art (as with the Bull of Crete/Marathon). Theseus is allowed to join Heracles' famous expedition against the Amazons, where before they had merely been the setting for yet another of his womanizing forays (for Antiope), not a war. And he is prominent in a new tale which was surely inspired by Athens' own support of the Ionian Revolt against Persian rule in 498/7 BC, when an Athenian expeditionary force joined the Ionians in burning the lower town of the Persian capital at Sardis. The revolt came to nothing but Athens made much of her role. Historically, the burning of Sardis provoked the Persian invasion which came to grief at Marathon in 490 BC. In myth, and on vases, this was mirrored in a new story of an Amazon invasion of Attica and attack on Athens, repulsed by Theseus and Athenian heroes [223].

Heracles had appeared at Marathon, as did Theseus in the story and in the painting made later by Polygnotus for the Painted Stoa in Athens, and they share the honours on the Athenian

222. Attic red figure cup by the Codrus Painter, from Vulci. The Cycle of Theseus' adventures. Centre – dragging the Minotaur from the labyrinth at Knossos. Around, starting at the top – wrestling with Kerkyon at Eleusis, chopping Procrustes on his own bed, beating Skiron with his footbath while the man-eating turtle waits below the cliff, with the bull at Marathon, seizing Sinis to tie him to a pine tree, confronting the wild sow and its guardian Phaia. The same scenes decorate the outside of the cup. After mid-5th c. BC. W. 32.5cm. (London E84)

223. Drawing from a volute crater by the Niobid Painter, from Ruvo. Theseus, at the centre, fights the Amazons with his companions. The Amazon behind him looks friendly but is beside an Amazon chariot, so is hostile. The Amazons are dressed variously as Greeks, Scythians with patterned sleeves and trousers, and with a Persian cap. About 460 BC. (Naples 2421)

Treasury at Delphi which celebrated the victory. They also share the honours on metopes on the Temple of Hephaistos in Athens of the mid-fifth century. Heracles' popularity in Athenian art declined, but not much, and Theseus' rose dramatically, though never quite to eclipse the older figure. Heracles was after all a national hero, and only an Athenian hero by adoption but totally naturalized, and his association with Athena, the city goddess, was more important than with any of the politicians who may have exploited the connection.[20]

So did Athens' leaders use the potters' quarter as a tool of political propaganda? Of course not. Heracles was not a 'Peisistratid emblem' but, with Athena, an Athenian emblem. Architectural sculpture, being state-sponsored, might profess messages. The vase painters simply depicted scenes which found a response in their public because they were of stories which poets, priests and politicians had used to glorify and justify civic events and successes, in the usual Greek manner, using or inventing myth to suit each occasion. Opponents of the general thesis discussed in this section have an easy time of disposing of the idea of deliberate propaganda on the vases, which no one, I think, has ever argued. They have a less easy time with, or ignore, the evidence which is abundant for Theseus in the fifth century, and which makes projection back to Heracles in the sixth almost inevitable, especially since it depends even less on vases, and more on architectural sculpture and even texts, than does the Theseus connection.[21]

Elsewhere in Greece it has not been possible to trace so easily any comparable treatment in art rather than in literature. Architectural sculpture is relatively sparse in the interesting cities and vases fewer and less informative than Athens'. But certainly the Heracles of Peloponnesian art, in an area where his descendants lived, as not in Athens, is a very different fellow, more traditionally heroic in aspect and much less the lion-skinned, club-wielding, burly hero of Attic art;[22] while Theseus is largely ignored and Amazons often have different connotations, as natives of Anatolia. But even in the eighth century we found that Athens had taken a different view of the uses of art to that of the rest of Greece. It *was* a special place and Atheno-centricity is largely justified if we are to understand the full range of the Greek achievement.

Having, I hope, demonstrated that the vase scenes may reveal civic messages that can help us understand the use of myth in antiquity, and the expectations and response of the ordinary citizen, it is necessary to sound a note of caution. Just as comparable use of myth in vase scenes cannot as easily be proved outside Athens, so too it cannot be assumed that pottery decoration is likely to reveal much else of deep social significance when it comes to comparative studies around Greece, other than what it may tell about the public for which it was devised and made. The pot scenes are but one part of the visual experience of the Greeks that happens to have survived particularly well. If, in geometric Athens, the scenes on pottery made for funerals is informative, we do not need to expect comparable information from the geometric pottery of other areas; indeed, that of Argos is very different and possibly not designed primarily to express views about the dead or his status.[23]

The later pottery of Athens is more informative about relevant attitudes to myth locally; then to the social occasions on which much pottery was used; then to much that seems to do with the lives of women. To argue profound social changes from this alone is unwise, though the exercise may be suggestive if taken with other evidence. And no similar pattern can be detected elsewhere. In the archaic period Corinth's range of production and the choice of vase scenes seem to have been more wholly commercially motivated. Laconia and Boeotia made decorated pottery mainly for the table. East Greece offered a fuller range, but it was not on painted pottery that informative figure scenes were presented to the public. The changes in pottery decoration within one society can be revealing, but may simply mirror changes in potential use of the more imposing products, as between Athens of the eighth century and the seventh, where a change in burial manners, which rendered the big grave-markers redundant, may or may not betoken a profound social change. Such criteria are of no help in determining whether behaviour in other parts of Greece was similar or not; for this other archaeological and historical data are required.

### Athens and South Italy. Theatrical Messages?

Athenian vases travelled far and in great numbers, though we shall see that this did not much affect their painters' choice of scenes. In South Italy the production of red figure was brisk but seems to have been much more locally oriented, and the differences in the subjects chosen from those of Athens should prove an interesting reflection on the different societies and their use of the vases. Many have thought that the finer large vases of South Italy, especially Apulia, were decorated under the strong influence of the theatre.

That the theatre should serve as a common reference point for life viewed through myth is a viable proposition. The Athenian fifth-century plays by Aeschylus, Sophocles and Euripides, which certainly dwell on the dilemmas of the day, exercise the usual role of myth in Greek life, though more subtly than most. There is good evidence too that the theatre was an important element in Greek life, if only as the occasion for a major religious holiday, although the impact of its content on the ordinary man may not have been so great, given the subtlety of some of the messages; certainly not as great as the message of a hymn or speech, not flashed past his consciousness in the trappings of the theatre and at a rate of several each day during the dramatic festivals. The performances were rare and fleeting occasions, probably evoking little more than an immediate response from the emotions, rather than working on the narrative-consciousness of the audience, and only engaging intellectuals and other writers more deeply. We think we can understand Greek tragedy; we spend a lot of time studying it and have plenteous comparanda from antiquity. It is still very remote from us in manner and content, and by trying to understand it in terms of modern theatre, or even presenting it as modern theatre, we are attempting far more than, for instance, trying to understand Homer in reading or recitation.

In Athens there is far less reason to suspect any overwhelming role for the theatre in the choice of vase scenes. Some do become

*210*

popular after the same subject had appeared on the stage, perhaps in a winning title, but seldom immediately or in sufficient numbers or detail to suggest direct influence, and there are no visual clues. A story may have become popular for various reasons, and as a result attracted the attention of both writers and painters without direct influence from one to the other. Thus, the story of Boreas and Oreithyia was a subject for both plays and vases [224] after the Persian Wars, both media probably inspired by a new cult for Boreas after his (the North Wind's) help to Athens in wrecking two Persian fleets.

More importantly, the purpose of the stage presentations was very different. Many were profound psychological studies of contemporary problems seen through the stories of myth, as I have remarked. Such messages were not for vase painters, who simply told stories which might bear messages devised for them in other popular media, though some could do so with more originality, sympathy and subtlety than others. There are indeed some stage scenes on vases, just as other occupations and crafts are the subject for portrayal there, but not 'stills' from a production. At any rate, on the stage there were never more than three speaking actors involved, while the painter could have as large an active cast as he wanted or his vase could hold.

Exceptions are representations of satyr-players – human actors wearing trunks with tails and erect phalloi attached, and presumably masks though these are not made specific, enacting scenes of myth or with other mythical and divine figures. These must be inspired by the satyr plays presented at the main Athenian dramatic festival, each playwright offering a trilogy of tragedies

**225.** Attic red figure hydria by the Leningrad Painter. Satyr players, their phalloi and tails attached to their trunks, dance forward with pieces of a throne, to set up on a dais. The dance is accompanied by a pipes-player in the usual musician's enveloping robe, beating the time with his foot. About 475 BC. (Boston 03.788)

226. Attic red figure calyx crater by the Niobid Painter, from Altamura. Top – Pandora at the centre being dressed by Athena; at the left Zeus and Poseidon, at the right Ares, Hermes and a goddess. Below – a chorus of men dressed as Pans dance to a pipes-player. About 460 BC. H. 49.5cm. (London E467)

227. Attic red figure column crater. A singing, dancing chorus, in masks; words issue from their mouths but they are nonsense. They seem to be invoking the apparition of a man, also singing from what might be a tomb monument. Early 5th c. BC. (Basel BS 415)

and one satyr play. They treated mythical subjects in a generally scurrilous manner, a mode which we come close to in the far more sophisticated texts of Aristophanes' Old Comedy of late in the fifth century. Some scenes can be related to titles of satyr plays [225]; hardly any texts have survived except in scraps. But the suspicion lingers that while the 'real' satyr has a function in Dionysiac scenes, serving his master, a satyr-player might be used by a painter simply as a comic commentary in other scenes, and in this class also include action with 'real' satyrs (without costume). There are certainly many scenes with 'real' satyrs parodying

*212*

**228.** Drawing from a Sicilian red figure calyx crater, from Lentini, of the Manfria Group. The stage has incense burners and stairs at the front, columns behind. A comic Heracles, in lionskin, accosts a priestess, probably Auge, who had taken refuge at an altar by a goddess' statue. A man and an old woman observe without intervening. After mid-4th c. BC. (Lentini)

mythological occasions. No examples give any physical allusion to a stage beyond the costume, which is undoubtedly theatrical, but had been used earlier for religious occasions of worship for Dionysos.²⁴ The flexible use of such figures is demonstrated by scenes such as that on [*226*]²⁵ where dancers dressed as Pans perform for a piper. And there are a few other performance scenes on Athenian vases whose location and occasion often remain obscure [*227*]²⁶ though some are clearly associated with a ritual.

In South Italy, in all the local wares that have been identified, there is a comparable phenomenon, but here the stage is represented in graphic detail: not a formal theatre like that of Dionysos in Athens, or at Epidauros, or at several western sites, but a low stage with a curtained front and central steps leading on to it [*228*]. This is something far more makeshift, as for a travelling troupe. The scenes, all fourth-century, used to be referred to as *phlyax*, after a recorded type of western Greek performer who also acted burlesques of myth, but whatever the relationship, dates and subjects do not fit. The scenes are far more easily taken as illustrations of local performances, however edited, of Athenian Comedy. The padded costumes and masks, here explicit, are right, and so are the subjects, including both the distorted myth of Old Comedy and the genre subjects of fourth-century Middle and New Comedy, with the stock types of miser, braggart, crone, etc. [*229*]. It might be objected that Old Comedy was only intelligible to an

Athenian, since it was so full of topical references, but this is not true of all the plays, and editing would have been simple, as for any modern English pantomime, to suit the audience.[27]

The large vases of Apulia pose a different problem. For the most part the potters' output can be seen to have served the expected needs of any Greek community, and in Apulian as in other western Greek wares we can see some concession by shape and decoration (mainly a matter of local styles of armour) to the taste and behaviour of neighbouring native settlements, in which the vases also circulated.[28] But the big volute craters of the Ornate Style seem destined for Greek graves, and some graves were dug with separate compartments to receive them. The vases could hardly have been used for a symposion, unless perhaps at some funeral feast, but this is difficult to envisage, and we have noted that several shapes, and not only the largest, were made bottomless, decidedly not for use. Western Greek metal versions of the shape are smaller and without figure decoration. One wonders who viewed them and when, except at burials. If they were bespoke for particular burials we are at a loss to determine what provoked the choice of one scene rather than another, and might have to find an occasion for their committal to the grave some time after the actual burial. The design and execution of such vases must have taken days and, if some scenes are thought to have specific importance for a particular burial they could hardly come from stock.

Some of the decoration of the craters is funerary in character, heroizing the dead [156]; these need not have been bespoke, but were surely expensive. Many, however, also or only present big tableaux of mythological events, acted by groups of figures which commonly centre on a central *naiskos* (like that in the funerary, heroizing scenes); this may serve as a palace or temple for the action, and might in itself be taken to indicate some common inspiring factor, such as standard stage furniture. The upper frieze usually has relevant deities observing the action [157, 159]. Since many of the scenes are of subjects for Athenian tragedy – rather inevitable given the range of subjects both in tragedy and on the vases – it has often been assumed that they deliberately celebrate or are determined by the staging of a play in the west, rather like a glorious playbill. The western Greeks were held to be somewhat stagestruck, and they certainly seem to have generated a more than usual proportion of other objects related to the theatre – clay masks and figurines of actors, etc. One of the apparent clues to this may, however, have been overvalued: the way Athenian prisoners at Syracuse were favoured if they could recite passages of

**229.** Paestan red figure calyx crater by Asteas, from S. Agata. Stage front. An old man is being dragged off a chest – a miser being parted from his wealth? A mask hangs above. After mid-4th c. BC. (Berlin 3044)

Euripides. This seemed to show not only local taste for such matters but also wide knowledge of the plays among the Athenian soldiery. But the Athenian army was a civilian one, and to judge from the number of plays put on for single festivals in Athens, it seems almost as though there must have been at least as many actors and choristers in Athens as there were potters! It would have taken only one or two actor-soldiers to generate such a story.[29]

**230.** Campanian red figure bell crater. The setting is as for a stage, with projecting wings, but the figures are not in stage dress. At the left Artemis in her temple; centre, Orestes and Pylades; at the right the priestess, Orestes' sister, Iphigeneia greeting them. An episode from the story of Iphigeneia in Tauris. Mid-4th c. BC. (Paris, Louvre K404)

In effect the association of the scenes with plays is no less difficult than it has proved to be with the Athenian vases. The so-called *phlyax* vases show the stage in all detail; why, then, do not the big vases, on which there are no explicit masks or necessarily theatrical dress, yet plenty of opportunity for such display, for example on vase necks? The best answer must be that since they often show a variety of episodes of a story they could not pretend to a single view, as did the comic scenes; and tripods shown in the wings on some, or an altar in the lower frieze, have been associated with stage prizes and furniture. This is not much of an answer, and although it could well be that some literary composition was inspirational, the vases cannot be taken as a sure indication of the content of staged myth, nor therefore to have been chosen for this presumed origin. Just one Sicilian vase looks as though it could show a pillared stage set with actors – an exception that points the rule; but a Campanian, with what looks far more like a stage building, has 'ordinary' protagonists, as in any myth scene, not dressed as actors [230].[30] The artists of all media drew on the common stock of myth, elements of which could become popular for reasons which had nothing to do with any one medium, written, performed or visual.

The debate continues, between the 'philodramatists' and the 'iconocentric', but necessarily allowing the Ornate Apulian vases a special role as burial gifts, which might in some way determine the scenes of myth upon them, as it certainly does the other non-specific heroizing subjects.[31]

**231.** Drawing from a Boeotian Cabirion cup. Hera, Aphrodite and Hermes, probably from a Judgement of Paris. 4th c. BC. (Boston 99533)

**232.** Fragment of an Apulian 'Gnathia' crater, from Tarentum. A tragic actor contemplates his mask. After mid-4th c. BC. H. 18.5cm. (Würzburg H 4600)

It looks rather as though direct stage influence on the subjects of vase scenes might have been confined to the comic: the satyr-players in Athens, the ex-*phlyax* vases in South Italy. In classical Boeotia there is some comparably scurrilous treatment of myth on vases associated with the sanctuary of the Cabiri, where similar burlesques may have been performed in its theatre [110, 231].[32] Reflection of any other literary genre is quite lacking though there are scenes enough of performers as individuals [232],[33] and occasionally even a snatch of song in their mouths on archaic vases.[34]

### The High Life

Homeric heroes sat down to eat and drink and so did most Greeks, probably most of the time. But towards the end of the seventh century the practice of reclining for a feast was introduced from the east, at least for special occasions, and the formal Greek symposion was born. Soon special rooms were designed for it, to accommodate a predetermined number of couches, set against the walls. The idea was eastern, probably deriving from nomad practice of reclining on beds, but formalized in urban courts. Its practice in Greece was soon developed in an idiosyncratic way and became by the classical period virtually ritualized, when it could also be the occasion for political or philosophical discussions; these were probably the exception, and the vases suggest that eating, hard drinking, singing, dancing and sex were the usual programme. We have seen that it was a frequent subject on vases, notably those which might themselves be used in a symposion. It was not an altogether élitist practice but most Greeks probably enjoyed a reclining feast rarely, perhaps only at festivals, since many sanctuaries were provided with dining-rooms for recliners. But all the middle-class houses at fourth-century Olynthus had small symposion rooms (*androns*).[35] In a domestic symposion the couch is indistinguishable from a bed for sleeping, which was also used for the laying-out of a body [13, 14, 250]: already the symposion furniture begins to carry implications of far more important matters, and will in time characterize the heroic. Indeed, in the sixth century there is already a heroic connotation for the recliner when he appears alone, as might an oriental monarch, receiving homage. This is not a true symposion (the word implies company) but is more in keeping with the origins of the practice and on Greek vases is reserved for Heracles receiving Athena [111], Achilles receiving Priam, and occasional other kings (Phineus).[36] The couches take up a lot of room on a vase, but not all the recliners shown 'on the ground' are necessarily to be thought deprived of them through lack of space, and there are picnic parties with drink, especially where a Heracles takes a break from mythology to relax with Hermes or Dionysos.[37] There are also some women-only drinking parties, for courtesans in the lightest or no attire, and without couches [118].[38]

The first symposion we see on a vase was a mythical one, attended by Heracles, made in Corinth about 600 BC [233]. The trappings are there already: the three-legged side tables for food, a variety of cups. Incidentals often shown in such scenes are the dogs tethered to the couch legs, baskets hanging for food, arms on the wall, attendant musicians of either sex and cup-boys; and later, on Athenian vases, the discarded shoes and walking sticks, a basin for the over-indulgent. The Corinthian scenes create a stereotype for the rendering, even to the objects on the tables, a recurrent trio of pieces of meat (?) or strips of meat from the spit, small loaves,

233. Corinthian column crater, from Caere. A symposion in the palace of King Eurytios (right on the second couch from left); behind him his son Iphitos, then Heracles with the daughter of the house, Iole, standing between them. There will be a quarrel over who is best archer. Heracles wins but is denied his prize, Iole, so kills them all. Early 6th c. BC. H. 46cm. (Paris, Louvre E635)

and a cup. The Laconian scenes are similar though simpler, and the Athenian generally simpler still in the matter of table furniture. We look at this again in Chapter 7 [269].

In many respects the depiction of the symposion in Athens and elsewhere was determined by these Corinthian models, but also reflects surely the newly adopted behaviour throughout Greece. Sometimes, on Athenian vases, the layout of the room is suggested by showing one couch end-on, at a side wall [234]. There is a lot of informative incidental detail as well: the food and dishes on the side tables, party games, the presence of girl pipers and small boys, clutching jug and sieve to serve the wine, the occasional courtesan (hetaira).[39]

One Corinthian scene has a floorshow, for which the average symposion room allowed no space. The figures are naked women and dressed men, komasts, who deserve a closer look [235].[40] (Komasts are named from the *komos*, a revel of music, food and drink.) They wear what seem to be close-fitting costumes and often look pot-bellied (a wine belly rather than padding, I think). On other vases they are shown dancing a ribald measure with a lot of bottom-slapping and gesturing which suggest a pattern for the dance not unfamiliar on bucolic occasions elsewhere. They appear first on Corinthian vases, in the late seventh century, and are probably to be taken as professional entertainers. The occasional presence of a crippled komast (like an Hephaistos)[41] and even of scenes with komasts who seem to be conducting a lively Dionysiac procession returning Hephaistos, drunk, to Olympus,[42] suggest that

234. Attic red figure cup by Douris (signed), from Vulci. Symposion. The food has been cleared and the side tables carry only wreathes. Boys bring jugs of wine. At the right a couch is seen back-on. More jugs and cups hang on the wall. Early 5th c. BC. (London E49)

235. Drawing from a Corinthian amphoriskos, by the Tydeus Painter. Symposion and komos. A man and woman on the couch at the left, embracing; a boy at the standed crater at the right. Between, a dance of dressed komasts and naked women. Before mid-6th c. BC. (London B41)

236. Attic black figure skyphos by the KY Painter. Two komasts. About 580 BC. (Athens 1109)

237. Attic black figure amphora by the Swing Painter. A chorus of men on stilts. After mid-6th c. BC. H. 41.4cm. (Christchurch 41/57, N.Z.)

they could turn their revel into an enactment of myth, at a certain fairly basic level and for an appropriately vinous occasion. Many see here the beginning of Greek drama, always closely associated with the dance and Dionysos, probably rightly. Komast presence at symposia is, however, exceptional.

Similar komasts appear on Athenian vases through the second quarter of the sixth century [236].[43] Are they simply copying the Corinthian scenes or were there Athenian komasts too? The latter is probably true, and the komast dancers who appear on some East Greek, Laconian and Boeotian vases are also probably local performers; indeed the practice may have come from the east.[44] But in Athens there are some female komasts, and others grow tails and clearly imitate satyrs, enhancing the dramatic aspect of their performances and adding the satyric element which was equally essential in the development of Greek drama, as we saw in the last section of this chapter. Apart from the komasts there are several scenes of the second half of the sixth century of choruses of mummers, dressed as animals or otherwise resembling a circus act rather than any enactment of myth [237].[45]

With the introduction of a form of democracy in Athens in 510 BC the professional komasts disappear, and the drunken dancing is done by the symposiasts themselves, without any special dress or dramatic connotation [238], since the formal drama, including the satyr play, was by then well established in Athens. These amateur komasts offer the painter an opportunity to display some skill in depiction of acrobatic behaviour (compare the satyrs on [273]). One special class of komasts appears through and just after the late archaic period. They appear to be men dressed as women – with turbans, long dress (chitons), soft boots, parasols, even earrings [239, 240]. But all the items of dress are also male oriental – Lydian – from an area whence Greece took lessons in extravagant behaviour and welcomed several famous bon viveurs and performers, such as Anacreon who was brought to Athens by its tyrant family, and died there, in old age, choking on a grape pip. They may look feminine but their behaviour and beards do not, and we need not look here for transvestism, which is a more serious matter.[46] The *komos* is very seldom depicted at the symposion, but must be thought to take place either later, en route to another party as is often implied by the wine gear being carried, or in an adjacent room or courtyard, probably where the crater was set.[47]

Satyrs have been mentioned more than once and are the most plausible of all Greek monsters, almost too plausible for their

238. Attic red figure cup by Douris, from Vulci. Komasts carry their cups as they dance from one party to another. Early 5th c. BC. (London E54)

239. Detail of an Attic black figure kyathos by Psiax. A lyre player in short skirt, boots and wearing a turban from which protrudes a cock's comb. The long-armed lyre is a 'barbitos'. Late 6th c. BC. W. 9.5cm. (Malibu 77.AE.102+78.AE.5)

240. Detail of an Attic red figure column crater by the Pig Painter. Komasts, with a parasol, castanets (*krotala*, at left) and a lyre. They wear feminine snoods and enveloping chitons. About 470 BC. (Cleveland 26.549)

frequent and effective reflection of man at his weakest and least competent. They demonstrate the alternative or flip side to the high life. They have no myth but their physique can be borrowed for real but rustic figures of myth, as Marsyas [146] and Silenos, and they can be given names [66], just as their more serious female companions, the maenads, who are not monsters in appearance, only behaviour (tearing live animals), and only apparently victims, since the satyrs virtually never have their way with them [199, 241].[48] But the satyrs are serious immortal attendants of

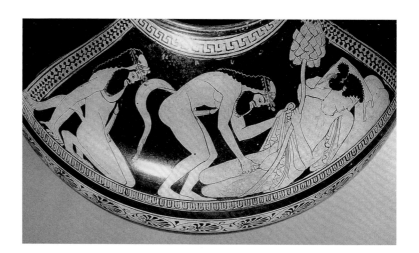

**241.** Attic red figure hydria by the Kleophrades Painter, from Vulci. Satyrs investigate a sleeping maenad, still clutching her thyrsos. Early 5th c. BC. (Rouen 25)

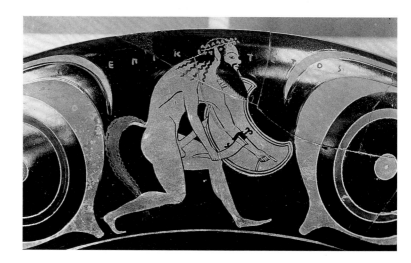

**242.** Detail of an Attic red figure eye cup by Epiktetos (signed). A satyr goes to battle, with light shield and drinking horn. About 520 BC. (London E3)

Dionysos, even when he goes to war [*119, 242*], and they too can eventually achieve a form of family life (even as does Pan). They appear with Dionysos often in Attic art for their drinking interests as much as for their sexual or theatrical. Yet in some archaic scenes Dionysos is attended by mortal youths, not imitating satyrs [*79*], and yet again the mortal and immortal are juxtaposed where the deity (like a Heracles) has at least as much of the earthly about him as the Olympian.[49]

It may seem a pity to define high life in terms of drinking parties and the celebration of Dionysos, but the vases distort the evidence in favour of this view because they are the appropriate setting for so many scenes of party-going. Otherwise, we might take the many athletic scenes as reflecting also the life of the more leisured classes [*116, 243*],[50] or the rare scenes of an upper-class finishing school [*244*],[51] as well as the instances of homo- and hetero-sexual behaviour [*245*],[52] not much of which is seen to

243. Detail of an Attic red figure cup by the Foundry Painter, from Vulci. The trainer belabours two practising wrestlers who are gouging eyes – about the only disallowed move beside biting. A discus in its bag hangs over them. Early 5th c. BC. (London E78)

244. Attic red figure cup by Douris (signed), from Caere. School scene. Lyre exercises at the left, then reading from a scroll on which is written 'Muse, I begin to sing about wide-flowing Scamander . . .' – the Scamander a river at Troy but these are not Homer's lines. There hang on the wall a basket, an animal-skin pipes-case with side pocket for the mouthpiece, a lyre and a cup. Early 5th c. BC. (Berlin 2285)

245. Attic red figure cup by Peithinos (signed), from Vulci. Courting pairs of youths and boys. The equipment hanging and in their hands is an oil bottle, sponge and strigil (for scraping down). About 500 BC. (Berlin 2279)

take place in a symposion setting. The hunt too comes to be regarded as a suitable indicator of a high style of life but on the vases is generally of a suburban character, for hares, and otherwise is heroically enhanced to embrace real country life, the chase in the wild, and this becomes an indicator of regal behaviour, as it was in the east [*138*].[53] My emphasis on the parties in this section must not be taken to reflect on any diminished importance for these other subjects, which I do not discuss more fully here.

### *Whose Choice?*

Analysis of the subject interests of several late archaic vase painters in Athens shows that they had individual favourites, often repeated, with variants.[54] This suggests that for the most part the choice of subject lay with the painter, and the subjects involved do not indicate that they were chosen to serve any special demand in either the home or the export market, although they were of course conditioned by what these markets expected, and once they had arrived outside Greece they might give rise to local interpretation. To this extent we are entitled to privilege what we can define about the choice of the painter over whatever we may surmise about the response of the customer. But among the subjects we may find some, so outside the usual range for any painter, that they must be judged special commissions.[55] Such must have been Myson's amphora showing Croesus on his pyre [*246*], it is so far from his usual range.[56] There are many more which were clearly chosen for a purpose, often on specific shapes, and there were even some painters who specialized in such work, though generally they were simply additives to the painters' usual stock, designed for special needs or occasions. Myson again, for example, made a special small crater showing Athena on both sides, signing as both painter and potter, for himself to dedicate on the Acropolis in Athens.[57] Obvious examples of commissioned subjects are the Athena and sport scenes on the Panathenaic amphorae, made to contain the prize oil for athletes in the Panathenaic Games [*73–76*]. Others, with which this section deals, are somewhat less obvious, and deal mainly with subjects suitable for vases which are to be dedicated or used for ritual purposes, and we also address the question of whether there was any deliberate choice of scenes for export.

Where there was already a rich selection of decorated pottery which might be used for dedication an element of choice in scenes bought could be exercised. Thus, on the Acropolis of Athens, there is a very high proportion of scenes with Athena, without most of

**246.** Drawing from an Attic red figure amphora by Myson, from Vulci. The Lydian King Croesus on his funeral pyre pours a libation to the gods while it is being lit. Early 5th c. BC. (Paris, Louvre G197)

them being outside the repertory used to decorate vases for the home or export market. But there was also much besides that was deliberately made for offering.

One class which was certainly for dedication, or normally so, is the clay plaque, usually rectangular and pierced for suspension or fixing to a wall or tree, very rarely two-sided.[58] Some, of course, might be simply decorative, even for the home, just as we imagine painted wooden panels may have been, but most are found in sanctuaries and are appropriately decorated. We have already remarked those made in Corinth's potters' quarter, mainly in the sixth century [*173*]. Several of these depict the deities, Poseidon and Amphitrite;[59] others show potters at work, soliciting divine patronage, or, where a disaster like a flare-up of the kiln seems to be shown, to avert evil. This mishap is one alluded to in the pseudo-Homeric Hymn for the Potters, 'he who peeps over, may his face be blackened'. But several have scenes which we might as readily expect on vases.[60] There is a series of small plaques from the Demeter sanctuary at Eleusis, mainly without figure scenes but just tripods or the like. Among the earliest is a single find, late geometric by the Athenian Analatos Painter, from the Apollo sanctuary area at Aegina, and inscribed with the donor's name. It

**247.1,2.** Attic clay votive plaques from the Acropolis, Athens.
*1.* Black figure. *2.* White ground. Both with Athena. Early 5th c. BC. H. 10 and 6.7cm. (Athens, Acr. I, 2585; II, 1038)

**248.** Corinthian clay votive plaque, fragment, from the Acropolis, Athens. The Birth of Athena. Zeus is gesticulating, and the hands behind him are those of a goddess of childbirth (compare [59]), The goddess Athena, fully armed and with spear raised, emerges from his head. The inscription ZEU[s] is more Attic than Corinthian in letter forms; perhaps bespoken by an Athenian in Corinth. Before mid-6th c. BC. H. 5cm. (Acropolis I, 2578)

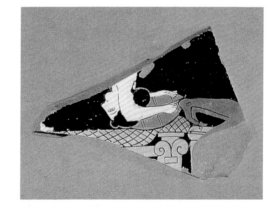

**249.1,2.** (*left below*) Attic red figure plaque fragments by Paseas. A long rectangle with at least three couches occupied by couples making love. Unlike ordinary red figure, the women are painted white, with incised detail, and the ruddled background does not extend below the top of the couches. Late 6th c. BC. H. of larger fragment 6.8cm. (Oxford 1984.131/2)

**250.** Attic black figure funeral plaque, to be affixed to a tomb monument, from Cape Kolias (Attica). The laying-out of a woman in the courtyard of her home – door pillar at the right. Relationships are inscribed: from the left, husband, brother, three aunts in all (one 'on the father's side'), mother (by the head), sister at the right. Note the children at either end of the bier (a small sister by the mother). Other inscriptions are mourning (*oimoi*), nonsense, and unexplained. About 500 BC. W. 26.5cm. (Paris, Louvre MNB905)

showed warriors, just possibly marines, who appear on another of the painter's plaques, from Sunium.[61] The series from the Athenian Acropolis runs from late geometric to the early fifth century, but rarely done in red figure. An exceptionally high proportion of them show Athena, alone or in action and possibly copying one of her statues – the striding, striking Promachos seen also on the Panathenaic vases – or close variants; this is no ordinary narrative figure [247]. Others have more commonplace scenes, including some of trade (weaving). Some carry bespoke inscriptions but most have scratched names and dedicatory formulae. Someone bespoke a plaque from Corinth, with an Athenian scene (the birth of Athena), to dedicate in Athens [248].[62] Stray examples are found elsewhere in Greece, including a Wild Goat style one from Smyrna, a later one in Crete, and some Attic red figure at Eleusis.[63] An unusually colourful Athenian plaque, of unknown provenience, need not be excluded as a possible votive for the character of its scene [249].[64] We should take all these to be the equivalent of wooden votive plaques (a few of which have been found near Sicyon, in Corinthian style, one with a sacrifice scene),[65] made in clay wherever potters and painters were prepared to supply this alternative. In late vase scenes they are seen hanging from trees or at shrines, once on a late archaic vase beside a kiln alongside votive masks, probably also of clay [256].

Other painted decoration on clay plaques can be found at a larger scale for the metopes of archaic temples (mainly Corinthian style, seventh-century), and for series or single plaques [250] in

Athenian black figure to attach to tomb monuments; a near-complete series of these has survived, painted by Exekias [198].[66]

Plates could serve a comparable purpose. The shape presents some problems as we shall see, but from the sixth century on it seems primarily for display and almost all archaic ones are provided with a pair of holes for a suspension loop.[67] One in an Athena temple on Chios shows the goddess and must have been bespoke.[68] There are many from the Acropolis in Athens. The painter Epiktetos signs one (uniquely for him) as both potter and painter and it must be his own dedication.[69] It shows the striking Athena, but she is by no means the only subject for the plates, and a numerous late black figure series, by the Kleiboulos Painter, has different, though suitable, subjects.[70] In Classical Corinth there is a class of small plates, cups and boxes, many showing deities, perhaps on purpose for local dedication (the Wide Group) [109]. Some Laconian black figure cups showing a seated deity being approached are thought to be votives, but they joined the export market too,[71] as did some fine Athenian white ground cups, several of which show single deities.[72] One at least found a proper home – Apollo at Delphi [127]. Much might intervene between votive intention on the part of the potter and delivery to the appropriate deity.

Other bespoke pottery for dedication is identified only by painted inscriptions but may be either undecorated or at best decorated in a conventional manner. This applies to the Chian dedicatory cups made at Naucratis in Egypt, cups for Hera at

251. Attic krateriskos with added colour, from the Temple of Artemis at Brauron (Attica). Girls (naked?) run and dance in honour of the goddess. Late 5th c. BC. H. 21.5cm. (Brauron)

252. Attic red figure loutrophoros by the Kleophrades Painter, from Attica. On the neck mourners, one holding a loutrophoros-amphora. The laying-out of a dead youth. Below, in black figure, horsemen making the mourning-farewell gesture. Early 5th c. BC. H. 81cm. (Paris, Louvre CA453)

253. Attic red figure 'battle loutrophoros' by the Achilles Painter (main scene) and Sabouroff Painter (neck and lower body). On the neck an old man (father?), and on the other side a warrior. A fight on the body. In the frieze below a procession of mourners making the traditional gesture for the occasion. Mid-5th c. BC. H. 92.8cm. (Philadelphia 30.4.1)

Samos and Naucratis, and some mid-sixth-century cups for Athena at Athens.[73]

In what has been mentioned so far the shapes, including the plaques, do not go outside the range applicable for non-dedicatory purposes also. Other religious occasions are served by special shapes as well as decoration. In Attica shrines of Artemis receive rather angular little craters decorated with scenes of the running and dancing girls ('little bears') who worship her [*251*], as well as other myth scenes relevant to her story and cult.[74] For burials, we have met already the geometric grave-markers with their funeral scenes. Thereafter the loutrophoros shape is associated

**254.** Drawing from an Attic white ground lekythos by the Sabouroff Painter, from Eretria (where Athenians had settled). Hermes leads a woman to Charon's ferry over the Styx to the Underworld. Little souls (*eidola*) hover. Mid-5th c. BC. (Athens 1926)

**255.** Attic red figure pyxis (the photo unrolled) by the Marlay Painter, from Greece. Wedding procession from the bride's house (left). Young women carry a lebes gamikos (from the bridal bath), a box (linen?); a youth (best man) and woman (groom's mother) have torches beside the couple in a chariot. The figure greeting them is Hermes, so the occasion seems to blend mortal and divine. See *ARFH* II, fig. 243 for the lid, with Sun, Moon and Night. Mid-5th c. BC. H. 17cm. (London 1920.12–21.1)

with Attic burials and through the archaic period carries scenes of the laying-out and consignment to the grave [*252*]. In the classical period these *prothesis* scenes continue but there are also several with fighting scenes [*253*],[75] which we might regard as heroizing, for male burials, and many with marriage scenes, which probably relate to the concept of an unmarried woman becoming a 'bride of Hades'. We look at the shapes in Chapter 7. The tall lekythos shape in Athens had long been used in burials since it contains the needed oil. From around the mid-fifth century to its end, it is used exclusively for burials, painted with a white ground, showing scenes of tending the grave or others of the dead in life (as on classical gravestones), or of the journey to Hades over the Styx with ferryman Charon and his boat [*128, 129, 254*].

Athenian wedding rites with a heroic flavour appear on a pyxis [*255*], of a shape thought designed for women. Another vase shape with specific wedding connotations is the lebes gamikos, regularly though not always decorated with wedding scenes, either the procession or, in red figure, the decking of the bride and reception of guests and gifts [*135, 293*]. Shapes and decoration peculiar to Athenian customs and rites are not generally for the

**256.1,2.** Attic red figure cup by the Foundry Painter, from Vulci. Name vase. Work in a bronze sculptor's foundry. A – A boy works the bellows behind a furnace, melting bronze, while a man stokes it. Votive plaques and masks hang from goat horns above. At the right a man prepares the neck of a bronze statue to receive its waiting head. There are various hammers (one held by a youth) and saws, and two feet – sculptor's models. B – two men, master sculptors, it may be, watch the finishing of a bronze statue of a warrior, in a shed. It is being scraped down with strigils. Oil flasks and strigils hang at either side, and a metalworker's hammer and scraper. The men are elegant, with hairbands, walking sticks and soft shoes; the workmen naked or with loincloths only and caps. Photos in *ARFH* I, fig. 262. Early 5th c. BC. (Berlin 2294)

**257.** Apulian red figure column crater. An artist is painting the lionskin on a statue of Heracles. A boy at the left is heating the spatulae since the paint is burnt on (encaustic). Zeus, Nike and the 'real' Heracles at the right watch. After mid-4th c. BC. (New York 50.11.4)

export market, and exceptions may demonstrate a real Athenian presence overseas to use them, but the last-named shape certainly travelled.

It is not clear whether we should include with the bespoke scenes those few that depict sacrifice or crafts and trade.[76] They are not exactly 'everyday life' in the sense that we might take the wedding scenes or those depicting the adornment of a bride, though it is certain that these were intended for appropriate occasions, but probably not for specific ones. I do not imagine that the scene of a bronze workshop [256], for example, was made just for stock or advertisement, and the fact that many such scenes went for export ought not to blind us to the possibility that they were made for an occasion or customer; again, the question of a second-hand trade is posed. It is not altogether surprising that a vase painter should be interested in depicting his own or a cognate craft. The Apulian vase showing a painter of statues is unusual enough for us to believe it was bespoke; perhaps its painter worked in the sculptors' studios too [257]. It is difficult to see the appeal of more banausic activities such as the cobbler [258] or peasants pressing oil [259],[77] and both vases, with others like them, almost certainly were exported. I doubt whether rich customers found them very edifying.

If appropriate scenes could be chosen from stock in Athens for dedication, was the same done for the export trade, and was there

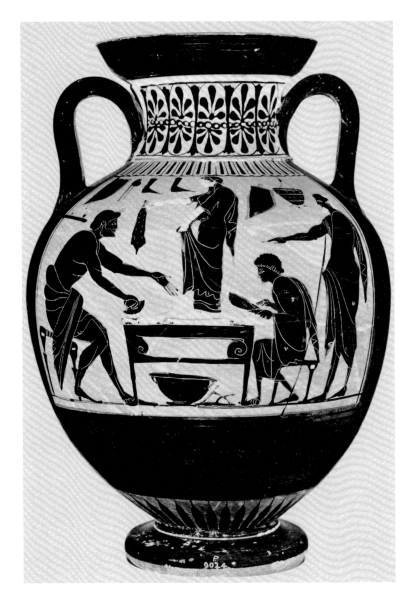

**258.** Attic black figure amphora. A shoemaker's shop. The customer stands on the table to have the leather soles cut round her feet. The boy seated at the right holds a sandal. Below the table is a basin of water, to soften the leather, and a sandal. Above is a shelf with tools (left), pieces of leather, an oil bottle, two lasts and a basket. On the other side of the vase is shown a foundry. Late 6th c. BC. H. 36cm. (Boston 01.8035)

**259.** Attic black figure skyphos. Two men help the boulders to press out the olive oil, flowing into a pot. About 500 BC. (Boston 99.525)

even a policy among some potters to supply special scenes for export? The first part of the proposition is acceptable, though counting scenes on vases found in Etruria with what seem to be appropriate stories (e.g., with Aineas, whose story had a western dénouement after his escape from Troy) can be deceptive, given that such a high proportion of vases with any identifiable scenes are from Etruria in any case, and there are none sent west from Athens with wholly Etruscan scenes; so it is difficult to prove. Moreover, the thought that scenes on Attic vases in Etruria or in any other export market reflect on Greek myth being used locally with a specific political rather than generalized social intent is hard to credit,[78] however they might have been read in Athens. That imported scenes might admit local interpretations and even generate a series of locally produced scenes does not imply that the models were either deliberately painted or chosen, any more than that they were understood in the same terms as those in which they were created.

Sometimes, however, when a foreign shape is adopted, it may carry themes of foreign inspiration, and be deemed more marketable in lands where it would be recognized. This has been explored already in Chapter 4, and examples given.

The second proposition, of the deliberate placing of scenes on ordinary vases for export, has little to recommend it. It was vases that were exported, not images.[79] If it had been true we would surely have had far more evidence for it, and in most cases where we do discern a special shape and style of decoration being made for the Etruscan market, the scenes do virtually nothing to suggest a deliberate choice. Correlations of the scenes on Greek vases with the Etruscan deity to whom some are dedicated are not convincing, so perhaps even the Etruscans, other than their artists, did not look too closely.[80] The Tyrrhenian amphorae made in Athens mainly for Etruria in the second quarter of the sixth century have a full range of colourful myth scenes of Attic pedigree [58, 59, 263], and are peculiar only in the artists' treatment of them, which does not go beyond that of their fellows working for the whole market. And the Nikosthenic vases of the second half of the century, copying even an Etruscan shape [187], have mainly banal scenes which Etruscans may have enjoyed, but were clearly not any sort of sophisticated choice for the market. Other Etruscan shapes copied – kyathoi – have standard Attic decoration and did not travel only to Etruria [188]. However, another series of late black figure stamnoi (the Perizoma Group), not an Etruscan shape but one which was sent to Etruria, show athletes in

260. Attic black figure stamnos by the Michigan Painter (of the Perizoma (loincloth) Group). Reclining men and women. Below, an acontist (with javelin), trainer and two boxers, a man practising a start for the footrace (stooping). Late 6th c. BC. H. 32.6cm. (Würzburg L328)

loincloths [260], which was not a Greek habit at all, though Etruscan.[81] In the fourth century there 'is brisk production of vases with scenes of Amazons or of Arimasps fighting griffins which reflect stories associated with the Black Sea. It could be that they were painted and chosen with this in mind, and therefore sent, or picked up by merchants for the northern circuit; but they were just as readily sent elsewhere, to the west and to Africa. These scenes appear also on a special type of crater which seems to copy a Black Sea shape [261].[82] This is nothing like Chinese and Japanese attempts at western themes and style on their export

261. Attic red figure bell crater (of Falaieff type – a collector who had two specimens of it), of Group G. Arimasps fight griffins on foot and from a chariot, with battle axes. Other side, *ARFH* II, fig. 414. Mid-4th c. BC. H. 43cm. (Paris, Louvre G530)

porcelain. However, when the only surviving scene of a Dionysiac ship being carried appears on an East Greek vase found in upper Egypt, at Karnak, where a similar ceremony for Amun took place annually, it would be wretched to claim a mere coincidence.[83] This must have been a matter of a commission or at least deliberate choice.

Finally, we should remember that we are dealing with what seems to be exclusively a male choice, whether for scenes or marketing. Women's Studies are comparatively new to classical scholarship and were partly ignored in the past largely through lack of evidence, although it has also been too easy to forget nearly half the population of antiquity.[84] The studies have naturally turned often to the evidence of the vases. What these show us is the male view of life, including women, not the women's view, and when we

*238*

suspect that the female customer may be in mind for the decoration of some Athenian later red figure, we have no means of knowing whether they dictated the content or mood to any real degree; most probably not at all. But male artists can be most perceptive observers of their world and partners, and need not automatically be judged unsympathetic.

*Moving Pictures*

Emotion as an ingredient for communication in images has been important in all post-antique representational western art, especially that of a religious or narrative character. Was it present in the art of the Greek vase painter, or did any emotional response depend wholly on the subject matter, conventional gestures and poses? The question seems little discussed but is potentially crucial to our understanding of viewer response. The only possibilities open are the communication of emotion through composition/subject and through expression.

A uniquely Greek method of indicating an emotional or spiritual element in any scene may be discussed first. It was to introduce a human figure, usually a woman, who personified that emotion or other abstract element in the narrative which would have been difficult to express otherwise. Examples are Apate (Deceit [*159*]), Dike (Justice), Eirene (Peace), Eris (Strife), Eukleia (Glory), Lyssa or Mania (Madness), Peitho (Persuasion). Others contribute to the mood of a scene – Eudaimonia (Happiness), Eunomia (Just Rule), Eutychia (Good Fortune), Hygieia (Health), Makaria (Happiness), Nemesis (Fate). They are female largely because the words they personify are feminine, and they embrace both good and bad. Several of these figures achieve divinity and receive worship, among them Eukleia, Peitho (representing the persuasive aspect of Aphrodite rather than the sex appeal), Hygieia, Nemesis.[85] On [*262*] Menelaos, at the sight of Helen's dishevelled beauty, drops his sword to indicate that he will not kill her; Aphrodite, sex goddess, is the intermediary with Eros flying to crown him, and her companion Peitho (Persuasion) turns away to the left.[86] The only comparable male personifications are figures like Hypnos (Sleep), Thanatos (Death), Geras (Old Age), Phobos (Fear), and they are generally active, not passive adjuncts like the females and like Eros' various alter egos, Himeros and Pothos.

The posture of the actors of a scene can often reveal more than their immediate role, quite apart from the conventional but expressive gestures. Frontality in anything as large as sculpture

262. Drawing from an Attic red figure oinochoe by the Heimarmene Painter, from Vulci. At the left Peitho (Persuasion) looks away from Menelaos who drops his sword and his intent to kill, at the sight of the beauty of his regained wife, Helen, who, dishevelled, takes refuge at a statue of Athena in Troy during the Sack. The agents of his change of heart are Aphrodite at the centre and Eros flying to crown him. Mid-5th c. BC. (Vatican 16535)

may impose a sense of awe but on the scale of a vase does no more than identify the subject as statuesque. A frontal face is different since in every person we meet we scan the face first and where, as in vase scenes, most are in profile, the rare frontal face challenges us. It is a successful bid for direct communication in a genre which is otherwise very much a spectator exercise. We can see that it is used for frightening faces, like the gorgoneion [214, 215], which in itself must have become such a cliché in Greek art and decoration that it no longer terrified. Other frontal faces bid for sympathy and are found where the actor is in danger – of rape if Cassandra, of imminent death if setting out for Thebes ([195] left). A comic effect is sought with mask-like heads of satyrs. Yet others are used to designate a sleeping figure – Alkyoneus, Ariadne being deserted – sometimes a dead one.[87] They invite the viewer to shed a tear, laugh or shudder.[88]

263. Attic black figure Tyrrhenian amphora by the Timiades Painter. The sacrifice of Polyxena, Priam's daughter, at the tomb of Achilles, by his son Neoptolemos. At the left Nestor ('of Pylos') and Diomedes; she is held out by Amphilochos, Antiphates and the Lesser Ajax ('of Ilion' = Troy); old Phoinix, Achilles' mentor, looks away. Before mid-6th c. BC. (London 97.7–27.2)

264. Attic black figure lekythos by the Beldam Painter, from Eretria. Name vase. Satyrs torture a woman, perhaps a witch, tied to a palm tree, extracting her tongue and burning her hair; at left out of sight others wield a pestle and a whip. Early 5th c. BC. H. 31.7cm. (Athens 1129)

It is difficult to say how impervious an ancient viewer might have been to the subject matter of an ordinary narrative scene – a bloody sacrifice of the innocent, for example [263], or torture [264]; less so than any enacted or described on the stage, I imagine.[89] A combination of scenes can have a programmatic message, like a play, but these are quite exceptional, like the Kleophrades Painter's commentary on the fortunes of war at the Sack of Troy [121]. The scenes of erotic activity might have proved arousing for some, but are mainly straight reporting.[90] However, from the fifth century on it is likely that the realism of the figures occasioned both the intent and effect of some degree of sexual response, not usually *per se*, but secondarily. It probably requires a degree of realism in art for any viewer to identify sufficiently closely with an erotic scene for it to be arousing. Most in earlier art, in Greece and the near east, are highly stylized and can be seen from their contexts to have a strongly religious, fertility content. Such scenes on Greek drinking cups have a purely pleasure context. In Greek art nudity for women is at first a matter of religion, designating fertility, or for pathetic effect, as for Cassandra on [121].[91] Only after the mid-fifth century does it become realistic enough to be exciting. The appearance of dwarfs and foreigners is reported, not laughed at.[92]

Response to humour and the attempt to elicit laughter is a different manner. From reading Aristophanes we can see that the Athenian citizen had a broad sense of humour, not without some appreciation of the subtle. Incongruity is one mode, and we too may smile at visual puns, like a siren's body turned into an eye [78], or the use of decoration as furniture. Animals behaving as humans [265] might conceal some dancing mummery. The phallos bird is only slightly more serious [266], a monster designed to suggest a comfort for women without the discomfort of a man's presence.[93] Satyrs are *ipso facto* funny regardless of their behaviour, which may be 'normal' for them and therefore sexually inspiring for male viewers (perhaps because they almost never seem successful), or incongruous when they go to war for Dionysos [119, 242]. We have noted the frontal satyr face and gesture of pleased dismay [199]. When they intervene in myth scenes which can have no reference to satyr play the intention is purely comic. The ex-*phlyax* vases show comic situations and should raise a smile at least as readily as they did a laugh in the audience [152, 228, 229, cf. 153]. And there is the incongruity of treating a vase as a figure, so that a cup looks like a mask when drunk from [307], or a jug a bird.[94]

**265.1,2.** Attic red figure cup, from Vulci. A – a satyr with Pan pipes (Greek ones are not graduated) for three dancing goats. B – bibulous komasts with monkey heads on a see-saw. The scenes probably reflect mummer dances. Early 5th c. BC. (Rome, Villa Giulia 64224)

**266.** Detail of Attic black figure kyathos. A naked girl rides a phallos-bird. Late 6th c. BC. (Berlin F2095)

267. Attic red figure lekythos. Ajax, his shield and scabbard set aside, his sword planted point-up in the ground before him, prays before falling upon it. Early 5th c. BC. (Basel BS 1442)

268. Attic red figure cup by the Brygos Painter. Ajax, impaled on his sword (his left armpit was vulnerable, like Achilles' heel), lies on the fleeces of the flocks he has killed in his madness, thinking they were the Greeks. His body is covered by his slave/partner, Tekmessa, a motif picked up later by Sophocles in a play. Early 5th c. BC. (Malibu 86.AE.286)

Conveying emotion through expression came slower even than accurate delineation of the human body. When Exekias manages a few wrinkles for the suicidal Ajax [82] he seems far ahead of his time. Fifty years later the same occasion still catches its mood from gesture and pose alone [267], and its sequel by the pose and action of the woman tending his body [268].[95] Later there are at best grimaces of the wounded [308] or dying; never really a smile or laugh. The 'archaic smile' is a sculptural device, not shown on the vases. Only in the red figure of fourth-century Apulia do we begin to see the occasional painter reproducing, often with some success, the facial responses to joy or alarm which we know the major painters of the day were achieving. Women's faces remain masklike, on vases as in sculpure, far longer than do men's, and the innovations, for men only, in Early Classical sculpture were temporary phenomena.[96] This different treatment of women is a very important point for understanding classical art and mens' role in creating it.

Our vase scenes were not intended to carry the emotional impact of an icon or altar-piece, for all that they often concealed comparable intentions. Other Greek arts, from the classical period on, were more ambitious in these matters, and set standards for centuries later in the west. This is where total and even exaggerated realism can score.

# Chapter 7:    Greek Vases in Use

There is nothing mystical about Greek vases. Some may have had special functions of a ritual nature, and this affected both shape and decoration, but the majority were functional, designed or developed for everyday use, and unusual in antiquity only for the nature of the figure decoration chosen for them. You have to ignore a great deal of the evidence to believe otherwise. A scene with a conversation piece – 'Look, a swallow': 'It's spring already' – is not fraught with otherworldly messages; though with some misplaced ingenuity it could no doubt be made to be.

Pottery was not the only medium for the dispensing or storage of dry or wet materials in antiquity, and we do wrong to try to press into some necessary service every Greek pottery shape known to us, or to assume that what seems familiar to us was used in antiquity as it is now. Woodpulp-paper and plastic may not have been available, but many other materials were: skin, guts and horns from animals, gourds and leaves, reed or straw for basketry, woven materials, wood, metals. 'Skeuomorphism' is a term that has been invented for the translation of a vessel (*skeuos*) shape into a different material, but is applied by some only to translation into cheaper materials, and this is only part of the rich story of the interplay of materials and forms. We must both make allowance for these translations in reconstructing the kitchen and dining table furniture of a Greek house, and look to them for the inspiration of some clay shapes.

Fired clay is, to varying degrees, porous, which makes for good cooling containers, since some liquid can evaporate through the walls. This could be to a large degree countered by painting the interior with the usual black gloss, and the practice is normal for 'open' vessels, indeed it becomes a useful criterion for the archaeologist determining shapes from fragments. To be totally impervious a real glaze was required, not known for this purpose in Greece until the Hellenistic period. Clay cups could also be impregnated with spices, we are told.[1]

Shape names are a problem. In this chapter I italicize the principal occurrence of words which we know were used for certain shapes from inscriptions on them or from explicit texts, but for the most part I use the conventional terms, most of them ancient words. Some of these are now known to be wrong (and I say so) or at best were used for some if not all the types of the shape discussed. Listing what might be ancient names alongside line drawings tends to systematize a subject where all is flexible and little yet properly determined. I have tried not to be confusing, but have stuck to generic types for the discussion, grouped by function, where known or reasonably surmised.

We need for a moment to consider the quality of our evidence. The vases themselves can mislead us through their apparent similarity to modern forms. Most vases we have are from graves or sanctuaries (votives). We need more from houses to be sure about what was used there. There were some well-stocked archaic houses in Old Smyrna, with fine imported Athenian, Corinthian and various decorated East Greek wares, also some fifth-century ones. The best later source is Olynthos, in north Greece, for the fourth century, since the site was abandoned and there was plenty of pottery, including much decorated Athenian, left on its floors.[2] Elsewhere we have little more than some country farms in Attica,[3] and deposits in the Athenian Agora which seem to be discarded from houses, especially during the clear-up after Persian occupation in 479 BC. Here, for instance, the dump in a well has been taken to reflect on the drinking ware for a house – two good (though mended) Euphronios cups, five lesser red figure, and over fifteen poor black figure for common guests.[4] Throw-outs of about 425 BC from a public dining area, with many of the vessels marked with the monogram *DE[mosion]* ('public') are largely decorated cups and craters, with some kitchen ware, but more than half the pottery is black or striped only.[5] In general such deposits contain a very high proportion of plain black pottery as well as kitchen ware, but always with a good range of the figure-decorated shapes with which we have become more familiar from graves, and even shapes which we might take as 'ritual', such as *lebetes gamikoi*.

Another source is the representations on the vases themselves, where they may be shown in use, and on a few where the shape is even labelled with its current name, which is seldom the one we tend to use![6] Another is the literary evidence for crockery. This is more difficult to manage since the Greeks were notoriously inconsistent in their use of what we might designate technical terms, and there are many names for vessels in classical authors whose shape we can only guess from their context. The desperate situation with regard to finding plausible names for shapes will have become apparent to the reader of earlier chapters. In about AD 200 a highly literate bon viveur, Athenaeus, wrote an account of party-going (*Deipnosophistai*, the 'Dinner Experts') which is heavily dependent on quotation from earlier sources. It includes a whole long section on vessel names, shapes and uses, and it would be fair to say that it confuses as much as it elucidates our naming problems for the sixth to fourth centuries, however useful it may be for later periods and lexicographers.[7] Finally, there is what we learn from various sources about Greek food and drink. For instance, there is good evidence to suggest that soups and stews were common dishes and we ought perhaps to try to accommodate them in the clay table ware.

The obvious place to start is with the vessels provided for drinking. Cups are the commonest decorated shape, and Greek cups seem to have been almost as much a national marker as the Greek language. Most early Greek cups are relatively deep and with outturned lips making a ridge within, which helps stop accidental spillage in handling. Corinthian kotylai have straight, upright rims, but are relatively much deeper. Greek cups have handles and flat bases, almost always. The remark may seem otiose, but it is not, since cups used east of Cyprus generally have neither handles nor flat or separate bases, but are roughly hemispherical or flattened (*phialai*). They are balanced on the finger tips, regularly refilled by the attendant who is normally shown at hand. This eastern habit died hard, down through Sasanian and later Persian periods. (The way eighteenth-century Europeans added handles to the shapes of Chinese tea cups is analogous.) When the Greeks borrowed an eastern cup shape, as they often did, they added handles and a flat foot of varying heights. It may be that the easterner tended to drink what might have been a stronger liquid in a single short gulp, with a quick refill, while the Greek, who considerably watered his wine, was more likely to need to set the cup down between whiles.[8] For the easterner there were little hoops on which he could balance the cup if it was set down, and we see something similar in use for some Greek cups of related shape for the brief period when they are depicted on vases (archaic Corinthian), perhaps just a piece of thick folded cloth to stop them rolling about. These cups are taken to indicate metal models, orientalizing, and show the fluting expected on metal originals and no handles. But there is none in the east exactly like them, they are more like half-gourds! They appear on tables beside other and plain shapes, handled, which are clearly meant to be clay and which match clay vases that have survived [*233, 269*].[9]

Greeks also fancied high stems to their cups, especially those whose otherwise rather flat and open bodies were copied from the

**269.1–3.** Symposion tables on Corinthian craters. Before mid-6th c. BC. (Paris, Louvre E634, 629 and 623)

**270.** Eastern open bowls and Greek derivatives, with handles and feet added. 6th c. BC.

**271.** Lucanian red figure skyphos. A naked woman beside a crater, holding a ladle and sieve, balances a saucer as target for the *kottabos* game, while a youth holds his cup in readiness for the throw. About 400 BC. H. 16.5cm. (London 1902.12–14.1)

east. It is a preference that goes back to the Bronze Age. This accounts for the Little Master cups and 'eye-cups' of archaic Greece [*270*; see *71, 72, 89, 307*], and some later forms which add handles and foot to an eastern type of lipped bowl popular through the Persian empire (Athenian 'Acrocups').[10] The wider, open bowls cannot have been very easy, or tidy, to drink from, especially given the considerable diameter of many of them – the standard is about a foot, but can be more – and it only lessens with the ongoing fifth century. Lipless cups, with no separate rim, mainly derive from the east and appear first for broad cups in east Greece (the 'bird bowls' [*41*]). Many folk now use the word kylix for the finer, stemmed cups, but kylix was a generic term in antiquity.

We may well believe that to a Greek his cup was as personal a possession as a favourite pipe might be today, and the better appreciated in a foreign environment, which is why any great concentration of Greek pottery, especially cups, overseas in the archaic period probably betokens the presence of Greeks. This is particularly evident in Greek mercenary establishments, in Palestine and Egypt,[11] and may be assumed for earlier concentrations of finds in the east, as at Al Mina in Syria.

From the many drinking scenes on vases we can see that the commonest way of holding the stemmed cups was by their feet, not their handles [*234*], except often when actually drinking. The handles are more commonly shown in use for the game of *kottabos*, when the lees of the wine are flipped at a target for prizes, or often no doubt at other guests, with a toast [*271*]. The targets are bronze dishes balanced on a stand, or floating in a basin, to be sunk.[12] Cup handles are usually horizontal but there are deeper

**272.** Attic black figure mastos cup. A mask and satyrs at a vine. Late 6th c. BC. H. 9.5cm. (London B376)

cups, often with high stems, which have vertical handles, and are called *kantharoi* (from the kantharos beetle, with spread wings). There are a very few one-handled cups, or handleless, like tumblers, copying an eastern shape or possibly wood, since it can easily be rendered by turning wood on a lathe. Some archaic and classical cups have knobbed or pointed handles [310], rather like wishbones, which could be their inspiration, attached to wooden bowls.[13] Some archaic standlets may be for cups.[14] Horn-shaped cups are rare, but notice the special Sotadean products of the mid-fifth century in Athens [190, 191]. And an archaic freak is the breast-cup, mastos, with a nipple at the base [272].[15]

The decorated cups tend to become smaller with the fourth century and many lose their stems. In the fifth century a common black shape is called a bolsal (a made-up name – Bologna + Salonica), with straight upright sides, certainly copying metal as do many black shapes from now on. Their undersides are cushioned, like the turning patterns we see on metal – and, earlier, on wood.

Symposion scenes on vases have proved a rich source of information about cup shapes and handling. We cannot always judge whether the model was thought to be metal, but virtually all the shapes are met in clay. Clay (and glass) is better to drink from than metal, which can interact with the acid wine. More silver cups have probably survived than bronze, but there could not have been many symposia with a silver service except among the most wealthy. Another difference is that the metal cups in Greece are not figure-decorated. Indeed, we shall find this a major difference between clay and metal vessels, and the very few classical figure-decorated metal cups all hail from, and were probably made, outside the Greek homeland – Thrace, other Black Sea countries and Anatolia.[16] This probably deliberate austerity, avoiding the

**273.** Attic red figure psykter by
Douris (signed), from Caere.
Satyrs celebrate. One at the left
is dressed as a Hermes.
About 480 BC. H. 28.5cm.
(London E768)

hybris of oriental luxury, is only abandoned with the Hellenistic period, when it is eastern imperial behaviour that is being deliberately aped by Greek nobility and even royalty: another reason, no doubt, for the demise of the painted, figure-decorated clay vessel in Greek lands by the end of the fourth century.

A few cup shapes have special connotations, not necessarily demonstrated by common clay versions rather than metal; some are apparent in myth contexts in vase scenes. The *phiale* was best known in Greece in metal and there are very few clay copies; they seem used for ritual purposes of libation rather than at the drinking party.[17] The *kantharos* was especially favoured in Boeotia, and in art it is seen to be a favourite shape for Heracles (who was born in Boeotia, at Thebes) and for Dionysos, the god of wine. Heracles is also seen to have in the classical period a special version which is called 'Sotadean' by us, *karchesion* in antiquity [122]: a shape which played a role in the deception of his mother by his father Zeus, impersonating her husband. In this form it is hemispherical, most like some Mycenaean cups;[18] other examples are more like tumblers with small loop handles.

The next most important vessel for the symposion is the crater, available in various forms throughout our period. It was used for the mixing of wine and water, the wine being poured in either from a wineskin or a storage/carriage amphora. A special shape appears in the archaic period, a cooler (*psykter*). These may simply be double-walled amphorae, with one space to be filled with cold water. In Athens from the later sixth century on there are examples with ballooning profile to give maximum cooling surface [273]. These are placed in a normal crater, filled with snow or well water. Exceptionally they may be one-piece [274, 275] with spouts low in their walls so that the coolant could be regularly renewed.[19] The wine has to be got out of the rather narrow mouth with a metal dipper, rather like a soup ladle [276].[20]

You got the wine from the ordinary crater by dipping in a jug (*oinochoe* 'wine-pourer'). (An exception is [277] where the wine would spurt out and up from the low spout.) The poet Hesiod warns against putting the jug 'above' the crater during the drinking (*Works and Days* 744), presumably on its rim, though it is shown there on many vases; perhaps it might have fallen off, and in his day the clay craters did not have broad rims. Column craters have convenient broad handle plates which could serve this purpose [54, 77, 227, 233, 257]. There are some clay vessels which are like footless kantharoi but with only one high-swung handle; they look like dippers and so are called kyathoi [188, 266],

274. Drawings of one-piece psykters with spouts for draining the coolant. (Market; Boston 00.331)

275. One-piece Attic black figure psykter, its outer wall (as a calyx crater) missing. Late 6th c. BC. H. 30.5cm. (Malibu 82.AE.125)

276. Detail from a drinking scene on an Attic black figure oinochoe by Kleisophos. A boy ladles wine from a psykter set in a calyx crater. About 530 BC. (Athens 1045)

*250*

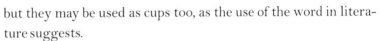

but they may be used as cups too, as the use of the word in literature suggests.

The essential crater shape is simply broad and open but can be elaborated in various ways: in the geometric period, with a high foot [14]. In later black and red figure we find it with a high neck and volute handles imitating metal ([62, 132, 156] volute craters); with handles set to support the heavy rim via a 'stirrup' or directly ([102] stirrup or column craters); and with straight splaying walls enlarging a cup type ([116, 226, 229] calyx crater). The bell crater copies a wood-and-leather bucket with lug handles [130], later with the usual loop handles [230]. The last is the commonest shape for the later fifth and fourth centuries. From depictions it seems that the craters were normally kept in a vestibule adjacent to the symposion room (*andron* – 'mens' room') or a courtyard, rather than the symposion room itself, and that they were the focus for song and dance (komos) after the serious drinking on the dining couches. Some bucket-shaped vases with horizontal handles, smaller than the average crater, are called stamnoi

(wrongly). They are seen in archaic East Greece, but especially in Athenian later black [260], and red figure. Some have Dionysiac scenes which seem to record a ritual involving wine-tasting by women [278]. Perhaps they are not true mixing vessels (which is what the word crater implies) but were for unmixed wine. They are not all decorated as seriously as the Dionysiac [279]! Stamnoi are often, craters rarely, lidded.

**277.** Attic red figure kalathoid psykter by the Brygos Painter, from Agrigentum. Alcaeus and Sappho, the early 6th-century poets of Lesbos. Early 5th c. BC. H. 25.3cm. (Munich 2416)

**278.** Attic red figure stamnos by the Dinos Painter. Detail showing women dressed as maenads dancing at a table before an image of Dionysos (basically a mask and clothes on a pole). One is dipping for wine in one of two stamnoi on the table. About 430 BC. (Naples 2419)

**279.** Attic red figure stamnos by the Siren Painter. A youth importunes two young women at their wash basin. About 470 BC. H. 36.5cm. (Once Hunt Collection)

**280.** Attic red figure chous. Children with go-carts, chous juglets and a bunch of grapes. Late 5th c. BC. H. 5.7cm. (London E536)

Jugs could hardly have been exclusively for wine, any more than cups were, and they must have been much used for any drink, even water. It is a necessary shape for any liquid, and so often provided with a pouring lip (trefoil). Some small round-bodied ones in Athens in the later fifth century regularly carry scenes of children at play [280], and larger versions generally have Dionysiac scenes. This shape may relate to the Dionysiac spring festival, Anthesteria, when there was a drinking competition, though the volume of even the larger jugs is too little to have made them competition pieces. The festival association gives them their name, chous/choes, *chous* being also a liquid measure of about three litres. The small ones might have been for children's graves – too young to participate in rites appropriate even to toddlers.[21]

The cups, craters and jugs represent a very high proportion indeed of all the decorated clay shapes, as well as many of the plain black. Closest in popularity is the water jar, with a vertical handle for pouring and two horizontal for lifting: the *hydria* or kalpis (without the offset shoulder). These are all vessels for liquids; so are vessels for oil, which will be considered later, after more reflection on table wares.

The tables that appear in those symposion scenes that depict the feast as well as the drinking that followed may tell us something. Sixth-century ones have plenty of food [233, 269]; later there is other evidence for 'second tables' for the dessert to go with the wine.[22] After the sixth century the scenes concentrate on the drinking which had become more ritualized. The symposia on Corinthian craters have already been mentioned for the depiction of what are clearly both metal and clay cups on the side tables [269]. Meat is shown in long strips hanging over the side of the table. The other regular course is of what look like small loaves, sometimes stacked in two layers. On the Corinthian tables they may appear on a thin flat board, probably a wooden charger on which they were brought to the table, or on what are more clearly plates, like the surviving clay ones, with wide slanting or upright convex rims.[23] A better plate profile is shown on the tables in some Laconian scenes of feasting.[24] The Athenian scenes show no plates, I believe, but put the loaves on a board or more often straight on the table.[25] Food could easily be served also on leaves. The plates are the only vessels other than cups and craters shown, and I shall return to the absence of anything that might have contained a soup or stew.

The plate has already engaged our attention in Chapter 6 in its role as a field for a votive picture. Its role in life was, it seems, to

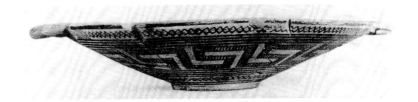

**281.1,2.** Attic geometric dish, from a grave (66) in the Kerameikos, Athens. Late 8th c. BC. Diam. 36cm. (Kerameikos 800)

carry comestibles and not to eat from, as today. The early plates have pairs of holes for suspension, but these are not found from the sixth century on, except for assured votives.[26] The archaic Corinthian, Attic and East Greek plates probably derive details of their shapes from wooden ones, of which some have been found on Samos,[27] and even copy the lathe patterning of the underside which is natural to the carpentry technique. It seems not a shape for metal until much later.

Antecedents to the plates are probably the late geometric dishes which have wider rising walls and narrow bases [281]. Attic examples regularly have recurved handles, and one thinks of little wicker platters as models, with handles made of a bent reed twisting in and out of the rim; it is certainly not a natural pottery or metal form. Flat versions might relate to Levantine platters, but most of these generally have more distinct and sometimes upright rims, of proportions that have more to do with Greek cups copying the east than anything [42, 43]. The eastern platters have neither handles nor suspension holes. But there were some Cypriot flat

**282.** Apulian red figure fish plate. The fish are a gurnard, bream, cuttlefish, scallop and small fish seen from below. 4th c. BC. W. 26.3cm. (Bochum, Ruhr-Univ. S 1191)

dishes with handles copied by Euboeans for carriage east in the eighth century, [28] and eastern shapes may lie behind Euboean versions made in the west, on Ischia. The standed dishes common in East Greek archaic pottery look like fruit or cake stands, and may well be so. [29] Fish plates are probably correctly so named. They start in Attica and are most popular in south Italy in the fourth century, their flat tops decorated with a variety of sea life, and a central hollow 'dip' [282]. [30]

Soups and stews were perhaps inferior fare for a feast and symposion, where steak was served, and no dishes for them are shown. Bowls which could have been used (*lekane* or *lekanis*, the latter word generally reserved for the lidded) [31] appear rarely in the geometric period, rather more often in the archaic; some are lidded, but I suspect that much that was fairly liquid was as readily consumed from a drinking cup of the stouter variety, and most of it probably from wooden bowls, not clay, or even from dipping into a common bowl from the kitchen. [32] Some *lekanai* hang on the wall at Corinthian symposia, [33] and the shape is well represented in archaic Attica and Boeotia [91]. The *lekanides* of later red figure are elaborate vases, attracting wedding scenes and the like, surely

*256*

**283.** Rhodian(?) flask imitating Cypriot, from Cumae. About 700 BC. (Naples)

not tableware but perhaps simply receptacles for other things. The shape generally carries flat, ribbon handles, recurved like those on the geometric dishes.

Olive oil was an important commodity in Greek life and trade. It travelled in skins or in the usual carriage amphorae, but it was dispensed in a variety of vessels, plain for ordinary culinary use, fancy for cosmetics. The industry for cosmetic uses derived from the east and Greeks learned, through import or experiment, to scent the oils with floral essences. The use of iris in Corinth is mentioned, and rose must have been popular; for the rest we guess. An Athenian alabastron is inscribed 'of iris'. For personal use a small container, *aryballos* or the taller *alabastron*, was used, and later the more substantial *lekythos* or askos; all these terms are conventional and cannot always be proved to follow ancient usage exactly or consistently but are appropriate. The essential eastern shape was spherical and made of skin – there are examples from Egypt. In the Levant the clay containers are spherical but given a tall neck and narrow foot, with a side handle for pouring and, a common feature in later periods in Greece, a broad flat rim which enables the user to spread the oil on to skin, like some modern glue dispensers [*283*].[34] The oil is thick and has to be shaken out, like hair cream.

The small Greek flasks were mainly for athletes, it seems, and were carried slung by a strap from the wrist, to be used after exercise, with the surplus then scraped off the body with a strigil, a common motif in athletic scenes on vases and in sculpture. The smell of oil in the gymnasia, said Xenophon, was sweeter than perfume on women.[35] The earliest are Corinthian of the later eighth century [*27*], although earlier small lekythos-jugs had probably served the same purpose before the trade orientalized.

**284.** Attic white ground alabastron of Egyptian shape, from Tanagra. A negro. Early 5th c. BC. H. 16.2cm. (London B674)

**285.** Apulian red figure alabastron by the Chini Painter. An Amazon, with light shield, two spears and a battle axe. Mid-4th c. BC. (Oxford 1945.55)

Through the seventh century they slim to an inverted pear shape on a pointed and impractical foot, but about the mid-century a stretched pear-shaped 'alabastron' is introduced, imitating the elastic body of a skin flask sagging full of oil, while the aryballos becomes quite spherical.[36] The real *alabastron* shape, which is cylindrical and with little lug handles, derived from the Egyptian stone alabaster vase and is later copied in Athens [*180, 284*] and East Greece,[37] along with another Egyptian aryballos shape, with broad flat base (in Athens). Some mid-seventh-century Corinthian aryballoi are exquisite, painted in extreme miniature, and with moulded or modelled lips in the form of animal or human heads [*31*]. It was common in various wares in the Archaic period to make these flasks in the form of animals or even human heads and figures [*286*].[38] Some have ring bodies,[39] and in the classical period in Athens some have acorn-shaped bases.[40] The classical alabastra are toilet vases for women and can be very elaborate, even given feet and handles [*285*]. The only metal versions of these small oil vases found so far are plain.[41]

Varieties of taller *lekythos* appear in the sixth century [*68, 69*], culminating in the cylindrical form which is dominant through the

**286.** Ionian figure vase: a heron. H. 13cm. (Cleveland 88.65)

fifth century, notably in its white ground funerary form in Athens ([*128*]). This is potentially more capacious, for use at table or in the laying out of a body, whence its common appearance in tombs – exclusively so for the white ground with funeral scenes (as used on [*128*]). But many of the big cylinder lekythoi disguise their contents by having a false inner wall for the oil, no bigger than the smallest aryballos; it is revealed in broken vases or by x-ray.[42] This deceptive packaging is familiar enough nowadays but a little surprising in antiquity. It may have been anticipated in Corinthian aryballoi.[43] In the fourth century the cylinder lekythoi of Athens are replaced by 'squat lekythoi', some of which can be large and elaborately decorated [*138, 160*], though most are small and just decorated with a head or an animal. By the Hellenistic period the oil flasks for deposition in tombs and probably most ordinary household purposes were small and plain [*168*].

With 'askos' we use the ancient name for a skin flask with a strap handle, and in clay they are small and disc-shaped, geometricizing the form out of recognition [*287*], though in South Italy especially some are made larger, and closer to the proportions and shape of the bigger skin vases. In time the disc version changes the position of spout and handle and becomes the *guttus*, used as a lamp filler [*288*].[44]

The sagging shape of the seventh/sixth-century 'alabastra' has been noted, as imitating full skin vases. This is also the origin of the shape of another oil vase, developed in Athens in the later

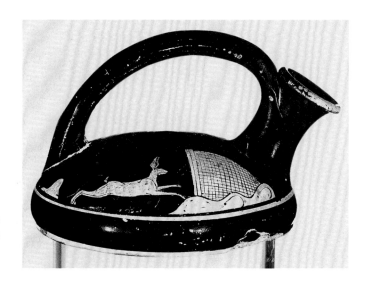

**287.** Attic red figure askos. A hare chased by a dog (on the other side of the vase) into a net. 5th c. BC. (Oxford 1979.20)

**288.** Calene black guttus, with moulded shell. 3rd/2nd c. BC. W. 10cm. (Once Castle Ashby)

sixth century, called (wrongly) a 'pelike'; this remains popular into the fourth century. It has two handles and several late archaic ones carry scenes of the retail dispensing of oil via funnel and flask [289].[45] It regains popularity in the fourth century [136]. Another sagging profile is that of the 'olpe' (really a name for an aryballos), Corinthian of the seventh/sixth century and attracting some elaborate decoration; the 'Chigi vase' is one [30]. It is generally treated as a type of *oinochoe* but is about as effective for pouring thin liquid as many modern wide-mouthed coffee pots; it is possibly, in function, the predecessor of the pelike.

From the sixth century on there appear low vases, sometimes on stands, with inturned and overhanging lips. These must be to

**289.** Attic black figure pelike. Retailing oil. At the left a youth fills a flask from a funnel for a customer. The pelikai on the ground hold the oil. The seller says 'O father Zeus, may I get rich!'. Late 6th c. BC. (Vatican 413)

prevent the accidental spillage of something precious, probably something like rose water or scented oil. They appear in scenes where women are dealing with clothes or wedding gifts (as on [*292*] right). They are commonly called *plemochoai*, but *exaleiptra* may be their real name [*290*].[46] They used, wrongly, to be called 'kothon', which is a name for a Laconian cup.

A variety of boxes were made in clay, mainly cylindrical, and generally lidded. A name for such in antiquity was *pyxis*, which reveals its commonest medium – boxwood, and many clay shapes are very clearly copying turned wooden models [*291*]. But among

**290.** Attic plemochoe. About 500 BC. H. 18.5cm. (Cape Town 13)

**291.** Attic red figure pyxis by the Thaliarchos Painter. A komast. Late 6th c. BC. (Athens 1710)

the earliest are the round wool-basket shapes of the geometric period, whose origins must lie in basketry [9 middle].

The *amphora* (Latin; Greek *amphoreus* or *amphiphoreus*) has yet to be discussed and is in some ways the most puzzling, yet taken as a 'Greek vase' archetype. Given that its only common feature is the two vertical handles at the neck (and we use the term too for horizontally-handled ones in the geometric period [4, 7, 13]), it seems to promise a multiplicity of uses, from the massive custom-made geometric grave-marker, to the Panathenaic prize vase, as well as the myriad plain storage and carriage amphorae, which, to judge from their narrow necks, were for liquids [50, 51]. The quality of these plain vases can be judged from the fact that they were recycled in Egypt and even imported empty, to serve for water storage.[47] The name means nothing more than 'carried on both sides', viz., two-handled, and we know that the actual shape could be called by other names (e.g., *kados*, which is yet more commonly a bucket). Otherwise the shape is common to all wares and in none, I think, does its decoration betray its use – no emphasis on vinous or athletic scenes, for instance, which might indicate use for wine or oil. Yet they were surely used for both, though perhaps not for export since most decorated examples have inconveniently wide mouths. In drinking scenes we see only the plain carriage amphorae in use. You can get a hand into the mouths of most examples, and there is a very wide range of dry, or at least not liquid objects (like olives, or dried figs or fish), which they might hold. They might have been exported with such contents, and many do have lids, or a groove within the lip to accommodate a plug of some sort. They could then be reused as containers for other things – rather as Chinese ginger jars are today.

**292.** Fragment of an Attic loutrophoros-amphora. Eros hovers between bride and groom, holding a loutrophoros-hydria for her, loutrophoros-amphora for him. The bride is taken by the wrist in the ritual gesture. Presents include a box (left) and a plemochoe (right). Late 5th c. BC. H. 13.5cm. (Oxford 1966.888)

Vases for ritual purposes identify themselves by their decoration, already considered, and their shapes. The *loutrophoros* may be properly so named, at least in the classical period when it can be identified as a funeral vase and sometimes grave-marker, in clay or stone, though the word is better applied to its carrier. It starts as an ordinary amphora or hydria, and the differentiation by sex, male or female respectively, is maintained from the geometric period to the fourth century. The Eros on [*292*] clutches one of each type for the bride and groom at either side. At an early date it begins to become tall, thin and impractical, intended, if anything, for carrying water (which is what the name implies) for the bridal bath.[48] *Lebes gamikos*, for warming the bridal bath water, is applied to a cauldron of orientalizing type, usually on a stand [*293*]. In later red figure, with or without a foot, it is most commonly decorated with marriage scenes, as [*135*]. The *lebes* or *dinos* is the same basic shape, requiring a built-on stand or a separate tripod, and was used to keep liquids warm, or as a crater at feasts. The bail-vase, with a bucket-handle, is too rare a shape to declare positively funerary, for all that one example gives a very full account of preparation for the grave.[49]

Some everyday shapes acquire also special functions. A *dinos* or *hydria* is often found to serve as a recipient for the ashes of the dead. The *hydria* may also be a prize vase, but these special functions are commonly, though not always, reserved for metal specimens. A Corinthian aryballos, calling itself an 'olpe', was made as a

293. Attic black figure lebes gamikos. A wedding procession by chariot. A divine connotation (so for Peleus and Thetis? – see [61,62]) is given by the presence of a kitharist (as Apollo), a wreathed man (as Dionysos). On the foot Peleus wrestles with Thetis, giving credence to the identity of the marriage above. About 500 BC. H. 39cm. (London B298)

294. Corinthian aryballos. A piper (Polyterpos – 'pleases all') and dancers. The inscription names the vase an 'olpe' – 'Pyrvias leading the dance; to him an olpa'. Early 6th c. BC. H. 5.3cm. (Corinth C-54–1)

295. Three miniature Corinthian kotylai, out of a total of over 170 found dedicated to Demeter and Kore at Taucheira (N. Africa). Early 6th c. BC. H. 3cm. (Tocra)

prize for the dance-leader [294].[50] The Panathenaic amphora as prize vase is a special case, designed to contain oil from Athena's sacred trees, and has been described in Chapter 1. The shape is a version of the carriage vase [50]. Painter attribution enables us to see that batches were commissioned from potter/painters, a case of state patronage.

Size matters. Most wares include series of miniature vessels, sometimes of ritual shapes, often just plates and cups, which served as dedications [295] and sometimes as grave gifts, in place of larger specimens or metal vessels. There were also the outsize – cups so large that they could never be lifted if full or drunk from; some are over 70cm across. These are for display, often as dedications or special gifts, and one cannot escape the thought that many were treated as works of art.

Most other, minor shapes from the potteries are copies of various vessels and objects in other materials – little bags for knucklebone toys, eggs (funerary), sieves, little dishes like salt cellars (from the fourth century on), 'dips' (*oxybapha*), lamps, even dice.[51] In Athens are found 'official' clay measures for liquids or grain, even water clocks (*klepsydrai*) to time public speeches, marked *demosion*, 'public', or the abbreviation *DE*.[52] And there are

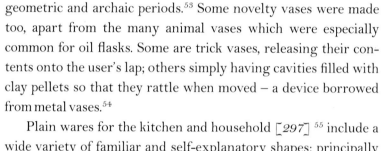

296. Attic geometric box with model granaries, from the tomb of a rich woman in Athens. About 800 BC. W. 44.5cm. (Agora P27646)

297. Kitchen pots. Casseroles and braziers. 5th c. BC. (Agora P21948/21958, 14655/16521)

clay models of granaries [296], carts, houses and shrines in the geometric and archaic periods.[53] Some novelty vases were made too, apart from the many animal vases which were especially common for oil flasks. Some are trick vases, releasing their contents onto the user's lap; others simply having cavities filled with clay pellets so that they rattle when moved – a device borrowed from metal vases.[54]

Plain wares for the kitchen and household [297] [55] include a wide variety of familiar and self-explanatory shapes: principally broad-bodied jugs and casseroles, some frying pans, water basins (*lekanai*), even babies' potties and feeders, and knee-covers for carding wool, which may also be figure-decorated (*epinetra*) [298],[56] as may sprinklers [299] or siphons.[57] Many of the oven wares are handmade, not from the potter's wheel, since the clay is then more heat-resistant without the particles being all aligned one way. Aegina had a reputation for the production of kitchen ware, its only important contribution to this story, apart from the assumed activity of its merchants. The massive barrel-shaped *pithoi* are for storage, not necessarily or indeed normally for liquids since they are difficult to manage and seem to have no drainage spouts, although useful where there was a big industry like that in the Minoan palaces. They are just as useful for holding folded clothes, and, since wood was expensive for chests and boxes and there were no cupboards, they could serve a far greater range of purposes than we may be able to divine. Only in the archaic period did they attract decoration [45, 46]. Pandora's box was really a *pithos*, and perhaps one of those filled with Good and Evil that, Homer tells us, Zeus kept at his doorstep. But the use of the word simply implies storage, not size.

*266*

**298.** Attic red figure epinetron (knee-cover for carding wool) by the Eretria Painter, from Eretria. Preparations for an heroic wedding. From the left, Eros with boxes attends Aphrodite holding a necklace, seated Harmonia (bride of Kadmos) is attended by Peitho (Persuasion) and Kore (Maiden), seated Himeros (Desire) hands a perfume vase to Hebe (Youthfulness). At the front of the piece a scene of Peleus winning Thetis. Late 5th c. BC. L. 29cm. (Athens 1629)

**299.1,2.** Attic red figure sprinkler, from Athens. H. 14cm. (Kerameikos)

Apart from most of the kitchen ware and the storage/carriage vases, virtually all the shapes mentioned in this chapter were available in other media, and some, as we have seen, derive from other media. Most shapes and details come most readily to the potter's hand since they can be contrived plastically, while wood and metal depend on what can be carved, turned on a lathe (most like the finish possible with pottery), hammered or cast. A roll of clay from which to fashion a handle is more readily managed than a cylinder of metal, and metal handles tend to be cast or hammered flat, but the rivets which fasten these handles may sometimes be imitated in clay. Wooden vessels have lugs as handles, copied for early bell craters ([130] and on [277]). The metal vessels were certainly more expensive than the clay, indeed out of all comparison when gold or silver was involved.[58] But a high proportion of the clay vases used were also figure-decorated on their bodies, with scenes which were more than arbitrary: the principal message of a silver vase was its weight (= cost), so the silver vases sometimes record their weights in inscription, almost never their makers. I have noted more than once that metal parallels to clay shapes, even when they may be prototypes, are generally not decorated all over, as are the clay vases, but only with cast handles or the like, or for the big archaic craters with relief figures on the necks only, not the bodies. With the Hellenistic period this changes and the new overall figure-decorated metal vases are heralded by the great bronze Derveni crater.[59] In this respect the potters and painters were exercising a craft which had more to offer than utility, even if they seldom competed in terms of extravagance, and no other craft served such a wide range of activities at all levels of society.

# Chapter 8:    Pottery and other Arts

There was an essential unity in style between the arts in Greece in every period, a fact that has greatly helped art historians to chart their development. This is a matter that has to be demonstrated in many different media, but we should also acknowledge that there are minor local variations, and that a Corinthian or Ionian or Athenian style can, with care, be identified and defined. This is perhaps easier with pottery than with most other arts, since the appearance of the vases and their decoration must have mirrored much else in what I would call the visual experience of citizens, to the point at which one can speculate about the degree to which differences of visual environment in Greece can be detected and help contribute to our understanding of what it meant to be a citizen of one town rather than another.[1] The unity depended very much on the Greeks' rather odd indifference to the challenge of material, so that, after earliest days, they were minimally affected by whether they worked on or in clay, metal, stone or wood for figurative or decorative subjects. That clay was probably the cheapest of the materials, though requiring some skill to process into pottery, should not be taken to indicate that potting was always regarded as an inferior craft, despite the smoky and muddy environment in which it was made. The extraordinary qualities of clay, which can present itself as liquid or hard as rock, can be handled with full plasticity but also moulded or carved, and provides an essential tool in the preliminary stages of other crafts such as metalwork and sculpture, gives it a special place in the hierarchy of artists' materials. It is no accident that many different cultures have seen clay as the primal element: God formed man from the dust of the ground, Prometheus fashioned mankind from clay at Zeus' command, and there are comparable stories from China to Mesopotamia to Central America.

The stylistic unity of Greek arts did not altogether extend to the iconography of figure decoration, however, and each craft developed its own traditions, though never out of step with others and often borrowing whole motifs. This is a further demonstration of the independent role of the artists themselves, continuing traditions in the separate crafts, often within a family, no doubt. There were always regional differences, which were suppressed only when one centre began to dominate a craft, as Athens did with pottery decoration. This short chapter considers Greek pottery as one art among many, its similarities, differences, loans and borrowings, even its place as an 'art' in the modern sense.

The question of borrowed shapes has been considered already, the debt of many pottery forms to vessels in other media, and the continuing influences. It was not all one way, however, and forms natural to the potter were as readily copied by workers in less plastic materials, despite difficulties of execution, just as the forms in more prestigious media were themselves sometimes copied in clay. In many ways the closest of the other media was wood, since for vessel shapes and details both wood and clay were much affected by the use of a lathe or potter's wheel. All forms of moulding and casting are essentially modelling techniques, for clay, whatever the medium of the end product; even major sculpture in marble as well as bronze started from a clay model, at least after the archaic period. For smaller works wax was used.

It is natural to study development in style through treatment of the human figure. The geometric figures of the Dipylon Painter evolve naturally from the stick silhouette of earlier geometric art. Contemporary figures in the round, usually bronze, can often be more plastically rendered, betraying their origin in clay or wax, but some are nevertheless conceived in planes, of proportions much like those on the vases and with the same stylization of forms. It is even possible that in this instance it was the vase painter who showed the way.[2] The essential parts of the figure are emphasized – the broad shoulders, strong thighs – with helmets reduced to a crest, breasts to blips.

The orientalizing period homogenized forms in all media according to the observed foreign models. Many of the new motifs, floral and animal, may first have been adopted and executed in beaten or engraved metal,[3] and we should not assume that the vase painter led the way in devising narrative scenes. There is still an overall similarity of forms, however, the large head, short waist and long legs being characteristic of figures in both two and three dimensions even to the beginnings of monumental statuary in marble at the end of the seventh century. Through the sixth century the statues acquire more realism of detail and proportion without quite copying life directly. En route proportions are thought to have been affected in sculpture by observation of a canon of proportions derived from Egypt; if so, much the same canon was copied in painting, but the Egyptian element may have been exaggerated by scholars. It is in the vase painters' work, in red figure, that we see first a closer observation of live forms and posture which proves that there is a move towards fully representational art. It is not necessary to believe that the painter was the leader here, but it was a development certainly easier and cheaper to express and experiment with in two dimensions than in three, and draughtsmanship was surely a major element in the artists' gradual command of realism, as the archaic period gave way to the classical. Pre-classical sculpture and relief in stone must have started as drawings on the block sides. An interesting comparison can be drawn between the distinctive profiles of heads, in clay, stone, drawing or on coins, made in regions of archaic Ionia, and the profiles of heads painted on early red figure vases in Athens by artists who may well have immigrated from Ionia, such as the Andokides Painter.[4]

It is only with the later seventh and the sixth centuries that we can begin to consider whether the vase painter was seriously influenced by the subjects and compositions of other Greek arts. The relationship to minor metalwork, especially small relief bronzes as on shieldbands, is easy to observe and these are relatively plentiful, but it is here that we already begin to find different craft traditions in iconography; the comparisons with most shieldband reliefs should be with Corinthian vases, but there are many divergencies both from the Corinthian vases and from the better recorded Athenian practice.[5] East Greek bronze reliefs, which are few, seem to have more in common with experimental narrative in mainland Greek vase painting. With major sculpture there is nothing to compare closely; with architectural sculpture there is little enough since its messages of myth were devised for a different purpose. Only the rather uncharacteristic Heracles scenes on Athenian buildings seem to share the vase painter's world of images and narrative, as we have seen in Chapter 6, but this is a phenomenon which seems peculiar to archaic Athens, since classical Athens does not treat her hero Theseus in quite the same way on public buildings of the fifth century.

In the fifth century it is the ethnic and other characterizations by the painters that seem to presage that brief period of sculptural interest in depiction of age and emotion that is typified in the Olympia sculptures; but confined to depictions of the male only. These expressions of emotion were discussed in Chapter 6. Broadly, the early classical styles of the period are mirrored in the painting of the Niobid Painter and his followers, and the idealized realism of the Parthenon period is no less well documented on vases.

**300.** Drawing from Attic red figure calyx crater by the Niobid Painter, from Orvieto. Various interpretations have been offered. A war-weary (brow furrowed, sunken cheeks, teeth gritted) Heracles at the centre stood, in the painter's penultimate sketch, on a base. Athena stands behind him and various heroes attend, possibly a Theseus below. In the wings two figures wearing piloi – the Spartan Dioskouroi? – late for the battle of Marathon, which may be the occasion for this assembly as in Polygnotus' painting in Athens. Other side [125]. About 460 BC. (Paris, Louvre G431)

With such an outburst of activity we might expect the painter to be led by the subjects and styles of major works in a more closely related medium, indeed one which he might even have practised himself. The new style of narrative painting for walls or panels, apparently introduced to central Greece by Polygnotus of Thasos, certainly led to the adoption by painters of some new up/down compositions [125, 300], just as the colourful white ground scenes were probably encouraged by the appearance of wall paintings. The earliest extant example of the new composition on a vase may well be the closest we get to their actual appearance [300].[6] We know the wall paintings, their subjects and compositions, only from texts, but this suggests that their treatment of myth was very different in detail to that generally accepted and often repeated on vases. It was the compositions that were influential, not the details. Only towards the end of the century do some groups of vases with near-identical mass compositions of gigantomachy lead one to suspect, no more, that a painter was positively trying to copy a whole composition in some detail [301].[7] These are the exceptions that point the rule: we can only be sure that vase painters copy each other, not other arts, at least in iconography.

Several vase scenes appear to copy groups from the metopes and parts of the frieze on the Parthenon, and this has led scholars to believe that they are deliberate copies. But all are in their way generic groups that could have appeared at the time in various media, and not only on what were the less visible parts of the Parthenon (the frieze), where the figures and poses are the common stock of the classical Athenian world. It is a question of a

301. Drawing from an Attic red figure amphora by the Suessula Painter. Gigantomachy. Zeus with thunderbolt, Nike in the chariot and Heracles with bow at the centre; to their left, Athena, Apollo and Artemis; to their right, Poseidon, Hermes and a goddess. The giants wield torches and stones and wear animal skins. About 425 BC. (Paris, Louvre S1677)

shared idiom and shared principles of composition. It is of course possible that the frieze was studied, even that parts of its design depended on the contribution of draughtsmen in another medium, but all the evidence is against close copying of major art by vase painters. Thus, it is significant that the really diagnostic groups on the Parthenon, the parts of the frieze away from the cavalcade and sacrificial procession, are never copied. We should be wary therefore of reading too much into a very few parallels that look more than chance, beside the hundreds that are only generically similar. Nor are the subjects of the pediments copied in the form in which the sculptor presented them – the birth of Athena almost never, and the contest between her and Poseidon only later and in much altered form [139, 140]. Indeed, it is almost as though they were avoided. The metopes carry standard subjects but several groups are innovative in ways never picked up by the vase painters. We are easily deluded into thinking that all we have is all there was, and can promote apparent similarities to the status of model and copy. A good test is the shield of the Athena Parthenos statue in the Parthenon, the composition of which is well known from many ancient copies in relief. Although the subject, the Amazonomachy of Theseus, was well represented on vases, not one of them shows any of the novel and diagnostic groups from the shield, which one would have judged an obvious source of inspiration if the vase painter was indeed concerned to copy major sculptural or relief works in other media.[8] Indeed, many a major classical composition in sculpture has proved to be simply a sublime copy of a theme current earlier in other media, often even to minor details. The

302. Attic red figure stamnos. The Tyrannicides. Harmodios and Aristogeiton murder Hipparchos (an event of 514 BC), in poses inspired by the statue group set up in Athens soon after 479 BC (as *GSCP* fig. 3), where the figures stand side by side and no victim was shown. The painter makes the narrative explicit. Before mid-5th c. BC. H. 34.2cm. (Würzburg L515)

303. Detail from an Attic red figure vase by the Meidias Painter, from Ruvo. Late 5th c. BC. (Karlsruhe 259)

304. 'Aphrodite' from the east pediment of the Parthenon. 430s BC. (Oxford, Cast Gallery)

'inventor' is anonymous, and may be celebrated only in the works of more prominent artists. Where a famous statuary group is the inspiration for a vase painting, as apparently with the Tyrannicides [*302*], the composition is changed, keeping only the (stock) poses, and an extra figure, of the victim, is added to make a narrative where in bronze there were only the two assassins. Gradual and measured change was the keynote of Greek art in this period rather than dramatic innovation,[9] though it was rapid by ancient standards.

305. Detail from [136].

Towards the end of the fifth century, the painter skilfully manages to render in line the new sculptural treatment of dress with its sweep and folds and clinging drapery that define the figure beneath [303]. This seems deliberate, and is as far as a painter on clay can go in following new trends in major painting on wall or panel. In this case it seems a style well mirrored in sculpture, as we see it in the various female figures of the Parthenon pediments, especially the 'Aphrodite' [304]: compare [134]. We investigated in Chapter 1 the problems any such attempt to copy major art involved, and the inability of the pot-painter to compete. But in the fourth century, through sheer quality of line drawing he could do much to render the deep modelling of figures, facial expression, and even the sensuality of the female figure [305], as well as that of the male with which he had long been at ease.

This belated success with the female figure, which had nevertheless generally been better managed in drawing than sculpture, should require a brief digression on the male. 'Heroic nudity', dependent on classical models, is real enough for some later periods of antiquity and for the post-antique to the present day. In Greece male nudity, or at least the casual baring of parts of the body that most of us today keep concealed, was commonplace, and not merely confined to the athletics field. It is everywhere on vases, from the geometric on. It was not just an artistic convention, or foreigners would not have commented on it, with disapproval. It must have contributed to the artists' readiness to take realistic images of the naked male as a serious subject to be mastered. It may have predisposed them to use it more often than live practice might have warranted, and from the classical period on the balance tends rather in favour of the nude in scenes of myth, but no more than that.[10]

On balance the differences from the other arts are more expressive of the special role of pottery decoration as a reflection of the visual expectations and understanding of the ordinary Athenian citizen, than the similarities to other arts. These commanded a different audience because of their expense, or the same audience but in a quite different context, at a temple or in a graveyard.

Only with the Hellenistic period does the model of relief metal vases dominate the appearance of the decorated clay vases, and some metal vases become more generous with their surfaces in accommodation of figure decoration in relief. At the same time there disappears any serious interest in iconographic content, except, for a while, on the Homeric cups and for vignettes on other relief bowls. Clay vases have become just another part of the furniture, as uninformative for us, as no doubt for an ancient buyer, as a new kettle.

In retrospect, one must judge that in development of style the potters and painters were, so far as comparisons can be made, well in step with other artists. The major changes, from geometric to orientalizing, and from the formal to the idealized realistic (virtually black to red figure), echo other media, without it being possible to say that they were positively motivated by them, or were any more disturbed than they were by external factors (war, politics) except to the extent that patronage and trade might be limited. If we had no literary evidence it would probably have been impossible to detect from the archaeological record of objects (not sites) any trace of an outbreak of democracy or a Persian invasion or the devastating (for Athens) Peloponnesian War. The Persian empire was well supplied with Athenian vases, and Athenian

exports continued, somehow, through the war, perhaps with few if any Athenian carriers.

The broader issue of pottery in terms of Greek aesthetics is one that has been touched on in passing throughout this book, not that it is a craft from which one might expect too much enlightenment on the topic, although it commands an 'aesthetic' of its own. There are some aspects, however, worth dwelling on briefly: the human mode in pottery in terms of appearance rather than use; the role of proportion, even mathematics; composition and space; the relationship to the idealized realism achieved in other classical arts; and the question of originality.

The 'humanity' of Greek culture is something of a truism. At a fairly mundane level, they were not the only ancient (or modern) people who could see pots as persons, but they made more of it than most. Our own usage, speaking of neck, shoulder, belly, foot, for a vase, was theirs also, though they called handles ears. Occasionally the parallel is made manifest when eyes are painted on a vase neck (or under arched handle-brows). The East Greek artist of [306] has made a whole vase like a head, even hinting at ears, frown and nose, only the eyes being 'real', and using the ordinary decorative motifs of corner palmettes, tongues and leaves.[11] Pairs of eyes as decoration sometimes simply animate an object (as on ships' prows or, once, on a clay penis-vase),[12] but can also abet the transformation of a whole cup into something like a mask, so that when it is held to the mouth the eyes, ear-handles and hollow mouth-foot cover the face [307]. A whole head, moulded or modelled, may be set at the mouth of a vase, from the animal and human heads on early aryballoi, to the animal heads replacing the necks of larger vases. A spout can become a penis, genitals a vase foot, hands serve as handle attachments.[13] Whole flasks in the shape of men or animals are to be found in most periods, especially small ones, for perfumed oil [286], and look at the cup [96].[14] The whole phenomenon is a combination of visual wit and a matter of vitalizing the inanimate.

The 'architecture' of a Greek vase is a term often applied in descriptions. The proportions may seem almost mechanical and often to lack the natural flow of, for example, oriental ceramics. This effect is abetted by the practice of finishing the vases on the wheel, 'turning' as with wood on a lathe, creating sharp mouldings at rim and foot which seem as precisely articulated as the members of an architectural order. Scholars have in the past attempted to define the proportions and outlines of the finer vases in mathematical terms, and there has been a tendency to think that here, as also

**306.** East Greek handled bowl. About 600 BC. W. 10.8cm. (Bonn inv. 3004)

**307.** Drinking from an Attic red figure 'eye cup', the vase appearing as a mask.

in the design of metal vases, a geometric formula was being applied. At best there can be the application of a practical form of geometry, as where a volute, for a bronze vase as in architecture, is designed by the unrolling of a cord from a cylinder, or from a series of compass arcs. Any regular parabolas, such as form the outline of amphorae and other shapes, can be defined mathematically, which does not mean that they were created mathematically. The forms are truly 'natural', the eye approves and the potter's hands instinctively comply. There was no call for templates. In architecture, as for the Parthenon, a common proportion was applied to most aspects of the design, from ground plan to the detailing of ornament. In pottery the most we can observe is the popularity of certain proportions for certain shapes in certain periods, much being determined by function, and the changes are rung between stout and slender. When the fourth-century potter starts to let lips and feet flare more than hitherto, to turn over handles and apparently encourage a certain baroque sinuosity in design and detail,[15] it is an effect that we can follow in other arts only in ornament, rather than in composition or posture of statuary, for example. In sculpture at any rate the ideal classical proportions were related to life, which can only roughly be mathematicized in the Egyptian manner, into hands (only for horses now), feet, cubits (forearms), palms, fingers, and can still admit notable changes in the basic relationship of, say, head to height. And in architecture the forms of capitals and bases are never copied for vases. Pottery design fits with the rest of Greek art in any period and place without being bound to all the vagaries of fashion and details of execution in the other arts.

The principles and practice of composition were remarked in Chapter 1, especially the ability to fit a subject to a sometimes awkward field. This is a skill which seems to have been instinctive and has eluded many a forger. In the archaic period it was mainly a matter of managing to let the 'negative space' of a composition remain in perfect balance with the 'positive space' of the figures and with the frame imposed by the vase shape.[16] In the fifth century, when for some subjects circumambient space is a serious factor, notably for the 'spotlit' single figures, it is the contour of the vase that provides the frame in which the figure has to be set [119].

From around the mid-fifth century on, until the Hellenistic period, the sculptor was dedicated to creating a realism that was an idealized counterfeit of life; whence anguish among philosophers. It was an exceptional aim in the history of art, and it has bred

**308.** Attic red figure cup by the Sosias Painter, from Vulci. Name vase. Patroklos grits his teeth as Achilles binds his wound. About 500 BC. (Berlin 2278)

various successors in the west. The sculptor could expect almost complete success, at life size and in three dimensions, and smaller works, on their own or applied to furniture or even vases, could be judged in the same spirit. From the end of the fifth century, in two dimensions, panel painters were achieving much the same, with *trompe l'oeil* compositions, at least according to descriptions that have survived since the paintings have not. Where, in all this drive to realism, stood the vase painter? We have seen how in early days of red figure his brush techniques might be useful experimentally in creating realistic figures in terms of both anatomical detail and posture. Beyond that he could hardly go, except in terms of isolated figures, some of the very best of the early fifth century, where there are single figure studies which can vie for realism with those of any period. But for interacting figures the uncompromising black background denied any achievement of a realistic setting, and the white ground of wall painting, seen occasionally for multi-figure scenes on vases, was hardly better. On these the ground lines are perfunctory, and everywhere landscape or architectural indications are virtually ignored, or are at best simply symbolic of a setting: a single column for palace or temple, or a tree. The figures and scenes present surrogates of life and action, not veracity; they are not expected to do more, and in some ways the restriction abets their efficacy as bearers of messages or stories. Wholly realistic art is not by any means the best mode for narrative art, unless it moves and speaks. This is also why the roundness of a figure is only tentatively and rarely indicated by shading, and perspective is applied piecemeal to objects in a scene, if at all, not with the single vanishing point which Renaissance art and the camera have led us to expect. In this respect alone the vase is more like life, since we create new vanishing points as we turn our heads to scan a scene.[17]

En route to realism we have on the vases some fascinating instances of experiment. One is the way the eye is gradually rendered in a true profile view and not staring frontally from a profile head, as it had done in archaic art (compare [117] and [126]), and in most early non-Greek arts. We can even detect a premature attempt at this by an innovative painter [308] in the grand interior of a cup whose no less ambitious exterior stays with the old scheme for eyes.[18] It was perhaps a successful twisting three-quarter back view that Euthymides boasted of on [115]. Profile shoulders become realistic in the late archaic period, not spread frontally in the eastern and Egyptian manner, and the triangular upper bodies are given up. It takes a surprisingly long time to manage frontal breasts. Real foreshortening of limbs comes slowly, and for long the full extent of limbs and feet is indicated even for quite loosely composed postures. Real three-quarter views take some time to move away from a simple and rather incongruous juxtaposition of pure profile and elevation. Shields are a good test of this, sometimes simply side+front, but becoming pairs of arcs and eventually quite realistically foreshortened. But almost all these changes are accomplished within a generation around the start of the fifth century BC, as the artist looked about him and led the viewer remorselessly into acceptance of the real world in art.

Originality might be thought to have been at something of a premium in such a busy industry. Copying from the works of others was normal, and stock scenes are repeated often within a workshop or in the work of a single painter. But, as with the 'copying' from sculpture, it seems not to have been mechanical, and variants in figures and poses were regularly admitted except for the merest daubs (mainly latest black figure). There seems to have been no real effort in the better workshops to make true replicas. Where we do find two careful versions of the same scene by one painter minor variations are apparent, even though there may have been an attempt to make a replica, to create part of a 'set'. These are rare, and the same is seen when identical scenes are found on either side of a vase – the correspondence is close but not exact.[19] There were certainly no draft designs or pattern books to be copied, only other vases. Nostalgia plays a minimal role also. A Corinthian made a stirrup vase which seems to hark back to the Bronze Age shape, but is no copy.[20] In second-century Troy there are what seem to be clay copies of fifth/fourth-century volute craters, an altogether odd phenomenon possibly inspired by a chance find or an observed votive specimen.[21] In painting only the 'mannerists' of the fifth century cling to old stylistic forms, but this is a matter of continuation not revival. True archaizing is for other arts.

# Chapter 9:    Tricks of the Trade

Greek vases are not just a simple product of throwing, painting and firing. There remain several problems about their manufacture, and close attention to detail has revealed a number of interesting ways in which potter and painter tried to make their task the easier. This chapter is devoted to a number of these; they help us to appreciate better what we are looking at, and some of them show the vase painter as inventor and innovator in ways not readily paralleled in the pottery of other cultures. It records some short-cuts to success, and some accidents.

*On the Wheel*
Many of the larger vases, and even some smaller ones, were not thrown in one piece, but, say, neck and foot were made separately in batches, and then the parts were married up and fastened together with wet clay before being turned, decorated and fired.[1] The strongly articulated shapes obviously required this, but a measure of mass production was involved, and although a skilled potter can work to a very close programme of shape and size by feel, without measurement of height or weight, there are examples where the match was less than perfect, notably with lids, where of course there may have been replacements to find, or lids were switched in antiquity.

For the painting of interiors or for horizontal stripes the pot was naturally replaced on the wheel and slowly turned against the brush. Otherwise, dipping the pot in the paint was resorted to for plainer black wares, and could help with some interiors, swilling the paint around.

*The Colours*
The fine black gloss, especially on the Attic vases, has long and understandably been miscalled 'glaze'; it can be exceptionally brilliant but, being black, not very reflective. Producing it was no simple matter, but in the archaic and classical periods, and long before, it depended not on any pigment, but the careful preparation of a thin slip of the same clay as the body of the vase, sometimes with additives – potassia or iron oxide.[2] This fires red in an oxidizing (clean) atmosphere, but before the end of the firing a

reducing (smoky) atmosphere is introduced which turns the slip black, but not the body of the pot, and the firing is stopped before that too starts to turn red. It all calls for precision timing, and we can detect some examples where the potter was slow to 'switch off' and the whole pot has reverted to red, some parts glossy, some not, but experience generally told.

Corinthian red-ground vases of the earlier sixth century [*54, 55*] used a pigment to create an orange ground. But the better Athenian vases too, in latest black and early red figure, did not rely only on a slip of the pale red Attic clay for the background colour. It was enhanced with a pigment (probably a red oxide – *miltos*) which gave it a far deeper red, that looks unfamiliar since it has generally not survived well except in protected areas, under feet or handles. After its application the surface might be burnished with a cloth or something harder to give a smooth surface for the painting. The slip lay beneath the painting, yet its superficiality suggests that some may even have been added after firing, wiped over the vase surface but clinging only to the background and surviving only in stray corners. On some fine vases which carried this slip it has not survived completely, leaving a rather unpleasant mottled effect [*81*], like the patchy patina on many marbles.[3] The effect was far darker than present appearances might suggest, not at all like the bright colour of clean bronze or gold.

For a while in the late archaic period in Athens there was some deliberate firing of parts of a vase so that the gloss was a rich red – 'coral red' – even on the same vessel with the black gloss. Its earliest survival is in the work of Exekias on the background of the interior of his famous Dionysos cup [*309*], making it like reverse red figure, with the figures still black; it is not itself a ground, but a filled-in background like the black on red figure vases.[4] The technique called for some subtle preparation of the slips so that both the red and the black gloss could appear on the same vase. On a few vases an area of glossy white could also be introduced, other than as a ground for the figures [*310*]. From the Hellenistic period on the practice of firing for red became normal, culminating in Roman red wares, Samian, Arretine and the like, and may then have been deemed a rough imitation of metalware, like the decoration, but far ruddier than most ancient gold. Much Hellenistic is a rather unpleasant brown; the finest black is met less often and has a harder, metallic look.

A white ground was prepared from primary clay, like kaolin, not the secondary clays which are red, brown or buff. It too achieves a fine glossy finish on the vases of Athens of the later

**309.** Attic black figure cup by Exekias, from Vulci. Dionysos sails his ship, a vine at the mast, the dolphins around probably referring to his encounter with pirates when he turned them into dolphins. Ordinary black figure but the background has been painted coral red. About 525 BC. W. 30.5cm. (Munich 2044). *See Frontispiece*

sixth and early fifth centuries, but on earlier archaic vases it may be chalky in texture, and easily comes off. There are problems too caused by the different coefficient of shrinkage in clays of different composition, and on archaic Chian vases, for example, the thick white slip often flakes off. On Athens' white ground lekythoi the white was applied before firing, as was the black and brown painting over it, but in the main series which is exclusively for funerary use it is clear that, apart from the black and brown lines which are matte, the other colours (red, green, blue) were applied after firing, and are therefore even more fugitive.[5]

Gilding, with the thinnest leaf or paint, is practised occasionally in Athens in the late archaic period, which is seen to be one of considerable experiment in such matters, not always followed up; also in the fourth century, and on the plain black Hellenistic vases. Gold melts at a higher temperature than clay fires.

Real polychromy has not been much of a feature of this story except for the stray examples: orientalizing Knossos, some Protocorinthian, combinations of incision and added colour on an all-black ground: Rhodian Vroulia cups of about 600 BC, some later archaic Chian, Boeotian, and Attic.[6] In the fifth century there are the white ground vases with coloured figures, then more in red figure with the approach of the Hellenistic, and then generally

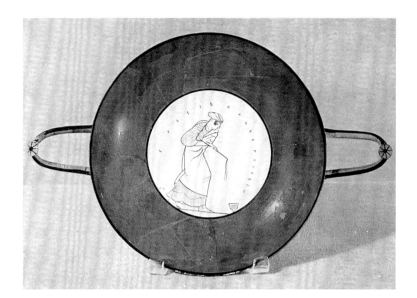

310. Attic 'merrythought' stemless cup with white ground tondo surrounded by coral red from the Sotades workshop, from Athens. A woman spinning a top. Mid-5th c. BC. Diam. 14cm. (Brussels A891)

following the lead of clay figures for vases on which moulded figure elements are prominent also [166]. But in black figure some very colourful effects could be achieved with the red and white additions, especially on Corinthian craters with their paler red ground. The rather monochrome or black-and-white appearance of most Greek vases and almost all Greek sculpture has unfortunately rather abetted the false assumption that Greek art has little to offer the colour-conscious. It does, however, often require a considerable act of imagination to replace it on the monuments we view, and even the vases may deceive in their present condition.

*Brush and Compass*

The invention of a multiple brush, which might be used on something like a fixed compass, or freehand, sometimes both in the same stroke [283], determined much of the characteristic decoration of Protogeometric vases [4–6, 26]. Freehand use was more of a ruse to duplicate simple patterns with minimum effort, and some use of it persisted even into the fifth century, for the linear 'rays' at the base of skyphoi.[7] A fixed compass was later used for shield outlines, etc.

The black 'paint' was applied with a brush. In a diluted mixture it is used in red figure to make a paler, honey-coloured line, much used for minor anatomical details and folds in dress, making a good contrast with the darker black. But by this time there was a special black line being used, the so-called relief line, which stands proud of the surface of the vase, catching the light [247.1], and can be far narrower than anything done with the

*285*

usual mix of paint, which tends to spread with pale edges. The relief line began in black figure, for some trivial detail, spear shafts and decoration-dividers, but in red figure it often defined the contour of the figures, as an incised line did sometimes in black figure, and could be used for inner painted detail of anatomy and dress, in contrast with the dilute line. How it was drawn has created problems for some. One theory, that it was applied by some sort of syringe, like icing a cake, can be dismissed; it would be impossible to manage a regular line every single time.[8] Another suggestion has been that the paint was not drawn on with a brush but laid on with a hair, dipped in the thick paint. This has won some support, but does not readily explain the way there is often a groove seen running the length of the line, which is explicable if we think of a brush tip dividing the paint it has deposited as it moves, but not from a hair which when lifted should leave no more than a ridge.[9] There is just one practice for which I can see the value of the hair. If it is made in a loop it can easily make the arcs connecting florals in subsidiary friezes [311], and seems the sort of practical labour-saving device that might appeal to any painter in a hurry with the most boring part of the decoration. This is a very different matter, however, from use of a hair freehand for the many very long or extremely short and curving lines which we see executed in relief all over the better late archaic red figure. For this it is easier to posit a careful mix of paint which can be taken up and fed into a long line by a thin brush [312].[10] This is also suggested by the way in which the true relief line gradually gives place during the fifth century to perfectly adequate thin black lines which are not in relief, suggesting that the problem of preparing

311. Painting arcs with a loop of hair.

312. Attic red figure cup in the manner of the Antiphon Painter. A boy is painting a cup; oil flask and strigil hang. Early 5th c. BC. (Boston 01.8073)

**313.** Apulian cup in the shape of a sheep's head. The neck may be cast from a metal cup; it shows a fight of Amazons and griffins. 4th c. BC. L. 20.8cm. (Oxford 1947.374)

and applying thick paint with a brush (for a dense, not dilute line) was readily mastered.

*Premeditated Decorative Forms*

Where so much of the subsidiary decoration was repetitive, one might have expected that the multiple brush would have been followed by other aids to a quick result. Only on the fine Caeretan vases of the late sixth century [*107*] has the use of a template been suggested, for the big ivy leaves.[11] It would not have been difficult to devise stamps which might have been used for the repetitive patterns of lotus and bud, maeanders, or the lines of squares that border so much in red figure, yet there are no signs of any. Such aids were, however, plentiful for work in relief, generally on plainer wares. In the archaic period the big relief pithoi and other shapes were decorated with stamped and moulded patterns [*45–49*], some of them figures, some patterns being applied with a roller like a cylinder seal, which had long been used for such purposes in the east. On the classical black vases small stamps were used to create palmettes, arcs linking palmettes in a chain, ivy leaves, and even occasionally figures, and there is 'rouletting' from a wheel [*144*]. Not, however, the 'tremolo' pattern created by a rocker, which was popular on jewellery and other metalwork and could easily have been employed to make a zigzag of arcs. Stamps with figures and ornament were also used in making the moulds for the relief Hellenistic bowls. Impressions from finger rings are found underfoot on some fourth-century and later vases made in Italy, perhaps a form of signature.

Moulded relief also appears on the archaic pithoi [*45*], readily adapted from the popular moulded relief plaques which were used for decoration and dedication at the time. In the classical period moulded groups, figures and animals, were made to decorate caskets and the like, copying the finer decoration in metalwork, and very similar, if not the same, moulds could be used to make appliqués for vases [*313*]. Xenophantos' fine lekythoi had hunting groups of Persians and monsters which could be reused and even renamed if need be on different vases, and the relief figures could act side by side with red figure painted ones [*138, 140*].

*Design and Composition*

The spheroid surface of an unfired clay vase is not the easiest field on which to create either a flowing or a miniaturist composition of figures. It would have been allowed to dry out to a fairly hard if not brittle state before being painted, but we can see from some dented

314. Attic black figure skyphos by the Theseus Painter, from Frankonisi. Heracles and the Bull, with Athena. The bull's body outlines have been sketched but the black not filled in, nor any white overlaid (which may have been intended). About 500 BC. H. 17cm. (Olympia)

315.1,2. Preliminary sketch in red figure. Detail of a vase by the Altamura Painter. The sketches beneath the shield show that the painter first planned to have the warrior face the other way; and how he sketched the figure without clothes (as did David for his Napoleon paintings and others). Before mid-5th c. BC. (London 1961.7–10.1)

specimens that accidents could happen. The run-of-the-mill painter needed no sketch or model for his work, but the better painters worked out with some care how the figures could be accommodated in the field offered. In black figure this was generally done by sketchy brush strokes which intimated the bulk of the figure, which could then be filled out to the desired outline [314].[12] The archaic Chalcidian painters of Italy went over the

silhouette twice, leaving thin, pale outlines. Might this have been a technique for fresco? There are a few examples of apparent erasure of the black paint, generally messy and darkening the vase surface.[13] Red figure compositions were often more ambitious, and for these the painter sketched his figures with short repeated strokes of a sharp implement. This might have been charcoal, which would have left a dark line that fired away. We can often detect this on the surface of the vase, and see how well the painter followed his sketch [315].[14] We can also see him here changing his mind about the position of an arm or leg, either with an adjusted sketch, or ignoring the original guide lines. He would then mark the outline to his figures with a stripe of paint of about 1/8 inch (3mm) thickness [316], [15] and on the better early vases the real edge is sharply defined by a relief line. The same rather sketchy preliminaries to the actual painting can be observed also in designs for painting on walls in other periods and places.[16] It might even suggest the origins of the earliest red figure artists. Other indications of change of mind can be relief lines on the black which are then not defined in white, as on the Niobid Painter's name vase [300], or of incised lines painted over.[17] There is nowhere any suggestion that a grid or other aid was used for determining proportions or for copying from some other drawing, at the same or at a different scale.

316. Fragment of Attic red figure crater showing the outlining of the figure and the background unfilled except for a careless splash of paint. Woman with phiale. Before mid-5th c. BC. (Berlin 3362)

# Chapter 10:    Tools of the Study

The title is a catch-all for a discussion of various aspects of the techniques of studying Greek vases of which the viewer might do well to be aware. It ranges from the application of real science, to the use and abuse of statistics and the problems of chronology.

*Science*

There are no areas of archaeological study and virtually none of art history which do not now depend to some degree on the application of scientific methods, in the narrower sense of what can be discovered in the laboratory or with equipment devised by the scientist, or of what can be achieved by the application of more than the simplest mathematics. Such methods have proved of prime importance in the study of prehistory, when man could not speak for himself through writing. In the historic period of archaic and classical Greece the same techniques can often be applied; moreover, their success can sometimes be judged since we have the possibility of testing much against other historical sources, and the theory may then be found wanting. The last forty years, since the advent of the so-called New Archaeology, have seen far wider application of such methods for classical antiquity, some with spectacularly useful results, some equivocal, some positively misleading in the wrong hands; all require an alliance of skills and interest between archaeologist and scientist, and mutual confidence based on mutual understanding of methods and aims.

The most obvious and productive application in our subject has been in the analysis of clays, fired and unfired. Each clay bed has its own 'signature' of composition, both in the proportions of the essential elements and in minor 'trace elements' peculiar to the location; and if the 'signature' is not exact in all respects, allowances can be made for variation. Composition may vary within a claybed, but not by much, and at any one time only one area within it may have been exploited and its composition be recognised in a fired vase. It would be a fruitless task to seek out every claybed of classical antiquity. They are potentially everywhere, and even those we know or strongly suspect to have been in use may not now offer us the composition sample used in antiquity. Of more use would be clay samples from datable kiln sites. So we analyse the

**317.** The author drilling a sample for analysis from the foot of the Northampton amphora *[105]*. (1973)

fired vases themselves, discreetly drilling out samples from inconspicuous areas *[317]*. Even when the results cannot be matched with a claybed, they can at least be matched with each other, to establish or confirm a group of probably common origin, that origin being determined by more traditional archaeological means – findplace, inscriptions, style. Generally a result such as 'A is not like B' is more reliable and useful than 'A is like B'.

Over the years different techniques of analysis have been used: first optical emission spectroscopy, then more expensive methods via neutron activation and atomic absorption. It has not always proved easy to correlate results since the proportions in composition recorded seem sometimes to be affected by the method, and in every case a standard has to be used against which to measure results. This has led to a lot of wasted effort and reduplication. There are also special methods to analyse for different qualities (as Mossbauer spectroscopy), or to study the clay itself microscopically, through thin sections, which is most appropriate for the coarser wares. But again comparability of results from different techniques is difficult, and at present much still relies on the individual judgement of the researcher (especially for thin sections). There has also been a move in some places away from presenting analyses for a good range of elements, up to ten, to what is considered more easily handled, as few as three, since the results can be more easily manipulated mathematically, or presented graphically. This seems a pity, and has not led to any more acceptable results, perhaps by ignoring the normally trivial which might yet unpredictably prove diagnostic in a special instance. Presentation of results by cluster analysis is also less helpful than simpler graphic presentation of each case, which can be judged for what is important and what is not by eye, even by the archaeologist's eye. However, new methods analyse more elements and the only problems will be expense, compatability between the methods, and the fear that the great corpus of analyses already made cannot be embraced in the study. There comes a point at which museum curators object to more holes in their exhibits; many a bronze, for example, is by now mainly a cluster of wax fillings. The whole programme, conducted now in many different centres, seems to lack clear definition of common goals, and rather pursues *ad hoc* exercises.

But there is no point in analysing anything which is not itself archaeologically intelligible in some way, and the tendency to analyse hundreds of undifferentiated sherds which cannot be readily related to classes or groups that are archaeologically intelligible is a waste of time and money (often public money). Far better analyse three vases of a recognised class, and then see how the results relate to each other, and to others, of the same or another period. This type of work has produced plausible results and adjusted significantly our views on the origins of several wares, a matter of considerable historical importance. It has also taught the archaeologist to what extent he may trust his 'eye': not always, but more often than not.[1]

Other scentific analyses are of more obvious application, for example to discover the composition of pigments, and possibly thus the origin of the raw materials. X-ray will reveal how a vase has been built up, and such things as concealed pellets (for trick vases) or interior containers (in the bigger lekythoi). It was science as much as trial and error that at last explained how the better vases were fired to create the black gloss. The most extreme technique is perhaps the study of fired clay *in situ* (from kiln sites) to determine the bearing of magnetic north at the time of firing, and so the date. Thermoluminescent dating ('likely to generate more heat than light', was an early comment) is too imprecise for our period except in the possible detection of forgeries. It could be that the profits are enough to encourage the forger to keep one step ahead of the laboratories. A computer has been enlisted to assist in the reconstruction of a multi-fragmented vase with half the pieces missing,[2] but the human eye and hand are not yet by any means superseded.

It is not impossible to imagine ways in which scientific analysis might help study of style. In its way the Morellian method of attribution, as practised on Greek vases and described in Chapter 2, is scientific but requires judgement by eye of what is important and what is significantly similar. However, it can hardly be worth scanning all vases to compare by computer the drawing of ears or knees, for instance. There are limits to the effort and expense this material can justify in terms of real results. For the geometry of shapes perhaps enough has been said in Chapter 8 to discourage too high hopes. It is possible to analyse how much of a given field the artists fill (the 'negative' and 'positive' space) – is it crowded or airy? This could help define painter preferences but I doubt whether it could do it more plausibly than is already done by eye.

*Statistics*

Statistical methods of analysis to demonstrate distribution or to suggest what is or is not diagnostic in an assemblage of pottery finds, or even of the decoration on vases, should be of great value. And it is, once it is realized that antiquity has never left us any body of material that can reasonably be called a random sample of the type and quantity to guarantee effective results, and we are virtually always denied any complete body of material. There is also the problem of the deceptive authority of any argument supported by figures, graphs, proportions, numbers, which thereby seems 'scientific' and reliable. Common sense teaches the truth of this, yet flimsy statistics are readily paraded. They can be useful only if the compiler is wholly honest about their sources and limitations, and spells them out, and if readers take note of them. Neither seems to happen often enough. I give a few examples of pitfalls.

The fallacy that what we have is all there was, remarked before in this book, still haunts some scholars. We considered what proportion of ancient production may have survived in Chapter 4. It is certain that some of the most productive sites have yet to be excavated or even located, while there is no major site that has been completely excavated. Yet it has been possible for assessment of import of Athenian vases to Italy to be based on only those specimens known to Beazley and attributed; this is an extreme case of misuse of figures, with ulterior motives. I remarked in Chapter 4 that at the last count there were over 350 sites in Italy that have yielded archaic Athenian figured vases; some are major sites but none of them completely excavated, some are casual finds from sites where hundreds more certainly lurk. Any new major find is likely to distort yet further any balanced view we might think to have about, for example, production or distribution. The single shipwreck off Marseilles with six hundred Attic black figure cups aboard is enough in itself to wreck many theories about numbers exported (Chapter 4). I have found it a salutary exercise when faced by any impressive statistical presentation of evidence, of whatever source, to consider what the effect would be on the figures if one major and productive find had never been made (if, for instance, the Athenian Agora had never been excavated, or Vulci had disappeared in an earthquake), or what the results would have looked like with the evidence of, say, thirty years ago. It is shameful too for classical archaeology to reflect on how much has been excavated but never published, or only published selectively, so denying us a proper perspective on what might otherwise seem a well-known site.

So where can such statistics be trusted? Sheer numbers are in their way comforting and might be thought to cancel some degree of imbalance in sources. Comparing shape preferences in Attic exports to various towns in and outside the Greek world, with overall production as known and what was left in Athens, there appeared to me to be intelligible differences to observe, although varieties of source could be a seriously upsetting factor.[3] There is also then the problem of oversimplifying categories to be compared, while overcomplexity can obscure basic trends.[4] Comparisons for major subject preferences between wares and even media has seemed equally suggestive.[5] In judging the subject preferences of individual painters I have thought that attributed vases numbering fifty or more might be safe, and am reassured mainly by the way in which intelligible patterns and comparisons between painters then emerge.[6] But it could easily happen that the figures are seriously distorted by an unjust proportion of finds of, perhaps, grave vases, or vases made especially for dedication. Thus, the massive find of black figure loutrophoroi and other 'special' vases from a shrine near the Acropolis, will distort all figures for production and survival of the shape, and for painter preferences.[7]

In all these matters, and especially where excavation material is considered proportionally, it is of vital concern that the items are properly identified and classified before comparisons are made.[8] Here I have mentioned mainly my own experience of such studies for research, for praise or blame. Frank avowal of, or even recognition of the limitations of such approaches are regrettably uncommon.[9]

The importance of the nature of our sources has been remarked and needs definition. We have no right to treat pottery from a sanctuary in the same spirit as that from a grave or from a house. There may have been, and probably was, a common stock from which almost all were chosen, but they *were* chosen, and therein lies the potential for profound differences in the excavated record. Fired clay is virtually indestructible, so all ancient vases still exist, somewhere. Thousands of fine vases were dedicated on the Athenian Acropolis in the eighth to fourth centuries BC. Very few have been found complete, a great many are known from one fragment only, and there must be many more for which excavation of the hill top and some areas of the slopes has yielded no trace whatever. Few could have been carried away, though it is possible that there were votive dumps nearby not yet found, and that these could contain material that had been kept apart for some reason on the Acropolis before disposal; much got washed away far from the hill. The fact that there are still so many pieces may seem reassuring, but for all we know one whole category of one period was kept in one place and then removed from modern sight. Too many towns are thought to have their history adequately mapped by what has so far been excavated without allowing for such contingencies. And the biggest filter of all was what happened before sherds worked their way to the modern surface, yet pottery from surface survey, subjected to the most elaborate mathematics, is thought an adequate record of what once lay below, even, incredibly, without the control of trial excavation.

Even the cemeteries for a single town may differ in composition, and it is rare if unknown for all to have been identified and excavated. From many major sites we have only a handful of graves. The published tombs from the Greek colony on Ischia are nearly all for children and not for the rich, who have yet to be located. A wise statistical study of them is highly suggestive but, in the circumstances, can prove nothing for the whole site.[10] Sometimes even the earliest material from a site, crucial to our understanding of its history, lurks undiscovered for years. The early history of Athens, its population and society, gets determined by the mainly pottery product of part of one big cemetery only, without serious consideration that there is evidence for cemeteries of all periods all round the city, and that for some periods other locations may have been preferred for important graves. But this touches on the uses of pottery to reconstruct social history, an enormous subject which I can allude to only, though it was a recurrent theme in Chapter 1. We read much today about 'the élite' in Greek cities but may be seriously wrong, and circular in our argument, to assume that the élite may be recognised by having finer pottery and other objects in their graves.

They may have preferred less in the grave and more in the cere-mony and above-ground memorial, or even have been buried else-where and out of sight (at sea, for example!). As for deductions about a 'classless society' from pottery and other grave goods – the animal kingdom has no classless societies. Our pottery studies can be used for many purposes, not all of them in touch with the real world.

Another problem is the question of objectivity and the dangers of being 'judgemental' about evidence. A whole chapter could be devoted to prejudices, obsessions, and their effects on scholarship and teaching, but I allude here simply to what might seem a reverse effect. Some studies avoid appearing to judge by taking each piece of evidence as of equal value. This makes for easier statistics and mathematics, of course, but in fact it is the most subjective and least reasonable of all judgements, to hold that all things are equal and no allowance should be made for what experience and observation would assign roles of varying value. This has affected studies based on decorative motifs on vases, and especially distribution maps where numbers of finds are not prop-erly correlated with relative areas dug and different types of source.

*Dates*

Dates have been given freely throughout this book, though often rather vaguely, and deliberately so. It is bad enough having to get used to counting backwards BC, without remembering too that each century BC meant nothing to an antiquity that could only count forwards and to no definable goal. (2000 BC went unre-marked.) If Christ had been born fifty years earlier many problems of 'which century?' would disappear, and as many new, different ones, be generated. In excavation we move backwards in time as we dig deeper. The evidence for the chronological sequence fol-lowed here has been set out in the handbooks.[11] It depends a little on the vases themselves since some, too few, carry names or allu-sions to historical events or are from the grave of an identifiable person or group, such as mass war graves. A few vases have been found in non-Greek contexts for which dates are supplied by eastern or Egyptian sources, or they accompany objects which are closely datable by other criteria, such as Egyptian scarabs naming kings. Very occasionally a vase scene plausibly relates closely to another, better dated, work of art which must precede it [*302*]. Some are found in situations where the effect of a dated historical event is evident – the founding or destruction of a town, and these can often be confirmed by Carbon-14 dating of accompanying debris, as at Sardis, destroyed by Persians in the 540s BC. One has to be cautious about identifying all destructions with recorded disasters. The warning model I proposed long ago was the Crystal Palace in London, destroyed not in World War I or II, but between the wars;[12] and, moreover, having already been moved from its original site, as were several Attic temples in the Roman period. A destroyed city may not remain unoccupied long, and a new foundation may be preceded by exploration or trade. It is possible to be defeatist about dating; or, worse, perverse by letting local problems obscure the overall pattern, which is by now well agreed. Much of the history of early Greece still depends on pottery dating.

Some more unusual sources which offer a date or a progression are the identification of names of pretty boys in the *kalos* inscriptions on Athenian vases of the later sixth and early fifth centuries, and other familial connections. The use of these for dating has fallen from favour in recent years, but the boys can sometimes be plausibly identified in their later careers. They were only of interest to their aged fondlers while they were still boys (*paides*), between about ten and fifteen years old. Sometimes inscriptions on different vases indicate father and son, both *kalos*, thus placing a generation between the appearances.[13] For some years around the mid-fifth century there was a fashion for naming their fathers too, which is a little odd, unless it guaranteed their civic status.[14] Little Leagros was much praised in the potters' quarter at the end of the sixth century [179]. When he fell in battle, a general, years later, demesmen who fell with him carried names familiar in the potters' quarter since the mid-sixth century as potters, painters, or favourite boys.[15]

All these observations create a close nexus, and all new finds in potentially historical contexts tend to confirm it. Sequences of pottery may of course be determined by observed progression of style in decoration and shape, which is not wholly subjective; by contexts with other pottery and objects in graves; and by sequences from stratified sites which have been excavated, observed and interpreted properly. It must be remembered that styles and conventions did not change overnight. On occasion we might feel another date for a vase could be more convenient for one reason or another, and uncritical reliance on such fallacious exceptions has led one or two scholars to propose radical changes, up or down, which may look plausible individually, taken out of context, but are totally negated by all else. Such attempts to upset the

**318.** Pottery on excavation. The British School at Athens' pot-mender, Stelios Katsarakis, mending the Sophilos dinos at the excavation at Old Smyrna, watched by the draughtswoman Audrey Petty, and Lilian Jeffery. (1949)

system radically have proved ill-founded, unscholarly, and sometimes virtually dishonest.

### Seeing Vases

Finally, how do we get to know about the vases? Watching them emerge from the ground may be exciting, but it takes time and trouble to make them presentable [*318*]. There are many in most major collections of Greek antiquities, displayed in varying ways. Fortunately they are robust and do not require any sophisticated display environment provided they have been properly cleaned. Some used to be polished to make the black look more like glaze, and some still are waxed, but the natural, hard blackness should need no cosmetics. There is generally proper regard to making repairs and restorations readily identifiable, and decoration is not faked. Actual modern fakes, however, are not uncommon, and with the legal sources (mainly old collections) drying up, the illegal are too easily filled out with the modern, few of which are very persuasive. Greek vases deserve our respect and attention, but the viewer needs to remember that he or she is not studying 'works of art' in isolation, but functional vessels which can illuminate for us much more than the practical uses to which they were put in antiquity.

The study is brisk and publication plentiful. There are many handbooks with varying generosity of illustration, and many more expensive monographs. More thought and publication is now devoted to studies beyond attribution and iconography, some with application of diligent observation and prospection for evidence, but some by writers barely conversant with the primary evidence. Enthusiasm is not enough.

Slowly, the advantage of placing this evidence for Greek pottery on the internet, for students rather than the public as yet, is proving of value. While the book is essential there is much basic information which can more readily be disseminated in this way. Thus, Athenian black and red figure vases are listed, as comprehensively as available traditional publications permit, with description and bibliography, by the Beazley Archive in Oxford, and are accessible on internet (over 70, 000 entries, and so far over 20,000 pictures also).[16] This is a continuing programme and service, being extended to other areas of Greek pottery and art (sculpture and engraved gems), with more appeal for the general public, but unfortunately still with no guarantee of continuing financial support (tycoon connoisseurs, please note).

# Epilogue

My first experience of Greek pottery was the study in Athens of material from old Greek excavations at Eretria in Euboea, and the freedom of the pottery shelves in the Athenian Agora excavations, generously accorded by the American School.[1] And my motivation towards the subject was largely the result of Rsobert Cook's lectures at Cambridge which I heard as an undergraduate in 1947/8. Eretria gave the opportunity to learn something about the stylistic and absolute chronology of a previously unstudied ware, about iconography, ritual shapes, and even allowed modest speculation about myth reflecting politics. The Agora was an exercise of self-education in understanding shapes, scenes and fragments. Shortly afterwards, publishing the Attic pottery from Old Smyrna initiated me into learning the techniques of connoisseurship. Since then, over some fifty years, I suppose at least a quarter of my research time has been spent on various aspects of Greek pottery, developing, according to no programme but following opportunity and speculation, many of the other subjects barely touched at first, and adding to them the experience of dealing with pottery from my own excavations and of working for a major iconographical source, *LIMC*. From all this I have come to learn the hard way, by observation and practice, that the study is a central one to classical archaeology and dare not be ignored by students of any other ancient medium, or indeed of any other classical discipline, from history to poetry, and I would barely exempt philosophy. In writing about the history and archaeology of Greeks overseas (*GO*) pottery proved a strong marker of both presence and influence. And I have learned much from trying to provide for students the well illustrated handbooks of which I had felt the lack as a student.[2] The techniques of study have been traditional, but the questions asked and answers sought have not been, and the flow of studies by others, dealing more closely with the social, political, and aesthetic aspects of such a well-represented medium, have been influential, as well as whatever was sometimes investigated as the result of what seemed an idle observation. Serendipity plays its part and I have changed my mind often over important issues.

There are certain disadvantages in an older scholar appearing to propound or embrace new ideas; he or she runs the risk of being disbelieved on principle and is readily misquoted or misrepresented. Moreover 'new' ideas rapidly become 'old' and apparently therefore to some minds redundant. A measure of 'affirmative action' is being applied not only in the choice of students but in scholarship itself.

I cite just two examples of new approaches which I have found useful, though not in the way they intended. Twenty years ago the principles of Structuralism, deduced from or imposed on the evidence of anthropology, were adopted enthusiastically by some classical archaeologists. Application of the principles has in general failed to convince in detail, [3] but even the rather mechanical process of categorizing opposites or complementaries has helped to distinguish better some of the ways in which Greek artists could combine or conceal what might seem contradictory messages. So too the definition of Greek attitudes to the non-Greek, the 'other' in both race and life, even the male/female; all stimulating when not taken to be prescriptive. They prompt the right questions, whether answerable or not.

A different current, also from over the Channel, had been to deny intelligible validity to anything but the text (or image) which at best can be judged, and in an incommunicable way, by the modern reader/viewer. This sophistry is, of course, absurd historically, but has helped focus attention back on to the viewer, and especially now the ancient viewer, who is our main concern. This may even bid to restore to favour attention to be paid to the creators, the artists without whom there would be no subject. This revival of old methods and even theories, though generally never acknowledged, can only be for the good. We are dealing with the visual experiences of ancient Greeks, not just their pots.

Several other pottery studies, based on theories generally devised to account for quite other situations, may prove fruitful but have yet to yield any substantial and acknowledged advance in our understanding of the subject. A common problem is lack of control of the primary evidence. This is not an easy study, and balanced, informed and instinctive understanding of shapes and scenes, even, and especially, in fragments, does not come overnight, nor, to some, at all. No area of pottery investigation, however theoretical or apparently remote from the clay, can be effectively conducted without intimate knowledge of the pots themselves. Only thus can the validity of the evidence they seem to offer be properly judged. Computerized evidence has simply set it at one further remove from scholarly control, except for ease of search and reference. The study has suffered at least as much as others from the academic hooligan and the academic buffoon.[4] More than most archaeological studies in classical antiquity, this cannot be dealt with in isolation; yet studies of isolated topics, lists and corpora, have proved crucial and necessary to the development of the whole, which I would define as a proper understanding of what our most prolific source of material information from classical antiquity can tell us about the life, motives and even thoughts, of those who made and used it.

The form of this book has been heavily influenced by my own interests. It therefore tends to turn often for demonstration to areas I have already visited and I make no apology for this, but I do not think the personal element can have obscured the relative importance of the various subjects involved. I have tried to refer to studies that may have been overlooked, though the handbooks (some rather old now) will generally be found to be well-referenced. Over the years the physical media for the study have changed. Monographs on particular wares and even painters are still published, and need to be. Catalogue publication remains an important source for an immensely populous field, and is by no means as easy an exercise as it may seem to those who have never attempted it. Subject monographs, iconographical or social (sex has proved a popular area), are still not uncommon, but the most notable features of recent scholarship have been the publication of conferences, exhibitions or of specially commissioned volumes on particular subjects. These have not always helped bibliographical tidiness; we turn to machines to catch references and often miss much or find that much is repetitive or, in this age of overactive publication, inadequate. My notes cite what I think will help the reader, and this is not always the latest comment, which may lack mature insights.

Possibly a small but significant and sometimes busy proportion of mankind finds great difficulty in seeing and 'reading' an image; a form of visual dyslexia which the computer age may do something to rectify. The situation in vase studies bears comparison with studies in Greek literature and life by those who cannot read Greek. This is a subject that requires the closest attention to detail as well as an eye for 'style' in the arts generally. But it is not the only traditional study in the classics and art history which has not been improved much by new approaches, except for the scientific described in the last chapter. New 'theoretical' studies are much promoted; but all study of the subject is based on theory of some sort, and theory which has stood the test of time and produced acceptable results, probably because it has been generated by close attention to the evidence plus a lively imagination to supply what must always be lacking. Too many studies, and not only in classical art history, are designed to prove a theory, not test it. 'Common sense is not enough'; but it remains essential in the formulation and execution of any academic exercise and is itself largely the product of experience, though we should take nothing for granted.

Nevertheless, the subject is essentially healthy, and I hope to have given something of its flavour to readers, scholars and others, for whom it may have remained, at best, on the periphery of their awareness of the evidence for classical antiquity, or even outside it. So it was once for me, a student who knew nothing more of ancient Greece than its texts.

# Acknowledgements

I am indebted to the following who read early drafts of the book and made valuable comments: Donna Kurtz, Elizabeth Moignard, Claudia Wagner. Several scholars have helped me with various matters: H.A.G. Brijder, Lucilla Burn, Nicolas Coldstream, Mary Comstock, C. Donnan, John Hayes, Alan Johnston, Norbert Kunisch, Irene Lemos, Adrienne Lezzi-Hefter, John Oakley, Mervyn Popham, Brian Shefton, Marion True. The maps are by Marion Cox, other new drawings my own.

The publishers and I are also indebted to the many museums and collections named in the captions for photographs. Other sources are named publications, the Beazley Archive and the publisher's archive of photos, and:
DAI Athens 7–9, 35, 46, 47, 133, 168; DAI Rome 154–156; French School, Athens 21; Hirmer Verlag 13, 15, 30, 44, 62, 65, 81, 88–90, 97, 118, 210; Photo Alinari 124.

A. Daneman 120; H. Giroux 184; C. Heinrich 282; W. Klein 10; C.H. Krüger-Moessner 72, 200; A. Lezzi-Hafter 192; C. Niggli 56, 122; M. Popham 26; J. Tietz-Glagow 229, 266; R.L. Wilkins 105, 113, 160, 307, 317. Author's photos 11, 16, 18, 24, 43, 48, 53, 57, 94, 109, 148, 211, 247, 248, 291, 295, 304, 313, 318.

# Abbreviations

| | |
|---|---|
| AA | *Archäologischer Anzeiger* |
| ABFH | J. Boardman, *Athenian Black Figure Vases. A Handbook* London, 1974 |
| ABV | J.D. Beazley, *Attic Black-Figure Vase-Painters* Oxford, 1956 |
| ADelt | *Archaiologikon Deltion* |
| AGAI | *Ancient Greek Art and Iconography* (ed. W.G. Moon) Madison, 1983 |
| Agora | *The Athenian Agora* I- Princeton |
| Ahlberg | G. Ahlberg-Cornell, *Myth and Epos in Early Greek Art* Jonsered, 1992 |
| AION | *Annali di Archeologia . . . Istituto universitario orientale, Napoli* |
| AJA | *American Journal of Archaeology* |
| AK | *Antike Kunst* |
| AM | *Athenische Mitteilungen* |
| Amsterdam | *Ancient Greek and Related Pottery* (ed. H.A.G. Brijder) Amsterdam, 1984 |
| Amyx | D.A. Amyx, *Corinthian Vase Painting* Berkeley/LA, 1989 |
| APP | *Athenian Potters and Painters* (edd. J.H. Oakley, W.D.E. Coulson and O. Palagia) Oxford, 1997 |
| Arafat/Morgan | K. Arafat and C. Morgan, 'Pots and Potters in Athens and Corinth', *OJA* 8 (1989) 311–346 |
| ARFH I | J. Boardman, *Athenian Red Figure Vases, the Archaic Period. A Handbook* London, 1975 |
| ARFH II | J. Boardman, *Athenian Red Figure Vases, the Classical Period. A Handbook* London, 1989 |
| ARV | J.D. Beazley, *Attic Red-Figure Vase-Painters* (ed. 2) Oxford, 1963 |
| BABesch | *Bulletin van de Vereeniging . . . Antieke Beschaving* |
| BCH | *Bulletin de Correspondance Hellénique* |
| Boardman, Diffusion | J. Boardman, *The Diffusion of Classical Art in Antiquity* London, 1994 |
| BSA | *Annual of the British School at Athens* |
| CAH | *Cambridge Ancient History* |
| Catania I, II | *I Vasi Attici ed altre Ceramiche coeve in Sicilia* (= *Cronache di Archeologia* 29, 1990) Catania, 1998 |
| Cook | R.M. Cook, *Greek Painted Pottery* (ed. 3) London, 1997 |
| Copenhagen | *Ancient Greek and Related Pottery* (edd. J. Christiansen and T. Melander) Copenhagen, 1988 |
| CPG | *Céramique et peinture grecques. Modes d'emploi* (edd. M.-C. Villaneuva Puig et al.) Paris, 1999 |
| CPP | *The Complex Past of Pottery* (ed. J.P. Crielaard) Amsterdam, 1999 |
| Culture | *Culture et Cité. L'avènement d'Athènes à l'époque archaïque* (edd. A. Verbanck-Piérard and Didier Viviers) Brussels, 1995 |
| CVA | *Corpus Vasorum Antiquorum* |
| EGVP | J. Boardman, *Early Greek Vase Painting. A Handbook* London, 1998 |
| Eye | *The Eye of Greece* (edd. D. Kurtz and B. Sparkes) Cambridge, 1992. |
| GettyJ | *Journal of the J. Paul Getty Museum* |
| Getty Vases | *Greek Vases in the J. Paul Getty Museum* |
| GO | J. Boardman, *The Greeks Overseas* London, 1999 |
| Green | J.R. Green, *Theatre in Greek Society* London, 1994 |
| JdI | *Jahrbuch des Deutschen Archäologischen Instituts* |
| JHS | *Journal of Hellenic Studies* |
| Johnston | A.W. Johnston, *Trademarks on Greek Vases* Warminster, 1979 |
| Jones | R.E. Jones, *Greek and Cypriot Pottery* Athens, 1986 |
| LCS | A.D. Trendall, *The red-figured Vases of Lucania, Campania and Sicily* Oxford, 1967 |
| LGV | *Looking at Greek Vases* (edd. T. Rasmussen and N. Spivey) Cambridge, 1991 |
| LIMC | *Lexicon Iconographicum Mythologiae Classicae* Zurich, 1981–1999 |
| Lissarrague | F. Lissarrague, *The Aesthetics of the Greek Banquet* Princeton, 1987 |
| Met.Mus.Bull. | *Bulletin of the Metropolitan Museum, New York* |
| Met.Mus.J. | *Metropolitan Museum Journal* |
| Noble | J.V. Noble, *The Techniques of Attic Painted Pottery* London, 1966,1988 |
| OJA | *Oxford Journal of Archaeology* |
| Para | J.D. Beazley, *Paralipomena* Oxford, 1971 |

| | | | |
|---|---|---|---|
| *Periplous* | *Periplous* (edd. G. Tsetskhladze, A.J.N.W. Prag and A.M. Snodgrass; Papers . . . J. Boardman) London, 2000 | *RVSIS* | A.D. Trendall, *Red Figure Vases of South Italy and Sicily* London, 1989 |
| *RA* | *Revue Archéologique* | Scheibler | I. Scheibler, *Griechische Töpferkunst* Munich, 1983 |
| *REA* | *Revue des Études Anciennes* | Schreiber | T. Schreiber, *Athenian Vase Construction* Malibu, 1999 |
| Robertson | M. Robertson, *The Art of Vase-Painting in Classical Athens* Cambridge, 1992 | Simon/Hirmer | E. Simon and A. & H. Hirmer, *Die griechischen Vasen* Munich, 1976 |
| *RVAp* | A.D. Trendall and A. Cambitoglou, *The red-figured Vases of Apulia* Oxford, 1982 | Sparkes | B.A. Sparkes, *Greek Pottery. An Introduction* Manchester, 1991 |
| *RVP* | A.D. Trendall, *The red-figured Vases of Paestum* London, 1987 | Trendall/ Webster | A.D. Trendall and T.B.L. Webster, *Illustrations of Greek Drama* London, 1971 |

# Notes

## Preface (pp. 7–10)

For the handbooks discussing the subject by progression of style see the list of abbreviations for: *EGVP* (for all wares down to non-Athenian black figure); *ABFH, ARFH* I and II (for the Athenian vases), *RVSIS* (for the South Italian). All are in the Thames and Hudson 'World of Art' series. *EGVP* chapter 8 and *ARFH* II, chapter 8 give very brief accounts of much that is discussed in this book. R.M. Cook, *Greek Painted Pottery* (ed. 3, 1997) covers the whole subject, except iconography, and is reliable, with a good chapter on the history of study of the subject down to a generation ago.

It is a good idea to approach Greek vases via books that are full in description, since these help the reader to learn how to look at the vases, rather than the summary and often faulty accounts in the many standard small books on archaic and classical Greek art, some of which are dangerously inaccurate. B.B. Shefton's commentary in *A History of Greek Vase Painting* (1962) is an excellent source but only found now in libraries; its German equivalent is E. Simon, *Die Griechischen Vasen* (1976, 1981). Otherwise, look for museum and exhibition catalogues with full descriptions, or essays devoted to individual painters, scenes or vases. In museums you are at the mercy of the curators and their labels.

Some conferences and other collections of essays are informative about a wide range of subjects, notably *Amsterdam, Copenhagen, LGV, APP, Catania* and *CPG*. B.A. Sparkes, *Greek Pottery. An Introduction* (1991) presents much basic evidence for some of the subjects discussed here; I. Scheibler, *Griechische Töpferkunst* (1983) is an excellent introduction, well illustrated, but unfortunately not translated, or indexed. The series *CVA* began in 1923 and now numbers over 300 volumes, with austere descriptions but, at least for the volumes of the last fifty years, comprehensive illustration; there is a plan to reissue the old volumes electronically. There is a *Summary Guide* to the contents of *CVA* (T.H. Carpenter

and T. Mannack, 2000). The *Kerameus* series (von Zabern, Mainz) has since 1975 published eleven monographs on individual painters or wares with complete illustration.

The Beazley Archive in Oxford has a website (www.beazley.ox.ac.uk) with a multimedia database of some 70,000 Athenian decorated vases, with pictures being added, and presentations about the discovery, study and collecting of Greek pottery. It is mainly for student use at present but broader programmes are in preparation.

References for Attic vases can be found via their museum numbers in Beazley's *ABV, ARV, Para*, and later references can be found in T.H. Carpenter, *Beazley Addenda* (1989) and on the Beazley Archive website (above). The same is true for the South Italian vases, using Trendall's lists. Other pieces can be traced through the handbooks, or references are given here to discussions.

## Chapter 1 (pp. 11–127)

The World of Art handbooks (see above) should be the major recourse for the reader requiring more information and illustration of what is discussed in this chapter. They contain a far fuller account of all the wares described here, down to the end of the 4th century BC. I cite them in the notes only where specific points are made or for particular illustration. I do mention articles and monographs where fuller series of pictures and useful discussion and descriptions can be found, but the student reader should turn to the handbooks.

**1** *GO* ch. 2 for the expansion east.

**2** On Protogeometric *EGVP* ch. 2, figs. 2–25, and a forthcoming monograph by I. Lemos, *The Protogeometric Aegean*. The Euboean *koine, eadem* in *Euboica* (ed. M. Bats and B. d'Agostino, 1998) 45–58.

**3** References in *EGVP* 276; several studies by N. Kourou.

**4** On sex differentiation by shapes, J. Boardman in *AION* 10 (1988) 171–179.

**5** M. Aspris, *Bonner Jahrbücher* 196 (1996) 1–10.

**6**  For Athenian Geometric, *EGVP* 23–28, figs. 26–75; more fully, J.N. Coldstream, *Greek Geometric Pottery* (1968) (*[18]* is 55,12), and on the period, *idem, Geometric Greece* (1977). C. Brokaw, *AM* 78 (1963) 63–73 on latest styles.

**7**  On non-Attic Geometric, *EGVP* 28–55, figs. 76–161.

**8**  *[20]* is D. Ridgway, *The First Western Greeks* (1992) 68, fig. 16. On the few Corinthian Geometric figures, C. Morgan in *CPG* 279–285; are some of the Thapsos Class which is close to Corinthian but not, as I believe (*EGVP* 49) but not Morgan (*CPP* 217–219), made there? It remains negligible at Corinth, has different shapes, iconography and distribution, for all the similarity of clay.

**9**  J. Boardman in *AGAI* 16–23.

**10**  A possible exception, an Eretrian like *EGVP* fig. 226, inscribed *thea* 'goddess' (*BSA* 47 (1952) 25, fig. 21e, pl. 5.C2).

**11**  *EGVP* 15, 28 on Euboean Geometric; *GO* 39–46, 165–169, 269–272, 276, on Euboeans east and west.

**12**  On Greek literature and its divergence from the east, from 'writing' to 'literature', a thoughtful essay by S. Averintsev in *Arion* 7.1 (1999) 1–39.

**13**  For the whole Orientalizing phenomenon see *GO* chs. 3, 7. For Euboeans and Al Mina see *GO* 38–46, 270–271; J. Boardman in *Ancient Greeks West and East* (ed. G. Tsetskhladze, 1999) 135–161.

**14**  I argue this in *Greek Settlements* . . . (edd. A.M. Snodgrass and G. Tsetskhladze, 2000). See also below, on cups, in Chapter 7.

**15**  For the Orientalizing groups, *EGVP* ch. 4, figs. 213–282.

**16**  For Protocorinthian, *EGVP* 85–88, figs. 163–186. The incising technique was not entirely novel for pottery: in XIII Dynasty Egypt: J. Bourriau in *Studies* . . . *W.K. Simpson* (ed. P. Der Manuelian, 1966) I, 101–116.

**17**  H.G. Payne, *Protokorinthische Vasenmalerei* (1933/1974) pls. 27–29; Simon/Hirmer, pls. 25, 26, VII (colour).

**18**  *EGVP* figs. 202–211. S. Morris, *The Black and White Style* (1984), arguing for some production also in Aegina.

**19**  D.C. Kurtz and J. Boardman, *Greek Burial Customs* (1971) chs. 3–5 (Athens), 9 (outside Athens), 11 (general offerings including pottery).

**20**  *EGVP* figs. 250–254.

**21**  Knossos, *EGVP* figs. 146–151 (PGB), 257–276. On the lack of evidence after the late 7th century, J.N. Coldstream and G. Huxley, *BSA* 94 (1999) 289–307.

**22**  *EGVP* ch. 5, figs. 283–361. R.M. Cook, *East Greek Vase Painting* (1997).

**23**  V. Karageorghis and J. des Gagniers, *La céramique chypre de style figuré* (1974).

**24**  *EGVP* 114, figs. 277–282.

**25**  Simon/Hirmer, pls. 18, 19.

**26**  J. Boardman in Papers . . . B.B. Shefton, forthcoming.

**27**  *Dädalische Kunst* (Hamburg, 1970) cat. C30. J. Schäfer, *Studien zu den griechischen Reliefpithoi* (1957).

**28**  M.E. Caskey, *ADelt* 18 (1963) 37–75, and *AJA* 80 (1976) 19–41, on the series. Another Troy vase, as *[46]*, with the horse on the neck but friezes on the body and

**29**  R.M. Dawkins (ed.), *Artemis Orthia* (1929) pls. 15, 16. References for early relief vases in *EGVP* 276.

**30**  E. Simantoni-Bournia, *La Céramique à Reliefs au Musée de Chios* (1992) pl. 2.

**31**  N.A. Winter, *Greek Architectural Terracottas* (1993).

**32**  A.W. Johnston and R.E. Jones, *BSA* 73 (1978) 103–141, on the SOS amphorae (our *[50]* is pl. 18b). On their contents, R.F. Docter, *BABesch* 66 (1991) 45–50.

**33**  V.R. Grace, *Amphoras and the ancient wine trade* (1979). Historical value, H. Parkins et al., *Trade, Traders and the Ancient City* (1998). For Egypt, see *GO* 280.

**34**  *Jahrbuch der Berliner Museen* 4 (1962) 3–16. *EGVP* figs. 3–17. For Athenian black figure, *ABFH*, and essays by J.D. Beazley in *The Development of Attic Black Figure* (1951; reissued in 1986 with more but poorer pictures).

**35**  The history of Corinthian vase painting was skilfully described by H.G. Payne in *Necrocorinthia* (1931), a book that has not been replaced, except by not altogether agreed studies of painter-lists, the latest being D.A. Amyx, *Corinthian Vase Painting* (1989). Other references in *EGVP* 278–279.

**36**  Corinthian black figure, *EGVP* 177–185, figs. 362–410. 'Mass production' in Corinth, J.L. Benson in *APP* 17–20.

**37**  For the monster head, A. Mayor, *OJA* 19 (2000) 57–63.

**38**  Amyx, 589,114.

**39**  M. Davies, *AK* 16 (1973) 60–70.

**40**  *[57]* is Amyx, 180–181; *idem* and P. Amandry, *AK* 25 (1982) 102–116; J. Boardman, *OJA* 1 (1982) 237–238. The Boeotian graves – P.N. Ure, *The Aryballoi and Figurines from Rhitsona* (1934) esp. pl. 2.

**41**  *EGVP* figs. 56–63. T.H. Carpenter, *OJA* 2 (1983) 279–293; 3 (1984) 45–56 – on dates and subjects. J. Kluiver, *BABesch* 67 (1992) 73–109; 68 (1993) 179–194 – on potter/painters.

**42**  L. Hannestad, *Acta Archaeologica* 62 (1991) 151–163.

**43**  *EGVP* fig. 410; Amyx, 273. For *[60]* *CVA* Robinson Collection I, pl. 48.

**44**  D. Williams, *Getty Vases* 1 (1983) 13–34.

**45**  *EGVP* fig. 46.1–7; *Bollettino d'Arte* Ser.spec. 1 (1981) for all details; Simon/Hirmer, pls. 51–57.

**46**  Simon/Hirmer, pl. 64. Egypt, *AK* 24 (1981) pl. 10.1–2.

**47**  G.M.A. Richter, *AJA* 36 (1932) 272–275.

**48**  On the painter, below, n. 52.

**49**  *EGVP* figs. 108–130, the cup sequence. For the Sianas, H.A.G. Brijder in *APP* 1–15.

**50**  *Getty Vases* 4 (1989) 95–112 *[74]*. *ABFH* ch. 7, figs. 295–308; J. Frel, *Panathenaic Prize Amphoras* (1973); J. Neils in *Goddess and Polis* (ed. *eadem*, 1992) 28–51. A comprehensive study, M. Bentz, *Panathenaische Preisamphoren* (1998). On imitations, P. Hannah in *Periplous* 80–88. Predecessors may be the 'Horse Head' amphorae: *EGVP* fig. 18; B. Kreuzer, *BABesch* 73 (1998) 95–114.

**51**  *EGVP* figs. 64–71; M. Tiverios, *Ho Lydos kai to ergo tou* (1976).

very fragmentary, from Tenos, E. Bournia in *Phos kykladikon* (*Eis mneme N. Zapheiropoulou*, 1999) 158–177.

**52** *EGVP* figs. 77–91. Much on Amasis in the catalogue and discussions in *The Amasis Painter and his World* by D. von Bothmer (1985) and *Papers on . . .* (1987).

**53** Beazley, op.cit. (n. 34), ch. 6; *EGVP* figs. 97–107.

**54** *EGVP* 109–113, figs. 181–230. The main source for the late lekythoi and skyphoi is E. Haspels, *Attic Black Figure Lekythoi* (1936), whose lists are subsumed by Beazley; her 249,9 is [85].

**55** *EGVP* figs. 268–272.

**56** *Clara Rhodos* 4 (1931) pl. 3. *ABFH* 64, 178, 188, figs. 309–314. J.B. Grossman, *Getty Vases* 5 (1991) 13–26. Six was a scholar who studied the technique.

**57** *EGVP* 185–213, figs. 412–436. C.M. Stibbe, *Lakonische Vasenmaler* (1972) is comprehensive for the black figure, and for subjects, M. Pipili, *Laconian Iconography* (1987). [89] is Simon/Hirmer, pl. XV (col.).

**58** *EGVP* 213–215, figs. 437–457; K. Kilinski, *Boeotian Black Figure Vase Painting* (1990), and (with J.-J. Maffre) in *Monuments . . . Piot* 77 (1999) 7–40 on kantharoi. The migrant painter: *ABFH* 19, fig. 32, and *EGVP* 214, fig. 438.

**59** Euboea – *EGVP* figs. 458–465. North – from a cemetery near Thessaloniki, *CVA* Thessaloniki I; near Aiane, *Ancient Macedonia* (VI Symposium, 1999) 537–562, cf. 1043–1045.

**60** *EGVP* 144–146, figs. 307–324. A. Lemos, *Archaic Pottery of Chios* (1991), is comprehensive. Recent on inscriptions, A.W. Johnston in *Periplous* 163–166.

**61** For the archaeology of Naucratis, *GO* 118–133; and A. Möller, *Naukratis* (forthcoming).

**62** *EGVP* 146–147, fig. 326–330.

**63** *EGVP* 147–148, figs. 331–339.

**64** *EGVP* figs. 299, 300 (black figure Wild Goat). Sarcophagi, *EGVP* 148–149, figs. 340–354; R.M. Cook, *Clazomenian Sarcophagi* (1981), comprehensive. Clazomenian black figure – *EGVP* figs. 340–348.

**65** *EGVP* figs. 290–304.

**66** D.A. Jackson, *East Greek Influence on Attic Vases* (1976); B.B. Shefton, *Getty Vases* 4 (1989) 41–72.

**67** A hundred years ago the poet Robert Service (*Songs of a Sourdough*; 'Dangerous Dan McGrew' et al.) was selling chamber pots to Siwash Indians in Canada as 'Etruscan vases' (J. Mackay, *Vagabond of Verse*). On Greek vases in Etruria, N. Spivey in *LGV* ch. 6.

**68** *EGVP* 217–219, figs. 468–482.

**69** *EGVP* 143, fig. 220.

**70** References in *EGVP* 280, cf. fig. 501.

**71** [105] is *CVA* Castle Ashby pls. A (colour), 1–3, Simon/Hirmer, pls. 16, 17 (colour). *EGVP* 220–221, figs. 485–492. S.L. Solovyov, *Ancient Berezan* (1999) 89, fig. 79.

**72** *EGVP* 221–222, figs. 494–499, J.M. Hemelrijk, *Caeretan Hydriae* (1984) for complete illustration.

**73** *EGVP* fig. 500; ibid., 219–222 for an account of the immigrant potters in Etruria, and illustration.

**74** *EGVP* 257–258; Amyx, 275–276. For [109] B.F. Cook, *British Museum Quarterly* 36 (1972) 113–115.

**75** *EGVP* 258, figs. 506–510; *Das Kabirenheiligtum bei Theben* I (G. Bruns, 1940), IV (K. Braun, 1981) for pictures.

**76** *EGVP* ch. 7, figs. 502–511, for the black figure aftermath.

**77** The fullest discussion of style is M. Robertson, *The art of vase-painting in classical Athens* (1992). D. Williams' articles in *LGV* ch. 5.1, *Culture* 139–160 and *RA* 1996, 227–252 are important contributions to understanding of early red figure production.

**78** C. Julier-Garbinier and A.-F. Laurens, *Topoi* 8 (1998) 731–748.

**79** *ARFH* I, figs. 1–10; *ABFH* figs. 160–166.

**80** *ABFH* figs. 168, 169 (Psiax); *ARFH* I, figs. 11–14, 54–78.

**81** On the Pioneers, *ARFH* I, 29–36, figs. 22–53; Robertson, ch. 2.

**82** An exhibition of Euphronios vases in Arezzo (1990) followed by Paris and Berlin, generated three excellent catalogues, and volumes of relevant essays.

**83** J.D. Beazley, *The Kleophrades Painter*, *The Berlin Painter* (1974); Robertson, 56–83. *ARFH* I, 89–111, figs. 129–161. D.C. Kurtz, *The Berlin Painter* (1983), also for discussion of Beazley's technique and the treatment of anatomical detail.

**84** On his Troy scenes, J. Boardman, *AK* 19 (1976) 3–18.

**85** E. Kunze-Götte, *Der Kleophrades-maler unter Malern schwarzfiguriger Amphoren* (1992).

**86** Monographs with complete illustration: D. Buitron-Oliver, *Douris* (1995); N. Kunisch, *Makron* (1997). The cup painters – *EGVP* 132–140, figs. 214–318; Robertson, chs. 3, 4.

**87** *ARFH* I, 9–10; D. Williams, *RA* 1996, 142–144; and see below, Chapter 3.

**88** J. Boardman, *Greek Sculpture. The Classical Period* (1985) chs. 3–5.

**89** For the painter, Robertson, 180–185.

**90** Early classical red figure – *ARFH* II, ch. 2, figs. 1–108; Robertson, ch. 5.

**91** J.R. Mertens, *Attic White-ground* (1977), 184–185 for [127]. *Archaiologike Ephemeris* 1970, pls. 10–12 (colour).

**92** For [128] *The Art of the Ancient Mediterranean World* (Nagoya/Boston, 1999) no. 177. *ARFH* II, ch. 4, figs. 252–284. I. Wehgartner, *Attisch weissgrundige Keramik* (1983) for a comprehensive study of shapes, technique and use; and in *Copenhagen* 640–651 on analysis of colours. On style, D.C. Kurtz, *Attic White Lekythoi* (1975). Achilles Painter lekythoi in Athens, O. Alexandri, *Leukes Lekythoi* (1998), good photos.

**93** The painter and his workshop, Robertson, 160–167.

**94** Mannerists – *ARFH* I, 179–193, figs. 319–349; J.D. Beazley, *The Pan Painter* (1974); T. Mannack, forthcoming.

**95** *ARFH* II, ch. 5, figs. 285–371. Robertson, chs. 7, 8.

**96** Thus, L. Burn, *The Meidias Painter* (1987).

**97** Wedding imagery, V. Sabetai in *APP* 319–335. The women on vases, Webster, ch. 17.

**98** As *ARFH* II, figs. 337, 367.

**99** *ARFH* II, figs. 387–391. M. Robertson in *Periplous* 244.

**100** 4th-century red figure, *EGVP* ch. 6, figs. 372–428; Robertson, ch. 9. H. Metzger, *Les représentations dans la* céramique attique du IVe siècle (1951), and *Recherches sur l'imagerie athénienne* (1965), for 4th-century iconography.

**101** For Xenophantos, M. Tiverios in *APP* 269–284; J. Boardman, *Persia and the West* (2000) 213–215, on fig. 5.93. On Classical relief wares, A. Greifenhagen, *Beiträge zur antiken Reliefkeramik* (1963); G. Hübner, *JdI* 108 (1993) 321–351.

**102** O. Palagia, *The Pediments of the Parthenon* (1993) 44, pls. 10, 11.

**103** Robertson, 236, with references.

**104** B.R. MacDonald, *AJA* 85 (1981) 159–168: the Suessula Painter, *ARFH* II, 168.

**105** *Getty Vases* 5 (1991) 13–17; essentially 'Six technique'.

**106** D.C. Kurtz, *Athenian White Lekythoi* (1975) Part Five.

**107** Ibid., 125, pl. 66.

**108** S. Howard and F.P. Johnson, *AJA* 81 (1977) 1–30.

**109** Stamped cups with figures, B.A. Sparkes, *AK* 11 (1968) 3–16.

**110** For the black vases of Athens, B.A. Sparkes and L. Talcott, *Agora* XII (1970).

**111** This is 'West Slope' (of the Acropolis) ware, but made all over Greece: S. Rotroff, *Hesperia* 60 (1991) 59–102. On Attic gilt black gloss, G. Kopcke, *AM* 79 (1964) 22–84.

**112** J. Boardman, *RA* 1987, 284, on the coin usage.

**113** *RVSIS* is the main source, summarizing Trendall's major books of lists and pictures. *The Art of South Italy. Vases from Magna Graecia* (edd. M.E. Mayo/K. Hamma, 1982) for excellent pictures and comment on subjects and technique.

**114** *RVSIS* 9–11 on shapes.

**115** As at Gioia del Colle: *Monumenti Antichi* 45 (1961) 151, 183.

**116** H. Lohmann, *JdI* 97 (1982) 191–249, for construction peculiarities and use in Apulian.

**117** H. Hoffmann, *Tarentine Rhyta* (1967).

**118** Questions of Athenians working in the west, M. Denoyelle in *APP* 395–405.

**119** A.D. Trendall, *Early South Italian Vase Painters* (1974) pl. 9.

**120** *RVSIS* 74–78, 81–83, 92–94.

**121** For [*151*] Trendall/Webster, II.1,6.

**122** G. Schneider-Herrmann, *The Samnites of the 4th century* BC *as depicted on Campanian vases and in other sources* (1996).

**123** For [*152,153*], Trendall/Webster, IV,35 and IV,30.

**124** *RVSIS* figs. 201–211. M. Schmidt, *Der Dareiosmaler und sein Umkreis* (1960).

**125** On the *naiskoi*, A Pontrandolfo et al., *AION* 10 (1988) 181–202.

**126** Trendall/Webster, IV.5,4.

**127** The fighting scenes with Persians, A. Stewart, *Faces of Power* (1993) 150–157, who is sceptical. *RVSIS* fig. 201, the vase fight; *The Oxford History of Classical Art* (ed. J. Boardman, 1993) 174–175, the mosaic. On this and the Darius vase, J. Boardman (forthcoming, *Prospettiva* Studi . . . M. Cristofani).

**128** The Hellenistic pottery of Athens, S. Rotroff, *Agora* XXIX (1997). For some 'West Slope' Corinthian craters, I. McPhee, *Hesperia* 66 (1997) 99–145.

**129** *CVA* Castle Ashby, pl. 57,97. Gnathia ware – J.R. Green, *Gnathia Pottery . . . Bonn* (1976); and in *Getty Vases* 3 (1986) 115–138 (124–126 for [*160*]).

**130** E.g., J. Boardman, *Greek Art* (1996) 248, fig. 252, Hesse Group; J.D. Beazley, *Etruscan Vase Painting* (1947) 208–209.

**131** Relief bowls, see especially S. Rotroff, *Agora* XXII (1982); P. Puppo, *Le coppe megaresi in Italia* (1995). U. Hausmann, *Hellenistische Reliefbecher* (1959); U. Sinn, *Die homerischen Becher* (1979). H. Gropengiesser in *Tainia* (Fest. R. Hampe, edd. H.A. Cahn, E. Simon, 1980) 307–332 for [*162*]. For the type of [*161*] *Agora* XXII, 21–22.

**132** R. Pagenstecher, *Die calenische Reliefkeramik* (1909), his no. 119 is [*163*]; M.-O. Jentel, *Les gutti et les askoi à reliefs* (1976).

**133** Sparkes, 54–57; A.H. Enklaar, *BABesch* 60 (1985) 106–151, 60 (1986) 41–65. Archaic and classical predecessors of the general type are being studied by S. Paspalas (including 'wavy-line' ware).

**134** R.A. Higgins, *Tanagra and the Figurines* (1986) 59, fig. 60 [*167*]. Cook, chs. 6, 7, for the plain and Hellenistic wares; also especially J.W. Hayes in *LGV* ch. 8. Glazed ware – H. Gabelmann, *JdI* 89 (1974) 260–307.

**135** V.R. Anderson-Stojanovic, *AJA* 91 (1987) 105–122 for unguentaria shapes.

## Chapter 2 (pp. 128–138)

**1** A *possible* exception for the man who *epoiesen* (erected or paid for?) a grave monument carved by another: L.H. Jeffery, *BSA* 57 (1962) 139–140. *ABFH* 11–12, Cook, 243–245, and Robertson, 3–4 on signature theories.

**2** Robertson, 112.

**3** G. Morelli, *Italian Painters* (trans., C.J. Ffoulkes, 1892) 78.

**4** 'The Study of Art History', *University Quarterly* 10.3 (May, 1956) 11. That what we detect is not quite the 'style' but the essential 'fingerprint', is demonstrated by R. Wollheim in *Art in Society* (edd. M. Greenhalgh and V. Megaw, 1978) 3–14.

**5** On changes of mind and subsequent justification, P. Rouet and H. Giroux, in *CPG* 145–153, 207–210.

**6** Thus M. Beard in *Times Literary Supplement* Sept. 12, 1986, 1013, a superficial and combative review regularly cited by the very few who also cannot understand Beazley's method. The technique was indeed developed in a period much influenced by the approaches of Darwin and Freud, but in application relied more on the former.

**7** Notably in A. Furtwängler on the Athena Lemnia, especially in *Masterpieces of Greek Sculpture* (1895) 18–19.

**8** M. Vickers' persistent association of him with the Arts and Crafts movement is quite misleading – as in *Artful Crafts* (1994) 82–83, misunderstanding (n. 37) Beazley's comment on bogus classicism; see J. Boardman, *RA* 1987, 295. Beazley may have met Berenson at E.P. Warren's house in Lewes.

**9** J. Sherwood, *No Golden Journey* (1973) for the life of

Flecker, with much on Beazley; J.M. Munro, *James Elroy Flecker* (1976) 26, 32, 54. A.L. Rowse, *Friends and Contemporaries* (1989) 287–297, speculates on the nature of the relationship. For Beazley's life and academic friendships in Oxford and Cambridge see B. Ashmole's obituary of him in *Proceedings of the British Academy* 56 (1970) 443–461, reprinted in *Beazley and Oxford* (ed. D.C. Kurtz, 1985) 57–71.

**10** Flecker had not been abandoned, though he did eventually marry in 1911 (and died in 1915). Both Flecker and Gow were with Beazley in Paris in 1910 when the latter was studying the pots in the Louvre. For Gow see F.H. Sandbach in *Proceedings of the British Academy* 64 (1978) 437–439; H. Lloyd-Jones in *Dictionary of National Biography*.

**11** *Classical Review* 34 (1920) 116–117.

**12** *JHS* 30 (1910) 38–69.

**13** D.C. Kurtz in *Getty Vases* II (1985) 237–250, describes fully Beazley's technique and its history; see also Robertson, 2–6, answering criticisms, and in *Beazley and Oxford* (above, n. 9) 26, 28. P. Rouet's forthcoming *Beazley and Pottier* discusses in detail the intellectual background to Beazley's work.

**14** *Japanese Prints* (ed. G. Fahr-Becker, 1999) 124, 99.

**15** The drawings are from various sources. I have not come across such Morellian studies in the literature on the prints, probably because it is not needed with signed works.

**16** I. Scheibler in *CPG* 211–215 on other attribution criteria.

**17** Exekias' writing, L. Rebillard in *Phoinikeia Grammata* (ed. C. Baurain et al., 1991) 549–564. Epiktetos learned to spell properly late in his career: *egraphsen* instead of *egrasphen*.

**18** M. Beard in *Looking at Greek Vases* (edd. T. Rasmussen and N. Spivey, 1991) 16–17.

**19** A.D. Trendall in Kurtz (ed., above, n. 9) 31–42, on Beazley and South Italian.

**20** It is still possible to detect two hands at work on one geometric vase; cf. J. Boardman, *Gnomon* 1970, 495–496.

**21** M. Roaf, *Sculptures and Sculptors at Persepolis* (*Iran* 21, 1983), and Greenhalgh and Megaw (edd.), op.cit. (n. 4) 133–145. Application to Greek sculpture has proved less easy: B. Ashmole, *BSA* 24 (1919/21) 78–87; *JHS* 71 (1951) 13–28; *ProcBritAcad* 48 (1963) 213–233.

**22** M. Robertson in *Beazley Addenda* (edd. L. Burn and R. Glynn, 1982) xi-xviii, explains them.

**23** A pioneering work is H. Bloesch, *Formen Attischer Schalen* (1940), followed by many later works on other shapes, the study being much helped by the growing practice of publishing drawn profiles of whole vases or details of foot and lip.

**24** B. Cohen, *Met.Mus.J.* 26 (1991) 49–95, the graffiti.

**25** O.R. Impey and M. Pollard, *OJA* 4 (1985) 157–164.

## Chapter 3 (pp. 139–152)

J.D. Beazley's 'Potter and Painter in ancient Athens' (1944) is little dated: now in *Greek Vases. Lectures by J.D. Beazley* (ed. D.C. Kurtz, 1989) ch. 3. Arafat/Morgan give a valuable if speculative survey of potters' life and work in Athens and Corinth, and the excavation evidence for their working quarters. Important other recent discussion of the Attic scene by D. Williams in *Culture* 139–160. *CPP* has valuable essays on production and consumption, relevant to this and the following chapter, but could not be taken full account of for this book.

**1** Scheibler, 100–107 for a good selection; *EGVP* fig. 409.1–6; Noble, figs. 75, 231–238.

**2** The Athenian potteries, Arafat/Morgan, 321–322; E.-B. Valavanis, in *The Archaeology of Athens and Attica under the Democracy* (ed. W.J. Coulson, et al., 1994) 45–54, with map: there were several 4th-century potteries west of the Areopagus. J.M. Camp in *Culture* 225–241 on the placing of the Agora; also, J.K. Papadopoulos in *Greek, Roman and Byzantine Studies* 37 (1996) 107–128; D.Harris-Cline, *AJA* 94 (1999) 310–320.

**3** J.D. Beazley in *Proc.Brit.Acad.* 30 (1944), reprinted in *Greek Vases* (ed. D.C. Kurtz, 1989) ch. 3; D. Williams in *Culture* 141–142; C. Wagner in *Periplous* 383–387.

**4** Cook, 234–236, and *BSA* 56 (1961) 64–67; Sparkes, 21–24.

**5** F. Blondé and J.Y. Perrault, *BCH* Suppl. 23 (1992) 11–40. And generally on the location of kilns, F. Villard and F. Blondé in *CPG* 107–120.

**6** *Arch.Ergon Makedonias* 7 (1993[1997]) 171–182; *RA* 1998, 386.

**7** More recent practice by seasonal pithos-makers has been described: R. Hampe and A. Winter, *Bei Töpfern und Töpferinnen in Kreta, Messenien und Zypern* (1962); *Bei Töpfern und Zieglern in süd-Italien, Sizilien und Griechenland* (1965).

**8** J. Boardman, *JHS* 76 (1956) 20–21.

**9** Robertson, 292–295; P. Valavanis in *APP* 85–95 (Panathenaics). For potting in families also Plato, *Republic* 467a.

**10** M.M. Eisman, *AJA* 82 (1978) 394–399, for details about [175]; also J.-J. Maffre in *Thasos* (edd. Ch. Koukouli-Chrysanthaki et al., 1999) 270–278. All are figured in Scheibler, 80, 83, 105, 111.

**11** L. Hannestad in *Copenhagen* 222–230; Webster, 1–3; Cook, 262; Johnston, 50–51.

**12** *Pax* 679–681, 688–692, *Nubes* 1065–1066, *Equites* 1304; *Ecclesiazousai* 248–253 (Kephalos). W. Miller, *Daedalus and Thespis* (1932) 690–693 for these and other texts.

**13** D.W.J. Gill in *Pots and Pans* (ed. M. Vickers, 1986) 19–23.

**14** Diodorus 19, 2, 7; 20, 63, 4.

**15** Athenaeus 28b (Kritias; West, *Iambi et elegi graeci* II, 52, B2).

**16** Plato, *Hippias Major* 288d, 289a.

**17** J. Boardman, *Greek Emporio* (1967) pl. 34.241; *EGVP* fig. 440.

**18** A.-F. Laurens in *Culture* 165.

**19** P.V. Stanley, *Münstersche Beiträge zur Antiken Handelsgeschichte* 17 (1998) 29–50.

**20** F. Canciani, *AK* 21 (1978) 17–22.

**21** Strabo 304 remarks the practice 'in old times'. On the foreign names on vases see now D. Williams in *Culture* 143, 151–155.

**22** D.A. Jackson, *East Greek Influence on Attic Vases* (1976); B.B. Shefton, *Getty Vases* 4 (1989) 41–72. An unusual instance, the copying of the Chian chalice shape: Sophilos, *ABFH* fig. 8; N. Malagardis in *Phos kykladikon* (*Eis mneme N. Zapheiropoulou*, 1999) 215–216.
**23** Our [*43*], Rhodian? plate; Athens, Acr. 2134 (Doric Athenaiai; *ABV* 347); Louvre E 732 (Keian on Attic?; *LSAG* 297); New York L68.142.8 (Samian on Attic; *Met.Mus.Bull.* 1969, 432–433, and cf. Douris' signatures); Berlin 1147 (Sicyonian on Corinthian; *NC* 169; F. Lorber, *Inschriften auf korinthischen Vasen* no. 46); uncertain variety of Corinthian on the Chigi vase [*30*], ibid., no. 13.
**24** G. Schaus, *AJA* 83 (1979) 102–106; and in *Cyrene* II (1985) no. 153; by the Naucratis Painter. Compare the Libyan (?) name painted in an Athenian cup found in Cyrenaica: J. Boardman and J.W. Hayes, *Tocra* I (1966) 169, no. 1040, fig. 51, pl. 76.
**25** H. Immerwahr, *Attic Script* (1990) Appendix 1.
**26** A. Seeberg uses this to suggest that painters might be the senior partners, not potters, which seems unlikely: *JHS* 114 (1994) 162–164.
**27** J. Boardman, *Iran* 36 (1998) 5.
**28** In *Greek Settlements*... (edd. A.M. Snodgrass and G. Tsetskhladze, 2000).
**29** Herodotus 4, 152. Aegina used Corinthian and Attic vases. E. Walter-Karydi in *APP* 385–394 for early Attic black figure. S.P. Morris argued that the apparently Protoattic Black and White vases found there were made locally, but her case has not been widely accepted: *The Black and White Style* (1984).
**30** A Sostratos scratched his name on an early 6th-century Ionian cup taken to Ischia: Ischia 281908, Tomb 782; and one dedicated a Chian bowl at Naucratis at about the same time (*EGVP* fig. 311); while at the end of the century one is hailed on a Pioneer vase together with Euthymides (*ARV* 33,8). An attempt to reconstruct his family of merchants through the 6th century, M. Torelli, *Parola del Passato* 37 (1982) 318. Also on him, M. Cristofani in *CPG* 345–349.
**31** J.R. Green, *JHS* 81 (1961) 73–75, argues that this is a metal workshop, and he may be right. I. Kehrberg, *Hephaistos* 4 (1982) 25–35, mounts some arguments against.
**32** Cf. *ARFH* I, fig. 297; the man says 'keep still'.
**33** Robertson, 31–32; Arafat/Morgan, 320; A. Schäfer, *Unterhaltung beim griechischen Symposion* (1997) 54–55, thinks it could refer to both art and dancing.
**34** J. Frel in *AGAI* 147–158 on this vase and on Euphronios and his fellows. On the Leagros kalos inscriptions, J. Boardman in *Euphronios* (edd. M. Cygielman et al. 1992) 45–50. Webster, 21–25, thought the *kaloi* were bespoke by the customer, which seems most improbable; the demonstrable common factor is the painter.
**35** J. Maxmin, *Greece and Rome* 21 (1974) 178–180.
**36** Webster, 15–18, for associations of potters and painters.
**37** *EGVP* 28; J-R. Gisler, *Archaiognosia* 8 (1993/4) 11–95; N. Kourou in *Euboica* (edd. M. Bats and B.

d'Agostino, 1998) 167–177. Did he work at Oropos?
**38** *EGVP* 214.
**39** *ABFH* 14–19.
**40** B.R. MacDonald, *AJA* 85 (1981) 159–168.
**41** *Papers on the Amasis Painter and his World* (ed. M. True, 1987) covers all aspects. And for Amasis as potter H. Mommsen in *APP* 17–34.
**42** *EGVP* fig. 440. *Oxford History of Classical Art* (ed. J. Boardman, 1993) pl. VII, signature at right.

## Chapter 4 (pp. 153–167)

An important study of early trade, especially à propos of Naukratis, is in A. Möller, *Naukratis* (forthcoming). The essential study on prices and merchant marks is A.W. Johnston, *Trademarks on Greek Vases* (1979), and see n. 2, below. Generally on pots and profit and important issues of trade, J. Salmon in *Periplous* 245–252. There are also important essays on pottery distribution and consumption in *The Complex Past of Pottery* (ed. J.-P. Crielaard, 1999), which appeared too late for further reference here.

**1** D. Williams in *Culture* 157–159.
**2** He gives a masterly survey in ch. 9 of *LGV*, based on his *Trademarks on Greek Vases* (1972), and in several articles: *Greece and Rome* 21 (1974) 138–152, summary; in *Papers on the Amasis Painter* (ed. M. True, 1987) 125–140; in *AJA* 82 (1978) 222–226 on lists of contents; in *CPG* 397–401; in *Periplous* 166–168.
**3** Johnston, 234–238, and in *BSA* 70 (1975) 145–167.
**4** I. Vokotopoulou and A.P. Christidis, *Kadmos* 34 (1995) 5–12.
**5** M. Torelli, *Parola del Passato* 37 (1982) 304–325.
**6** *GO* 206 with refs., 277; see above, Chapter 3, n. 30.
**7** *CVA* Bonn 1, 32–3, pls. 29–38; *ARV* 1180–2, Painter of the Athens Dinos; J.H. Oakley in *BCH* Suppl. 23 (1992) 195–203.
**8** D. Gill, *Papers of the British School at Rome* 43 (1988) 1–12.
**9** A. Yardeni, *Bull. Amer. School of Oriental Research* 293 (1994) 67–78. E. Lipinski, *Orientalia Lovaniensia Periodica* 25 (1994) 61–68.
**10** A.W. Johnston in *Il commercio etrusco arcaico* (Incontro Rome 1983 [1985]) 249–255; N. Spivey in *LGV* ch. 6.
**11** C. Dehl-von Kaenel, *Münstersche Beiträge zur Antiken Handelsgeschichte* 13 (1994) 55–83. R. Osborne, *Antiquity* 70 (1996) 31–44, on the non-opportunistic character of much early trade, even in pottery.
**12** T.B.L. Webster argued for this in *Potter and Patron in Classical Athens* (1972), still an interesting analysis of the subject, stimulated by the possibility of a statistical approach offered by Beazley's lists.
**13** J. Frel, *Taras* 12 (1992) 131–134. The Agora publication of black figure shows that Panathenaics might be painted within at any period (*Agora* XXIII, nos. 226–338).
**14** J. Gran-Aymerich in *CPG* 449–453.
**15** Much cited: Sparkes, 129, fig. VI.3; Scheibler, 147, fig. 129; A.W. Johnston, *AJA* 82 (1978) 222–226. The 'stamnoi' (7 obols each) are what we call pelikai; the

oxides and oxybapha are small (more than ten an obol) for vinegar (? – *oxos* = vinegar); the small lekythia (even cheaper) and lekythoi (half obol) we know as for oil, but the shape of the former (called *mik* = *mikra* = small) is not clear; maybe plain. The graffito probably indicates opportune packing of very small vases inside craters, stacked upside down, visibly showing what more there was in the batch (box, basket?).

**16** Scheibler, 146, fig. 127.

**17** Athenaeus 164f-165a, 229b (Alexis, *Phyg.* fr. 259 Kassel/Austin).

**18** E. Vanderpool, *Hesperia* 36 (1967) 187–189.

**19** On pot prices Johnston is the prime source. See also Sparkes, 129–131. The denunciation of Greek vases comes near to hysteria, but by far more disturbing is the treatment of evidence. The fullest statement of the troubled view is by M. Vickers and D. Gill (virtually the only believers by now) in *Artful Crafts* (1994). Thus, a red figure vase is diagnosed as being worth, by modern standards, 26p (40 cents). It seems to have been worth just under an obol in antiquity, that is, one-sixth of a working day's wage; which means that the standards Vickers and Gill employ, to make a true modern comparison, imply a modern working day's wage of just £1.50 ($2.40)! I review their book in *Classical Review* 1996, 123–126 (and see C. Rolley in *Topoi* 5.2 (1995) 517–522 *'un livre qui ne mérite que l'oubli'*). Also, D. Williams, *RA* 1996, 227–231, on details of the meretricious mathematics, and A.W. Johnston, *Acta Hyperborea* 3 (1991) 403–409.

**20** Boardman, *Diffusion* 304, fig. 8.11; not all the attachments were for masking mends.

**21** R.J. Hopper, *Trade and Industry in Classical Greece* (1979) 101.

**22** See above, n. 9; A.W. Johnston in *Periplous* 168–169. The imports included empty Greek pots, some of which are described as 'not coated', more likely to mean not treated with pitch or the like than 'undecorated', it seems.

**23** See last note.

**24** *OJA* 7 (1988) 31 refers.

**25** B.B. Shefton in *Catania* I, 85–98.

**26** Xenophon, *Anabasis* 7, 5, 14.

**27** Aristophanes, *Acharnes* 927.

**28** Scrap paper (failed plays) could be used by a grocer for packing: Chamaileon (fr. 43 Wehrli) in Athenaeus 374b; cf. Horace, *Epistulae* 2.1.269–270. Vase fragments (*ostraka*) were themselves used as scrap paper, for messages, voting slips, etc. Mr Pooter's son said of his father's diary ('of a Nobody') 'If it had been written on larger paper, Guv., we might get a fair price from a butterman for it' (Dec. 18).

**29** A.J. Parker, *International Journal of Nautical Archaeology* 24 (1995) 88–95 (cited, 89); and ibid., 21 (1992) 89–90, for examples.

**30** J. Boardman, *OJA* 7 (1988) 27–33 for comparisons with other cargoes.

**31** G. Trias, *REA* 89.3–4 (1987) 21–50 on the Athenian pottery in the Le Sec Phoenician wreck off Spain; of the red figure one-third were bell craters, more than half

cups. C. Campenon, ibid., 179–103, on the way export to Spain increased after around 400 BC but with fewer shapes and of poorer quality. B.B. Shefton in *CPG* 463–479 (Lancut Group).

**32** R.J. Hopper, *Trade and Industry in Classical Greece* 1979) 51–52.

**33** K. de Vries in *APP* 447, 453–454. There is a mass of Attic black figure also at Daskyleion: K. Görkay, *Asia Minor Studien* 34 (1999) 1–100.

**34** Repairs – Noble, 94; D. von Bothmer, *AJA* 76 (1972) 9–11; M. Elston, *GettyJ* 18 (1990) 53–68.

**35** *EGVP* fig. 479.

**36** Noble, 82, figs. 249–251; K. Schauenburg, *AA* 1974, 156–157.

**37** Volume of production – Cook, 262; J.H. Oakley in *BCH* Suppl. 23 (1992) 199–200.

**38** In an Oxford thesis by Margaret Curry (1993); and in *Periplous* 80–88.

**39** M. Bats (ed.), *Marseille grecque et la Gaule* (1992) 149–234, esp. 229–231.

**40** See J. Salmon, *Wealthy Corinth* (1984) 132 for thoughts on the volume of Corinthian pottery exported to Megara Hyblaea in Sicily.

**41** Their distribution in Italy: M. Cristofani and M. Martelli in *Catania* II, 9–25.

**42** Nikosthenes, *ABFH* 64–65; ibid., fig. 176, a chalcidizing cup, cf. *EGVP* fig. 480. On Etruscan shapes in Attic, T. Rasmussen, *AntK* 28 (1985) 33–39.

**43** *EGVP* fig. 478.

**44** *ABFH* fig. 220.

**45** N. Malagardis in *APP* 35–53 on the shape.

**46** H.A.G. Brijder in *APP* 1–4.

**47** *ARFH* II, 39–40; H. Hoffmann, *Sotades* (1997), with some rather bizarre interpretations.

**48** A. Lezzi-Hafter in *APP* 353–369.

**49** L. Burn, *Getty Vases* 5 (1991) 107–130.

**50** L. Todisco and M.A. Sisto, *Mélanges . . . l'école française de Rome* 110 (1998) 571–608, collect all these shapes.

## Chapter 5 (pp. 168–187)

For a good introduction to iconography in all media there is T.H. Carpenter's handbook, *Art and Myth in Ancient Greece* (1991), and the very full resources of the eight-volume *LIMC*; also a good range of essays and bibliography in *AGAI*. For myth in early art a useful compendium in G. Ahlberg, *Myth and Epos in Early Greek Art* (1992). The range of non-mythical scenes has attracted renewed interest in recent years, no little stimulated by C. Bérard et.al. (edd., 1989), *A City of Images*.

There is a very detailed (rather literary in approach) series of studies by K. Schefold; the first two volumes are available in English: *Myth and Legend in Early Greek Art* (1966), *Gods and Heroes in Late Archaic Greek Art* (1992); four others in German take the story down to Hellenistic.

**1** *ARV* 364,46; *CVA* Edinburgh, pl. 23.7–8.

**2** H.A. Shapiro in *Cultural Poetics in Archaic Greece* (edd. C. Dougherty/L. Kurke, 1993) 92–107.

**3** In *Myth into Art* (1994), an excellent guide to the problem, H.A. Shapiro starts from literary versions of several stories, but the art he cites shows clearly how great the divergencies could be, sometimes fundamental.

**4** M. Tiverios, *AM* 96 (1981) 145–161, pl. 44; J. Boardman in *Kotinos* (Fest. E. Simon, edd. H. Froning et al., 1992) 167–170.

**5** *CVA* Basel IV.

**6** D. Morris et al., *Gestures* (1979).

**7** H. Mommsen, *Exekias* I (1997) col. pl. 2.

**8** The Affecter: T.J. McNiven, *Gestures in Attic Vase Painting* (diss. 1982) 46, D12B, D15B; H. Mommsen, *Der Affekter* (1975) 57, e.g., pls. 16, 17, 73, 112, 101, 103. The figures are watchers of various scenes so the gesture may be expostulatory. In general on gestures, McNiven, op.cit.; G. Neumann, *Gesten und Gebärden in der griechischen Kunst* (1965).

**9** Boardman, *Diffusion* 124–145.

**10** C.B. Donnan, *Moche Art of Peru* (1978) 9. I am indebted to Professor Donnan for comment on the phenomenon.

**11** J. Boardman, *AK* 19 (1976) 13–14, pl. 1.3.

**12** On the iconography of corpses, M. Halm-Tisserant, *Ktema* 18 (1993) 215–226.

**13** The early scenes, Ahlberg, 35–38, 71–72, figs. 44–52, 107–109. J. Boardman in *Eumousia* (Studies . . . A. Cambitoglou, ed. J.-P. Descoeudres, 1990) 60, where another fighting formula with chariots is discussed as well as general principles, and *Praktika . . . Akademias Athenon* 72 (1997 [1999]) 641–661. *LIMC* I (1981) 185–193.

**14** Amphiaraos scenes, *LIMC* I (1981) 694–695, 706–708. Warrior departures, W. Wrede, *AM* 41 (1916) 221–374.

**15** J. Boardman, *GettyJ* 1 (1974) 7–14.

**16** J. Boardman in *Eye* 24–25, pl. 5a.

**17** M. Halm-Tisserant has useful studies on this matter, e.g., *AntK* 29 (1986) 8–22, *REA* 86 (1984) 135–170.

**18** For the patterns on sculpture see J. Boardman, *Greek Sculpture. Archaic Period* (1978) figs. 128, 129, 151, 155. Woven myth: Euripides, *Ion* 196–197.

**19** As on two-frieze calyx craters, such as our [226]: J.H. Oakley in *Amsterdam* 119–127.

**20** T. Seki, *Untersuchungen zum Gehältnis von Gefässform und Malerei attischer Schalen* (1985).

**21** Any which appear thus in this book are from the choice of the supplier of the print. I have chosen, where I can, views which show the vase as an object in a setting rather than as a catalogue entry, but there are few of these, often taken by the author in non-studio conditions.

## Chapter 6 (pp. 189–243)

**1** A. Schnapp, in *Copenhagen* 574.

**2** J.N. Coldstream, *Greek Geometric Pottery* (1968) 29–41; *EGVP* 25–28.

**3** For early figures see *EGVP* figs. 13, 15 (Euboean, archers), 21–23 (Cretan), 40, 41 (Attic).

**4** An Eretrian vase shows files of chariots with warriors mounting beside the charioteer – or dismounting in the later attested exercise of the *apobatai* (as on the Parthenon frieze): *AK* 42 (1999) 129, fig. 2 and pl. 22.2.

**5** On the shields especially, J. Boardman in *AGAI* 26–32. The later 'Boeotian' shield with smaller cut-outs and like a hoplite shield, but worn with a baldric, may be a parade shield and often shown for heroes (as [203]), as also on Boeotian coins.

**6** For Bronze Age and Egyptian motifs apparently echoed in the Geometric period, J.L. Benson, *Horse, Bird and Man* (1970); K. Sheedy, *AM* 105 (1990) 117–151.

**7** J. Boardman, *JHS* 86 (1966) 1–5.

**8** K.F. Johansen started discussion of this piece, identifying it as from the *Iliad*: see G. Ahlberg, *Myth and Epos in Early Greek Art* (1992) 28–29. Later writers are less optimistic but some still struggle to make a story of it.

**9** On the twins, J. Boardman in *AGAI* 25–26, *EGVP* 54; Ahlberg, 32–35: note their isolation in her chronological survey, p. 39. A.M. Snodgrass, in an otherwise uncontroversial divorce of Homer from early art, clings to both shields and twins: *Homer and the Artists* (1998) 28–33 (20–22 on our [209]); his fig. 10 is the *least* plausible of the alleged twins – there are no 'two torsos' at all and the formula is exactly that for horse teams, not deemed monstrous.

**10** A good mixture on the later Attic plate, *EGVP* fig. 201, which is more like metalwork than most.

**11** J. Boardman in *Le Bestiaire d'Héraclès* (edd. C. Bonnet et al., 1998) 29–30 on this and other sources for aspects of Heraclean iconography.

**12** *GO* 77–79 for eastern origins of these monsters.

**13** Eastern inspiration, J. Boardman, *Archaic Greek Gems* (1968) 37–39; in Corinth, M. Halm-Tisserant in *Copenhagen* 211–221. For [214], H.G. Payne, *Necrocorinthia* (1931) 80, fig. 23A; for [215] *Para* 104.

**14** J. Boardman in *Eumousia* (see Chapter 5, n. 13) 57–62.

**15** M. Davies, *JHS* 106 (1986) 182–183; J. Boardman in *LGV* 83–84.

**16** C. Jubier-Galinier in *Le Bestiaire d'Héraclès* (edd. C. Bonnet et al., 1998) 79, pl. 8.

**17** I. Scheibler thus argues for certain preferences for the decoration of Attic belly amphorae, though the function-application is here less obvious than it is for, e.g., pelikai and the use of oil: *JdI* 102 (1987) 57–118.

**18** I am yet to be totally convinced that the 'Athena' head on Corinthian coins is not really an armed Aphrodite, who was a far more important deity in the city.

**19** An abortive speculation as early as *BSA* 47 (1952) 38, and with H.W. Parke finishing an article left by T.J. Dunbabin at his death, in *JHS* 77 (1957) 276–282. The main statement is in *RA* 1972, 57–72 (Phye), followed by *JHS* 95 (1975) 1–12 (Kerberos, music, athlete); *RA* 1978, 227–234 (tripod, stag); *Catania* I, 26–30 (Priam Painter); in *Eye* 1–28 (Amazons, Theseus); in *Studien zur Mythologie* (Fest. K. Schauenburg, 1986) 127–132 (on the pyre); in *Fest. Nikolaus Himmelmann* (19) 191–195 (at sea); above, n. 11 (animals). The most serious objector has been R.M. Cook in *JHS* 107 (1987) 167–169, answered in *JHS* 109 (1989) 108–109 and see *Amsterdam* 239–247.

**20** Theseus taking over from Heracles and the Amazon stories, J. Boardman in *Eye* 1–28. For 5th-century Theseus, D. Castriota, *Myth, Ethos and Actuality* (1992) *passim*.

**21** To deny the proposition because Trojan War episodes cannot readily be associated with tyrant policy is poor method: B. Knittlinger, *Die att. Aristokratie und ihre Helden* (1997); cf. *AJA* 103 (1999) 142–143. The War offered no paradigms for Athenian civic behaviour, except possibly in the figure of Ajax, borrowed by Athens from Aegina to become an Attic tribal hero: possible intimations in art, J. Boardman, *AJA* 82 (1978) 11–25.

**22** J. Boardman in *Philolakon* (Studies . . . H.W. Catling, ed. J.M. Sanders, 1993) 25–29.

**23** J. Boardman in *AGAI* 15–25.

**24** E. Simon, in *Eye* 123–148 for Aeschylus' satyr plays and vases: her pl. 36b is [*225*]; Aeschylus' satyr play *Thalamopoioi* ('Interior Decorators') is invoked. Trendall/Webster, ch. 2; J.R. Green, *Theatre in Ancient Greek Society* (1994); and with E. Handley, *Images of the Greek Theatre* (1995) ch. 3. A good account of the scenes now by R. Krumeich in *idem* et al., *Das griechische Satyrspiel* (1999), where texts and subjects are also discussed. Earlier men-satyrs: *EGVP* fig. 487.2, *ABFH* fig. 247. A satyr-player holding his mask, *Hesperia* 68 (1999) 257, fig. 2.

**25** For Pandora, J. Boardman in *Mouseion* (Fest. O. Alexandri, forthcoming).

**26** *CVA* Basel III, pls. 6–7.

**27** Trendall/Webster, ch. 4; A.D. Trendall, *Phlyax Vases* (1967); O. Taplin, *Comic Angels* (1993); J.R. Green, *Theatre in Ancient Greek Society* (1994).

**28** *RVSIS* 264–266.

**29** On actors in Athens, E. Csapo and W.J. Slater, *The Context of Ancient Drama* (1995) ch. 4A.

**30** *LCS* 321,702; Trendall/Webster III.3,31.

**31** Trendall/Webster is devotedly philodramatic. Green, *Theatre* – an invaluable guide to the whole subject of theatre and art in all periods, and in *BICS* 41 (1996) 17–30, is more careful but sure of a stage connection: 'Tarentines, and perhaps others, turned to the theatre as a measure, a yardstick, in much the same way that people turned to the Bible in later ages. Theatre, and the stories it told, was the common reference point'. L. Giuliani, ibid., 71–96, is more iconocentric but believes the mythological narratives played a role in funeral addresses; also his *Tragik, Trauer und Trost* (1995). Green, *Theatre* fig. 3.6 for the Sicilian vase with stage columns (= *RVSIS* fig. 429; Trendall/Webster III.2.8, cf. III.6.1, another Sicilian, with stage); ibid., III.3.44 for the stage scene in Würzburg. See M. Bieber, *The History of the Greek and Roman Theater* (1961) for a good range of pictures, vases and other. On seeing and depicting theatre, J.R. Green in *Greek, Roman and Byzantine Studies* 32 (1991) 15–50.

**32** *EGVP* 258. And note the few Attic polychrome vases with comic scenes of the late 5th century, *ARFH* II, 223,

fig. 429; M. Crosby, *Hesperia* 24 (1955) 76–84.

**33** Best on the Attic Pronomos vase, *ARFH* II, fig. 324; Trendall/Webster, II,1.

**34** Lissarrague, ch. 7 and in *Periplous* 193–194.

**35** *CAH Pls. to Vols. V/VI* (1994) 121–128.

**36** For important essays on the symposion and bibliography see O. Murray (ed.), *Sympotica* (1990; J. Boardman, ibid., 122–134 for the furniture), and Lissarrague. A well illustrated study of all aspects of the vases and symposiac and Dionysiac behaviour in *Kunst der Schale* (edd. K. Vierneisel/B. Kaesar, 1990). Achilles at feast for the ransom of Hector, *ABFH* fig. 241, *ARFH* I, fig. 248. Phineus, *EGVP* fig. 479.

**37** *LIMC* IV (1988) 817–820.

**38** And Euphronios, *ARFH* I, fig. 27. For more dignified parties for seated ladies on black figure, S. Pingiatoglou, *AM* 109 (1994) 39–57.

**39** For the *hetairai*, J. Frel, *Rivista di Archeologia* 20 (1996) 38–53.

**40** H.G. Payne, *Necrocorinthia* (1931) pl. 38.1.

**41** *EGVP* figs. 385, 390. A. Seeberg, *Corinthian Komos Vases* (1971) collects; T.J. Smith, forthcoming, on komasts in general.

**42** T.H. Carpenter, *Dionysian Imagery in Archaic Greek Art* (1986) ch. 2.

**43** *ABFH* figs. 21–23, cf. 61.

**44** *EGVP* figs. 321, 336, 343 (East Greek); 414, 429, 433 (Laconian); 441, 442, 444, 449 (Boeotian). On the Laconian, T.J. Smith in *Sparta in Laconia* (edd. W.G. Cavanagh and S. Walker, 1998) ch. 7; *eadem* on komasts at the symposion in *Periplous* 309–319.

**45** *CVA* New Zealand I, pl. 8; Trendall/Webster, I,10.

**46** Discussed by D.C. Kurtz and J. Boardman, *Getty Vases* 3 (1986) 35–70. M.C. Miller's arguments (*AJA* 103 (1999) 223–253) for transvestism from the very beginning do not withstand close scrutiny of the figures nor allow for the otherwise totally male behaviour; these are not men behaving like women or even, in many cases [*239*], dressed like them, nor is there any ritual context.

**47** Placing the *komos*, C. Bron in *Copenhagen* 71–79.

**48** For satyr and maenad names, A. Kossatz-Deissmann, *Getty Vases* 5 (1991) 131–199.

**49** Lissarrague *passim* for satyrs, and in *Periplous* 190–197. T.H. Carpenter, *Dionysian Imagery in Archaic Greek Art* (1986) and . . . in *Fifth-century Athens* (1997).

**50** E.N. Gardiner, *Athletics of the Ancient World* (1930) remains the most valuable account; fuller is J. Jüthner, *Die athletischen Leibesübungen* (1965–8); and there is now a whole periodical devoted to the subject (*Nikephoros*), while collections of essays and exhibitions mark each modern Olympic Games.

**51** F.A.G. Beck, *Album of Greek Education* (1975).

**52** K.J. Dover, *Greek Homosexuality* (1978).

**53** A. Schnapp, *Le chasseur et la cité* (1998).

**54** See J. Boardman, *Catania* I, 21–23 for sample lists of the later 6th century, and in *LGV* ch. 4, for choice of scenes.

**55** Webster, ch. 2, on commissions.

**56** On the historical significance of the scene, J. Boardman in *Eye* 15–16.

**57** *ARFH* I, fig. 168.

**58** Early examples, and the general practice, J. Boardman, *BSA* 49 (1954) 183–201.

**59** *EGVP* fig. 409.6.

**60** Ibid., fig. 409.5, signed by the known painter Timonidas, cf. fig. 375.

**61** *EGVP* figs. 193, 192.

**62** Acr. 2578; *LIMC* II (1984) Athena no. 343, pl. 743.

**63** J.M. Cook and R.V. Nicholls, *The Temples of Athena* (1999) pl. 20b-c. Crete – *EGVP* fig. 273. Eleusis and other late, see J. Boardman, *JHS* 76 (1956) 24–25.

**64** A. Greifenhagen in *In Memoriam . . . Otto J. Brendel* (edd. L. Bonfante and H. von Heintze, 1976) 43–48.

**65** *EGVP* fig. 411, for the sacrifice (as J. Boardman, *Greek Art* (1996) fig. 112), and *Enc. dell'arte antica* VI (1965) 200–206 for others.

**66** J. Boardman, *BSA* 50 (1955) 51–66 for discussion; and H. Mommsen, *Exekias I. Die Grabtafeln* (1996).

**67** The shape reduced to a simple disc for what must be a dedication to Artemis: *LIMC* II, no. 407, Artemis with torch, bow and dog, late Attic black figure.

**68** J. Boardman, *Greek Emporio* (1964) pl. 60.785.

**69** Acr. 6; *ARV* 78, 102. The Epiktetos plates are not pierced for suspension, nor most later ones in Athens.

**70** D. Callipolitis-Feytmans, *Les Plats attiques à figures noires* (1974) 266–276.

**71** *EGVP* 187, fig. 434; M. Pipili, *Laconian Iconography of the Sixth Century B.C.* (1987) ch. 3, esp. 63.

**72** J.R. Mertens, *Met.Mus.J.* 9 (1974) 91–108.

**73** Naucratis – *GO* 123–124; *EGVP* fig. 307. Athens – Acr. 1812–3, 1923–30; inscribed pre-firing 'sacred to Athena'. C. Wagner's Oxford thesis, *Dedication Practices on the Athenian Acropolis. 8th to 4th centuries BC* (1997) is my major source for Acropolis finds.

**74** *EGVP* fig. 317; *LIMC* Artemis no. 1034; L. Kahil, *Hesperia* 50 (1981) 253–263.

**75** J.D. Beazley, *Philadelphia Museum Journal* 23 (1932) 4–22.

**76** For sacrifice scenes, F.T. van Straten, *Hiera kala* (1995); P. Cloche, *Les classes, les métiers, le trafic* (1931); J. Ziomecki, *Les représentations d'artisans sur les vases antiques* (1975).

**77** Cloche, op.cit., pl. 10.2.

**78** M. Torelli, *La Società Etrusca* (1987); L. Cerchiai, *Ostraka* 6 (1997) 129–134.

**79** F. Lissarrague, *REA* 89.3–4 (1987) 261–269.

**80** A. Maggiani, *Vasi attici figurati con dediche a divinità etrusche* (1997).

**81** *ABFH* fig. 219.

**82** 'Falaieff' craters, *ARV* 1469–1470; one is from south Russia, the others have no provenience; for the metal model see Boardman, *Diffusion* 220, fig. 6.47.

**83** *GO* 137–138, fig. 162.

**84** A balanced discussion with bibliography by G. Clark, *Women in the Ancient World* (1989).

**85** H.A. Shapiro, *Personifications* (1993); some 5th-century usage, A.C. Smith, *JHS* 119 (1999) 128–141.

**86** Shapiro, op.cit., 192, takes Peitho to have had some effect, but her pose, place and gaze tell otherwise, and the asymmetry draws attention to her exclusion.

**87** The comic satyr – ⌈66.1,199⌉, *Periplous* 192. *ARFH* I, fig. 95 (Alkyoneus); *LIMC* I, Alkyoneus nos. 7, 11, 12, 25; III, Ariadne no. 52.

**88** Y. Korshak, *Frontal Faces in Attic Vase-Painting* (1987).

**89** P. Blome in *Ansichten griechischer Rituale* (ed. F. Graf, 1998) 72–98 on horror pictures.

**90** M. Kilmer, *Greek Erotica* (1993) – Athenian red figure only.

**91** B. Cohen, *Source* 12 (1993) 37–46 on naked Cassandra.

**92** V. Dasen, *Dwarfs in Ancient Egypt and Greece* (1993). F.M. Snowden, *Blacks in Antiquity* (1970); on *EGVP* fig. 499 their stalwart appearance contrasts with the paler cowering Egyptians.

**93** J. Boardman, *RA* 1992, 227–242; ⌈266⌉ is 228, no. 3.

**94** *EGVP* fig. 335.

**95** *LIMC* I, Aias I, nos. 105, 140. K. Schefold, *AntK* 19 (1976) 71–78; M. Davies, *AK* 16 (1973) 60–71.

**96** R. Osborne's description of a woman's 'weight of pain' and 'agony' is abetted by his inadvertent choice of a picture of a Hellenistic replacement in the Olympia pediment to demonstrate it: *Archaic and Classical Greek Art* (1998) 173–174, fig. 100. The features of the real 5th-century women in the pediment are quite unmoved even while being attacked by centaurs. On 'expression' in heads, E. Moignard in *Periplous* 198–204.

## Chapter 7 (pp. 244–268)

**1** Athenaeus 464a-d.

**2** On the nature of the site J. Boardman in *CAH Pls. to Vols. V/VI* (1994) ch. 5.

**3** The Dema House and Vari House, 5th and 4th centuries BC respectively: J.E. Jones et al., *BSA* 57 (1962) 87–100; 68 (1973) 373–397.

**4** Brief report, K.M. Lynch, *AJA* 103 (1999) 298. See also Arafat/Morgan, 336. A smaller deposit, mainly of cups in both techniques, *Hesperia* 65 (1996) 242–252. On domestic sources for pottery, S. Rotroff in *CPG* 63–73.

**5** S.I. Rotroff and J.H. Oakley, *Hesperia* Suppl. 25 (1992).

**6** M.L. Lazzarini, *Archeologia Classica* 25/26 (1973/4) 341–375.

**7** Athenaeus is best consulted in the 7–volume Loeb Library edition, with a good index. I cite him for passages since they are easier to find there and are in context, but I name source and date also, where known. W. Miller, *Daedalus and Thespis* (1932) 705–809, lists vase names in the dramatists. M.G. Kanowski, *Containers of Classical Greece* (1983) is the fullest account of names and shapes, but shaky in some details; see also Noble, ch. 1. M.I. Gulletta, *Lexicon Vasorum Graecorum* I- (1992–), see *Gnomon* 1995, 87–88; and F. Brommer, *Hermes* 115 (1987) 1–21 for names in 5th-century texts. All the handbooks have chapters on shapes and names.

**8** On this phenomenon, J. Boardman in *Greek Settlements* . . . (edd. A.M. Snodgrass and G. Tsetskhladze, 2001). Shallow bowls of eastern type are used by some East Greek komasts (*EGVP* figs. 336, 337); also in Laconia, which had strong links east, ibid., figs. 413, 414, 421, 433; T.J. Smith in *Sparta in Laconia* (edd. W.G. Cavanagh and S. Walker, 1998) ch. 7; *Kotinos* (Fest. E. Simon, edd. H. Froning et al., 1992) pl. 25.1; many are patterned and may be taken for metal.

**9** The Corinthian table ware: Payne, *NC* 211–212, figs. 96–97; O. Murray (ed.), *Sympotica* (1990) pls. 1a, 2a, 2b (= our [269]), 10a; *AJA* 73 (1969) pl. 40.22; *Greek Vase-Painting in Midwestern Collections* (ed. W.G. Moon, 1979) no. 16; *AA* 1999, 264, fig. 6, and others. P. Schmitt-Pantel lists some, not all of these, and vases cited in the following notes, in *Sympotica* 18–19, 27–30. Similar (or are they not for drinking – three for one symposiast and his girl?) in a Laconian scene (on Brussels R 401, *Kunst der Schale* (edd. K. Vierneisel and B. Kaeser, 1990) 316, fig. 54.1); see also last note. The small flattish objects which rise at one end to a point or flat top and are arranged in neat rows are not identified: possibly bite-size pieces of meat, or fruit, or . . . ? They are almost invariable on archaic tables where anything at all is shown, but not much in Athens (small on *ABFH* fig. 161.1). One seems to be held by a woman over a bread oven (B.A. Sparkes, *Greece and Rome* 28 (1981) 175, pl. 3a), but should be flat if really ready for baking. Cf. *LIMC* IV (1988) Herakles nos. 1504, 1522, pls. 545, 546, for what seem similar titbits.

**10** M. Miller, *Athens and Persia* (1997) 144–146, figs. 53–56.

**11** J. de la Genière in *La Colonisation grecque* (Coll. Éc. Fr. de Rome 251, 1999) 121–130.

**12** Lissarrague, 80–86; E. Csapo and M.C. Miller, *Hesperia* 60 (1991) 367–382, for the toast (and lyrics sung by symposiasts in scenes). For a human target (the head) Aeschylus (fr. 94, Loeb) in Athenaeus 667c. On throwing bread rolls (or bits of meat or bone?) at a party, J.D. Beazley in *Studies . . . D.M. Robinson* II (1953) 81, pl. 28. Anecdotes and descriptions of the game in Athenaeus 665d–667c.

**13** The 'merrythought' cups: D. Callipolitis-Feytmans, *BCH* 103 (1979) 195–215.

**14** *ABFH* 189, fig. 318.

**15** A. Greifenhagen in *Festschrift . . . F. Brommer* (edd. U. Höckmann and A. Krug, 1977) 133–137; *Jb. des Museums für Kunst und Gewerbe, Hamburg* 2 (1983) 179–181. The shape is also met in Corinthian.

**16** D. Williams, *RA* 1996, 232–240.

**17** A luxury red figure example by Douris, M. Robertson, *Getty Vases* 5 (1991) 75–98, and useful remarks by C. Cardon, ibid., 6/7 (1978/9) 131–138; a colourful Sotadean imitating the eastern, *ARFH* II, fig. 100.

**18** J. Boardman, *JHS* 99 (1979) 149–151.

**19** *Kunst der Schale* (edd. K. Vierneisel/B. Kaesar, 1990) 260, fig. 41.4,5. *EGVP* 218, fig. 477, a Chalcidian psykter-amphora, and there are Corinthian. Also a psykter-column crater, New York 1986.11.12 (Christies, London, July, 1986, no. 141), where the spout is strangely put on the shoulder of the vase, so that it cannot be emptied without removing the wine too. Our [275] in Schreiber, 222–223.

**20** S. Drougou, *Der attische Psykter* (1975), but she thinks the coolant was in the psykter. Schreiber,

218–223. [276] is from *ABV* 186 (Lissarrague, 96, fig. 77). In Plato's *Symposion* (213e–214a) Alcibiades drinks off a whole psykter (about four pints).

**21** *ARFH* II, 170, figs. 369 [280], 370. For the shape, J.R. Green, *BSA* 66 (1971) 189–228. R. Hamilton, *Choes and Anthesteria* (1992).

**22** A. Dalby, *Siren Feasts* (1996) 103–104. On second tables for dessert, and what goes on them, Athenaeus 639–653.

**23** The only alternative to platters and boards is the straight-sided basket for cakes (?) on the Corinthian crater, Hermitage B4462, *AJA* 73 (1969) pl. 39.

**24** *EGVP* figs. 413, 414; Pipili, fig. 105; all by the Naucratis Painter.

**25** On many Siana cups (as *ABFH* fig. 36) but platters for food are not shown on later Athenian vases, except for a board for the mysterious bite-size objects on *ABFH* fig. 161.1 (Andokides Painter).

**26** Not, thus, for the Lydos or Epiktetos plates, but for the Acropolis votives.

**27** *AM* 82 (1967) Beil. 61, 62.

**28** *EGVP* fig. 17.

**29** As in the symposion scene on a revetment at Larisa: *Sympotica* 130, fig. 15. Later versions, B.A. Sparkes in *Periplous* 320–329.

**30** *ARFH* II, fig. 371; *RVSIS* fig. 394; I. McPhee and A.D. Trendall, *Greek Red-figured Fish Plates* (1987); N. Kunisch, *Griechische Fischteller* (1989) – our [282] is pl. 5; and for identity of the fish, H. Metzger, *REG* 103 (1990) 673–683.

**31** *lopas* is probably a better word for bowls used at table. A. Lioutas, *Attische schwarzfigurige Lekanai und Lekanides* (1987).

**32** On eating 'from the pan', Athenaeus 228e–229a (various sources). On spoons, which are rare, see E. Zimi in *Greek Offerings* (ed. O. Palagia, 1997) 209–220.

**33** *Sympotica* (ed. O. Murray, 1990) pls. 2, 3; on 2a with four handles! *EGVP* fig. 36.

**34** These Greek copies were well distributed in the west in the generations around 700 BC.

**35** *Symposion* 2.4. M. Dayagi-Mendels, *Perfumes and Cosmetics in the Ancient World* (1989).

**36** The Corinthian aryballos sequence: *EGVP* figs. 163–166, 171–176, 184, 362–368; alabastra: figs. 182, 369–371. On the shape and uses, N. Kunisch, *AA* 1972, 558–567.

**37** *GO* 142, fig. 168; 153, figs. 194, 195.

**38** *EGVP* figs. 358–360 (East Greek; 360 is our [286]); 407, 408 (Corinthian). R.A. Higgins, *Cat. of Terracottas in the British Museum* II (1959) for a good selection.

**39** *EGVP* fig. 372.

**40** A. Greifenhagen, *RA* 1982, 151–162.

**41** Except in archaic Anatolia: Boardman, *Diffusion* 27, fig. 2.10; 218, fig. 6.45. A Lydian metal perfume vase, the 'lydion', was also made in clay and copied in various parts of Greece: *GO* 99, figs. 114–116.

**42** Noble, fig. 150; and in *Proceedings of the American Philosophical Society* 112 (1968) 371–378. Schreiber, 9, fig. 2.1 and 178–183.

**43** K. Wallenstein, *AA* 1972, 458–474, fig. 17, cf. fig. 16.

**44** *CVA* Castle Ashby pl. 59.104. On Calene gutti, K. Schauenburg, *RM* 80 (1973) 191–198.

**45** H.A. Shapiro in *APP* 63–70 (64 for [289]), drawing attention also to scenes relating to the Panathenaic Games, where oil was a prize. It is not clear why it was thought that Solon had forbidden men to take part in the trade of selling perfume: Athenaeus 612a, 687a. Some pelikai are painted within: Schreiber, 210–213.

**46** J. Boardman and M. Pope, *Greek Vases in Cape Town* (1961) no. 15. Archaic examples, *EGVP* figs. 386 – Corinthian; 441 – Boeotian.

**47** References in *GO* 280.

**48** On the sex differentiation, J. Boardman, *AION* 10 (1988) 171–179; fig, 32.1 is [292], also figs. 20.1, 21.1; and figs. 19–21, in use.

**49** D.C. Kurtz and J. Boardman, *Greek Burial Customs* (1971) 149, pls. 37, 38.

**50** M.& C. Roebuck, *Hesperia* 24, 158–163.

**51** Dice, S. Karouzou, *AM* 88 (1973) 55–65.

**52** *CAH Pls. to Vols. V/VI* (1994) 125–126.

**53** *EGVP* figs. 30, 130, 150, 244. [296], from the 'Rich Lady's' tomb for which see J.N. Coldstream, *Hesperia* 64 (1995) 391–403. Some other models, D. Williams in *Periplous* 388–396.

**54** Lissarrague, 48–52, with references. K. Kilinski, *AJA* 90 (1986) 153–158 (Boeotian). In Etruria, T.B. Rasmussen, *Bucchero Pottery from Southern Etruria* (1979) 121; *Ann.Mus.Nat.Varsovie* 11 (1967) 53.

**55** B.A. Sparkes, *JHS* 82 (1962) 121–137, on the Greek kitchen.

**56** *ABFH* fig. 263.

**57** R. Amedick, *Antike Welt* 29.6 (1998) 497–507. For [299], L. Ghali-Kahil, *Les enlèvements et le retour d'Hélène* (1955) pl. 68.1–3.

**58** On metal-to-clay shapes D. Gill in *Pots and Pans* (ed. M. Vickers, 1986) 9–30; and details, M. Vickers, ibid., 137–151, the more extravagant claims in which are answered, J. Boardman, *RA* 1987, 279–295, and D. Williams, *RA* 1996, 227–252.

**59** *Oxford History of Classical Art* (ed. J. Boardman, 1993) 185–186, no. 181. Contrast the many fine silver vases from the 'Tomb of Philip' at Vergina, none of which has figure decoration on the body, and all of which were found clean and bright.

### Chapter 8 (pp. 269–281)

**1** On visual experience in archaic Athens and Corinth, J. Boardman in *Culture* 1–14.

**2** M. Robertson, *BSA* 46 (1951) 151–159.

**3** *GO* 56–71.

**4** F. Croissant, *Les protomés féminines archaïques* (1983), notably pls. 41 (Oltos), 43–44 (Andokides Painter); review, *CR* 1985, 153–154.

**5** E. Kunze, *Archaische Schildbänder* (1950) explores the iconography thoroughly.

**6** M. Denoyelle, *Le cratère des Niobides* (1997) on observations after cleaning. Much discussed; e.g., E.B. Harrison, *Art Bulletin* 54 (1972) 391–402; E. Simon, *AJA* 67 (1963) 43–62. J.P. Barron, *JHS* 92 (1972) 20–45, argued that the body renderings in some of the large

scenes copy those of wall painting, but there are problems – they are simply more accurate; J. Boardman, forthcoming.

**7** *ARFH* II, 168, fig. 329, cf. 330.

**8** The shield – *GSCP* fig. 110. The nearest vase – *ARFH* II, 147, fig. 293.

**9** Parthenon echoes on vases reviewed by B.A. Sparkes in *Classicism to Neo-classicism* (edd. M. Henig and D. Plantzos, 1999) 3–17.

**10** Nudity in sculpture: *GSCP* 20–22, *GSLCP* 53–54; J. Boardman, *Greek Art* (1996) 158–160, 272–273, 293. N. Himmelmann, *Ideale Nacktheit* (1990).

**11** N. Himmelmann, *Das akad. Kunstmuseum der Univ. Bonn* (1984) 61.

**12** *EGVP* fig. 313, Chian archaic. Under-handle eyes, ibid., fig. 252.2.

**13** Aryballoi – *EGVP* fig. 176; neck-heads, figs. 243, 312. On the general phenomenon, J. Boardman, *AA* 1976, 281–290, with illustrations.

**14** *EGVP* figs. 262, 358–360, 407, 408, 448, 449. Compare with [96] the Attic cup with a relief satyr head: T.H. Carpenter, *Dionysian Imagery in Fifth-century Athens* (1997) pl. 39b.

**15** See the useful drawings of the changes in various shapes from 600 BC on by E.D. Breitfeld-von Eickstedt in *APP* 58–59.

**16** See B. Edwards, *Drawing on the Right Side of the Brain* (1992) ch. 7.

**17** G.M.A. Richter, *Perspective in Greek and Roman Art* (1970).

**18** *ARFH* I, fig. 50; Simon/Hirmer, pls. 117–119.

**19** As Noble, figs. 198–199 (either side); *ARFH* II, figs. 290, 291.1 ('replica').

**20** *EGVP* fig. 376.

**21** J.W. Hayes, *Studia Troica* 5 (1995) 177–183.

### Chapter 9 (pp. 282–289)

Noble and Schreiber are the major sources for techniques of manufacture; and see Sparkes, ch. 2, and J.M. Hemelrijk in *LGV* ch. 10.

**1** 'Scales' in the production of lekythoi and cups, probably overstated: H. Holzhausen and R.C.A. Röttlander, *Archaeometry* 12 (1970) 189–196. Calculating capacities: F. Beltov, *Hephaistos* 7/8 (1985/6) 125–151.

**2** W.D. Kingery, *Archeomaterials* 5 (1991) 47–54.

**3** In colour in Simon/Hirmer, pl. XXV, a mottled Exekias; and pl. XXVII, by Psiax, where it is well preserved, but contrast the lightness of the incised lines which have cut through it. On its use, Noble, 60–61; Schreiber, 48–52, and 39–48 on burnishing.

**4** Simon/Hirmer, pl. XXIV (colour).

**5** See Chapter 1, n. 92.

**6** *EGVP* figs. 259 (Cretan), 301–302 (Rhodian), 320, 323–324 (Chian), 453 (Boeotian); *ABFH* figs. 313–314 (Six technique).

**7** I discussed its use in *Antiquity* 34 (1960) 85–89. J.K. Papadopoulos et al., *AJA* 102 (1998) 507–529, have worked out how it might have been made, and prefer not to use the obvious word for it, 'compass', because it is not adjustable, but 'pivoted'. I would have expected the brush to have been braced at both ends for secure use, like rigid dividers, and it would certainly have needed to be in this form for freehand use. The potters' version was obviously invented for potter use but may have been inspired by combed work on other plastic media.

**8** By far heavier relief lines on English 20th-century Moorcroft pottery seem to have been applied in this way; and see Noble, 60, who suggested the use of a syringe for antiquity.

**9** G. Seiterle, *Antike Welt* 7 (1976) 2–10; Scheibler, 202, n. 31.

**10** *ARV* 342,19: 'May be the painter himself', says Beazley.

**11** J.M. Hemelrijk, *Caeretan Hydriae* (1984) 88–89, 105–110.

**12** U. Hausmann, *Hellenistische Reliefbecher* (1959) pl. 49.

**13** Alterations and erasure in black figure; V. Tosto in *Stips Votiva* (Papers . . . C.M. Stibbe, ed. M. Gnade, 1991) 233–239. *CVA* Oxford III, 11 and pls. 2–3, for a change of mind.

**14** P.E. Corbett, *JHS* 85 (1965) 16–28, on sketches for both black and red figure ([*315*] is his pl. 4). M. Boss in *Euphronios und seiner Zeit* (ed. I. Wehgartner, 1992) 81–89, and in *AA* 1992, 533–537 (Exekias), *APP* 345–351. There are even some underglaze inscriptions: Immerwahr, 174, n. 6.

**15** On these lines, N. Kunisch, *AntK* 37 (1994) 81–90.

**16** E.g., in Etruria: J. De Wit, *JdI* 44 (1929) 31–85; S. Steingräber, *AA* 1988, 71–79; L. Vlad Borelli, *Archeologia Classica* 43.2 (1991) 1179–1192.

**17** On [*300*], M. Denoyelle, *Le cratère des Niobides* (1997) 35–36. Incisions – J. Boardman in *BCH* Suppl. 38 (Hommage à L. Kahil, 2000) 51–52, figs. 4–5.

## Chapter 10 (pp. 290–299)

**1** Jones (1986) is the bible for this subject.

**2** M. Elston, *Apollo* July 1999, 26–32.

**3** In *Expedition* 1979, 33–40.

**4** Thus, my omission of stemmed plates for the Spina figures: M.P. Guermandi in *Spina e il Delta Padano* (ed. F. Rebecchi, 1994) 179–202.

**5** In *JHS* 95 (1975) 1–2.

**6** In *Catania* I, 21–23.

**7** A start on publication by Ch. Papadopoulou-Kanellopoulou, *Iero tes Nymphes* (1997).

**8** Problems in north Africa, J. Boardman in *Archaeology of Greek Colonisation* (edd. G. Tsetskhladze and F. De Angelis, 1994) 144–149.

**9** Timely remarks about dangers with statistics in vase study, by V. Stissi in *CPG* 351–355 (also *CPP* 83–113). L. Hannestad has made valuable comments on the application of statistics, e.g., à propos of the Athenian home market, in *Copenhagen* 222–230, and *Catania* II, 211–216; on export to Etruria, *Acta Archeologica* 59 (1988) 113–130; on Attic and the indigenous peoples of Italy in *CPP* 303–318. For some typical studies of local shape distribution, C. Scheffer in *Copenhagen* 536–546,

for lekythoi; E.G.D. Robinson in *GCNP* 251–265, all shapes. There are many more, not always too careful about explaining quality of source.

**10** D. Ridgway, *The First Western Greeks* (1992) part 2.

**11** *EGVP* 9–10, 271; *ABFH* ch. 10, 234; *ARFH* I, 210–211; *ARFH* II, 9–10; Sparkes, ch. 3; W.R. Biers, *Art, Artefacts and Chronology* (1992). Radical revisions proposed by some can be ignored. For the early period down to the 7th century, L. Hannestad and I. Morris support the traditional dates in *Acta Archeologica* 67 (1996) 39–49, 51–59. There is a move to raise dates in the early Iron Age but the sequence is assured and evidence yet to be fully evaluated.

**12** *Antiquaries Journal* 39 (1959) 198.

**13** J. Boardman, *AA* 1988, 423–425, where potting families are also located in generations.

**14** H.A. Shapiro, *Zeitschrift für Papyrologie und Epigraphik* 68 (1987) 107–118.

**15** J.K. Davies, *Athenian Propertied Families* (1971) 90–91; the *kalos* inscriptions, J. Boardman in *Euphronios* (edd. M. Cygielman et al., 1992) 45–50; the deme Kerameis casualty list, *Inscriptiones Graecae* I.2 (ed. 3) no. 1144 (=*Agora* XVII, no. 1). It conjures something like a regiment of 'Artists' Rifles'. V. Parker has tried to adjust Leagros' dates down (*AA* 1994, 365–373) but relies on an uncertain re-dating of his death, the false assumption that no one could be a general over 60 years' old, and timid mathematics.

**16** See Notes to the Preface. A comparable programme for South Italian pottery is in hand at Melbourne at the Trendall Archive in La Trobe University (Professor Ian McPhee). The Perseus project (www.perseus.tufts.edu) has a valuable Greek vase section, and various museums are at work on placing their holdings on the net.

## Epilogue (pp. 300–303)

**1** In the Agora, Homer Thompson, Eugene Vanderpool, Lucy Talcott; in the National Museum, Semni Karouzou, whose generosity to visiting students in such difficult days (1948–1950) was quite exceptional.

**2** These were in fact in conscious emulation of Franz Winter's *Kunstgeschichte in Bildern* of 1900, fascicles of which I had acquired secondhand and found an invaluable source of pictures but lacking narrative and detail.

**3** Notably, H. Hoffmann, *Sexual and Asexual Pursuit* (1977), the only serious iconographical attempt; but flawed, see J. Boardman, *Classical Review* 1979, 118–120; with after-shocks in *Hephaistos* 2 (1980) 107–111, 3 (1981) 23–25, 4 (1982) 177–178, where 'structural paradigm' seems set above observation and the truth.

**4** I deal with some of these problems of over-interpretation by the inexpert and the occasional academic buffoon in *APP* 259–261. The academic felon, who digs without publishing, is a more destructive animal: see *GO* 10–11.

# Index